Copyright © 2016 by Lani Sharp
All rights reserved. This book or any portion thereof
may not be reproduced or used in any manner whatsoever
without the express written permission of the publisher
except for the use of brief quotations in a book review.

Printed in Australia

First Printing, 2016

ISBN: 978-0-9945051-9-4

White Light Publishing House
6 Lincoln Way
Melton West, VIC, Australia 3337

www.whitelightpublishingau.com

❧ DEDICATION ❦

This book is wholly dedicated to my amazing Mum, the most inspiring and important Piscean in my Universe. Thank you Mum, for your faith, understanding of my many quirks, your unconditional love and above all, for always believing in everything I do. I love you.

ABOUT THE AUTHOR

☾ ★ ☽

Lani Sharp is a Natural Born Rebel who just also happens to be an Aquarian, who shunned 'conventional' astrology courses to pursue her own path in the wondrous, inspiring and ever-evolving field of cosmic forces and stellar influences. After failing to find a course or tutor that suited her needs, Lani set out on her own starry Magic Carpet adventure across the skies, partly to discover her own 'truths' about this ancient system, but mostly to prove that one can achieve absolutely anything, including and above all, their dream careers (or lifestyle), if they put their hearts and souls into it. A self-taught astrologer who takes the esoteric and spiritual approach to this much-loved popular art, she has been studying and effectively practising astrology since she was eight years old. When she is not writing about, channelling, practising or teaching astrology, she can be found living her dream life alternating somewhere between her home in Australia's stunning Tropical North or her second home in Victoria's beautiful Dandenong Ranges, enjoying tea parties with her highly imaginative Cancerian daughter, Allira, and their gnome and fairy friends, crystal-wishing, day-dreaming, believing in gnomes, pixies, angels, fairies, magic and miracles, honing her magickal * witchcraft skills, Moon-gazing, Sun-worshipping, Venus-channelling, Jupiter-drawing, assisting others to discover, unravel and follow their true spiritual paths … or of course walking across rainbows!

Not a mistake. Magick is a Wiccan variation of the word 'magic'.

ACKNOWLEDGEMENTS, CREDITS & GRATITUDE BLESSINGS

✯

I would love to thank the following people and entities for their amazing contributions, interest, support and faith in me as I wrote the manuscripts for each of the twelve astrological Sun signs. Firstly, the biggest thank you go to my Mum, Sandra, and my stepdad, Barry, for their unending support, love, advice, daily Skype conversations, acceptance of our geographical distance, and above all, their inner knowing that everything always comes together in the end. Your support of me and my dreams is appreciated beyond words. Secondly, gratitude to my wonderful partner, Travis, for his patience (no mean feat for a Gemini!), for supporting me every step of the way, and for his acceptance of my 'mad scientist' Aquarian mindset by never trying to break down the invisible 'laboratory' walls I built around myself while writing the books. I would also like to extend my enormous gratitude to the following: Allira, my little Cancerian 'crab' daughter, a soul in a billion, who also had to tolerate and operate within the bounds of her nutty professor mother's antics and focus throughout the writing of the books. Thank you to Nicola, my wonderful Facebook friend, for recommending White Light Publishing House, and of course to White Light Publishing House themselves, for pouring their faith and passion into my project from the very beginning - and an even bigger thank you to the wonderful people behind the company for publishing my work, Christie and Jess! Gratitude also goes out to my dear friends, both near and far, who have inspired in me so many ideas through simply being themselves - especially Amanda and Carlie. Amanda, you have always been my 'astrology buddy' and I have always enjoyed - and learned so much through - our discussions on all things astrology and star signs: the good, the bad and the ugly! Having someone like you off which to bounce thoughts and share ideas with, has always been immensely helpful and appreciated. I have saved my final thank you for The Universe, who always delivers to me exactly what I have asked for, without exception. The Universe is my ultimate *higher power*, my guiding light, my powerful driving force, my spiritual helper, my guardian angel, my eternal friend, my inner motivator, my sympathetic listener, my inspirational teacher, and the fulfiller of all my dreams, including this one, having my very first book(s) published, a long-held dream that stretches way back through the years to my days of being a mini dreamer, inquisitor and stargazer. The Universe has always believed in me, but perhaps more importantly, I have always believed in *IT*.

So to all of the above, I wish to say:

Thank you, thank you, thank you!

"There was a star danced,
and under that I was born"

William Shakespeare

"We were born at a given moment, in a given place, and like vintage years of wine, we have the qualities of the year and of the season in which we are born"

Carl G. Jung

INSPIRED BY ALL THE SIGNS

Aries imparted courage and boldness
And helped me dance away the pain
Taurus gave me hugs and comfort
And shelter from the rain
Gemini provided me with laughter
And taught me again how to have fun
Cancer nurtured and sustained me
By reflecting back my Sun
Leo reminded me there was joy
From within myself and above
Virgo awakened my healthy glow
By teaching me how to love
Libra gave me gentle hugs
And judged me not for a thing
Scorpio lent me some of his power
And took away the sting
Sagittarius showered me with gifts
Of words so wise and true
As Capricorn led the way up the mountain
My resolve and strength grew
Aquarius gave me the gift of friendship
And carried me as his brother
And Pisces swam with me to the depths
With a compassion like no other.

Special Note

Throughout the text of this book, and indeed the whole Lucky Astrology book series, I have capitalised the first letter of the word 'Universe'. This is because, quite simply, I feel it is a very special title for the higher power that I personally choose to be guided by, and have accordingly highlighted it as such.

You may also notice that I use the words 'he' or 'she', and 'his' or 'her', when referring to your own Sun sign and other zodiac signs, and never 'he or she' or 'his or her' together. The reason for this is for simplicity, for I don't wish the sentences to be too wordy and therefore the messages within them to be lost. As a general rule, I refer to all six 'masculine' zodiac signs as 'he', and all six 'feminine' signs as 'she', and this remains a consistent rule throughout this book and the whole series.

Your Sun sign, Pisces, is a feminine sign and will thus be referred to accordingly.

CONTENTS

	Page
ASTROLOGY	15
THE ZODIAC AND YOUR PLACE IN THE SUN	24
PISCES THE FISH	31
QUOTES BY PISCEANS	38
THE PISCES CONSTELLATION	42
THE PISCEAN SYMBOL	44
THE RUNDOWN & LESSONS ★	
THE ESSENCE OF PISCES	49
THE THREE DECANS OF PISCES	73
YOUR ELEMENT ★ WATER	78
YOUR MODE ★ MUTABLE	102
YOUR RULING PLANET ★ NEPTUNE	105
YOUR HOUSE IN THE HOROSCOPE ★	
THE TWELFTH HOUSE	124
YOUR OPPOSITE SIGN ★ VIRGO	130
MAGIC, DRAWING, ATTRACTION, SPELLS,	
RITUALS, WISHING & POWER	141
ASTROLOGY & MAGIC	146
PLANETS ★ DAYS OF THE WEEK	
& THEIR POWERS	152
YOUR NATAL MOON PHASE	156
SPELLS, MAGIC & WISHING WITH MOON PHASES	159
THE MOON IN THE HUMAN PSYCHE	
& NATAL CHART	166
YOUR MOON SIGN	169
YOUR BODY & HEALTH	179
THE CELL SALTS ★ ASTROLOGICAL TONICS	185

	Page
WATER SIGN PISCES & THE PHLEGMATIC HUMOUR	188
MONEY ATTRIBUTES	191
COLOURS ★ YOUR LUCKY COLOURS	194
LUCKY CAREER TIPS	211
LUCKY PLACES	218
GEMS & CRYSTALS	220
PISCEAN POWER CRYSTALS	231
YOUR LUCKY NUMBERS	246
YOUR LUCKY MAGIC HOURS OR TIME UNITS	256
YOUR LUCKY DAY ★ THURSDAY	261
YOUR LUCKY CHARM / TALISMANS	265
YOUR LUCKY ANIMALS & BIRDS	268
YOUR METALS	282
PLANTS, HERBS, SPICES, TREES, SHRUBS, FLOWERS, SCENTS & INCENSE	285
YOUR FOODS	292
YOUR LUCKY WOOD & CELTIC TREE ★ OAK & ASH OR ALDER	294
THE POWER OF LOVE	301
LUCKY IN LOVE? PISCES COMPATIBILITY	315
YOUR TAROT CARDS	334
LUCKY 13 TIPS	368
HAVE YOU PACKED YOUR MAGICAL BAG FOR THE JOURNEY?	371
A FINAL WORD ★ TAPPING INTO THE MAGIC OF PISCES	372

LUCKY ASTROLOGY

By Lani Sharp

PISCES

*Tapping into the Powers of Your Sun Sign for Greater
Luck, Happiness, Health, Abundance & Love*

"That which is above is like to that which is below, and that which is below is like to that which is above, to accomplish the miracles of one thing … the Father thereof is the Sun, the mother the Moon."

**The Emerald Tablet, Hermes Trismegistus
(circa 3000 BC)**

★ ASTROLOGY ★

Astrology: "Divination through the correlation of earthly events with celestial patterns"
'Real Magic', I. Bonewits, 1971

A BRIEF HISTORY

Astrology can be defined as the calculation and meaningful interpretation of the positions and motions of the heavenly bodies, and their correlation with human experiences. Its central concept is based upon this interconnectedness or correspondence between the stars and ourselves.

The word astrology is derived from the Greek word astron, meaning 'star' and logos which means 'word'. Astrology, therefore, literally means language of the stars. It is based on the ancient law known as 'As Above, So Below', otherwise known as the Law of the Macrocosm and Microcosm. The Macrocosm is the Universe, symbolised by the sky, the starry dome that we can see from the Earth; the Microcosm is us - humans, and all other life on Earth. 'As Above, So Below' is a well-known and deeply impressing maxim of Hermetic origin, inscribed upon the famed Emerald Tablet among cryptic wording by enigmatic figure, Hermes Trismegistus, around 5,000 years ago. These four powerful words are adopted by astrologers and believers in magic to explain, in very succinct wording, the meaning behind the art and science of celestial influences upon our Earthly affairs.

Astrology and many other magical and occult studies, propose that we are not separate from the Universe, we are part of it. The Sun, Moon and planets all follow exact patterns of movement and their motions can be measured precisely by astronomers. The basic idea of astrology is that all individual parts of the Universe, from plants to animals, cooperate with each other and work together in harmony.

Anyone can apply astrological knowledge in their daily lives, but it hasn't always been like that. At one time, astrology was reserved only for Kings and nations, and only the court astrologer/astronomer could cast and interpret horoscopes. Ancient astrology and astronomy used to be one and the same. To be an astrologer, you first had to be able to interpret the stars in some systematic way, and then track the movement of the Moon and the planets against the background of the constellations.

Astrology, the knowledge and language of the cosmos, goes back to the ancient kingdom of Babylonia and was adapted by the Mesopotamians, Greeks, Egyptians and Romans to incorporate their own deities (as indicated in mythology). It is upon a combination of Greek and Egyptian interpretations of astrology that our present knowledge is based.

In the ancient Mesopotamian world, as far back as 800 BC, people lived precariously beneath the open skies. The skies and the stars which filled them, were the real founders of astrology. Today we are aware that the Sun and Moon exert a profound influence upon our Earthly affairs, but for our primitive ancestors, the heavens, the stars and the planets must have been a matter of great and mysterious significance. Early humankind, its senses influenced by natural processes of ebbs, flows, growth, decay and cycles, tended naturally towards a physical explanation of the Universe. At first, the movements of the planets - and all celestial occurrences - were observed as omens affecting the Ruler and his nation; it was only in Egypt in the fifth century AD that the casting of horoscopes for individual people and the calculation of the planetary positions at the time of birth became widespread.

The first astrologers, the Chaldeans, mapped the stars and later passed this knowledge and wisdom on to the ancient Greeks, who, during the third century BC, developed astrology into a science with the use of mathematical aids and instruments to measure planetary movements. The Greeks were the first to cast individual horoscopes. And it was the Greeks who associated the four elements with the signs of the zodiac. The word "zodiac" can be translated from Greek to mean the "circle or path of the animals." The Greeks not only had names for the twelve Solar phases but had symbols for each, and many correspond with the ones we use today.

The Greeks passed on much of their knowledge to the Romans. During the second century BC, Roman astrologers were primarily forecasters who were consulted frequently by rulers of the church and state. By the early third century AD, astrology co-existed with early Christianity. This harmonious co-existence was possible because it was considered that celestial bodies could foretell events, but did not determine the future - indeed, the stars seen by the shepherds at the time of Christ's birth were only predictors of his arrival. After the fourth century AD, Christianity strengthened and the popularity of astrology declined as Christian reluctance to support 'pagan' or 'superstitious' beliefs became more prominent. The Middle Ages saw a revival in astrology, with courses being taught in universities and other educational establishments, and connections were made between the zodiac, alchemy, herbs and medicine. Astrology was once again able to exist alongside the Church, although many remained suspicious of astrologers.

Around the beginning of the fifteenth century, academics of the Renaissance movement examined the past for knowledge, and ancient philosophies, including astrology, flourished; this coincided with arts and science movements developing. The famous prophet and astrologer Nostradamus lived during this period. Leonardo da Vinci depicted aspects of astrology combined with geometry in his art. Writers and poets of the time, including Shakespeare, alluded to zodiacal influences in their work.

During this period, astrology had numerous practical applications. Agricultural calendars were introduced, indicating favourable planting times according to the phases of the Moon; health and illness were linked with movements of celestial bodies; and emotional states and mental health afflictions correlated with the planetary positions.

Eventually, new ways of thinking led to a split between astronomy and astrology, and by the seventeenth century, the realm of science had developed to such a degree that astrology was no longer taken seriously.

The study of the sky above us has been charted for more than 5,000 years. This fact is known because ancient 'horoscopes' imprinted on clay tablets have been unearthed, dating back almost 5,400 years ago. However, no one knows for certain just how, when and where astrology first began, although it is known that it flourished in ancient Chaldea, Mesopotamia, Babylon and Egypt.

Astrology is a science which has spanned many centuries and still remains extraordinarily popular, and its truths have the potential to speak to and *through* all of us. Long before today's interest in it, men of great vision such as Ptolemy, Hippocrates, Plato, Galileo, Jefferson, Franklin, Newton, Columbus and Jung respected its inherent truths, mythology and eternal knowledge. Furthermore, astrology predates many other 'sciences' - for out of it grew religion, medicine and astronomy, not the other way around.

The discipline of astrology is ultimately a study of the interlocking and interrelated forces of the twelve zodiacal forces, or constellations, that grace the heavens, as they pour their energies into the Earthly kingdoms below. As these various energies circulate throughout the etheric realm of our Solar system, these zodiacal entities and archetypes imprint their vibrational frequencies and harmonic resonances upon our bodies, minds, souls and spirits.

ASTROLOGY & THE INDIVIDUAL

Since the earliest period of the history of humankind, people studied the starry vaults of the heavens and conceived that their presence, movements and positions endowed planet Earth's inhabitants with Divine influence. There is much evidence that positions and movements of the planets as seen from Earth at the time of a birth are linked to personality characteristics of individuals. Human energy and emotional cycles are governed by the forces and networks of magnetic impulses from all the planets. Of all the heavenly bodies, the Moon's effects and power are the most marked and visible due to its close proximity to Earth. But the Sun, Venus, Mars, Mercury, Jupiter, Saturn, Uranus, Neptune and Pluto exercise their influences just as surely. In fact, scientists are aware that plants and animals are affected by natural cycles which are governed by forces such as fluctuations in barometric pressure, the gravitational field and electricity in the air. These Earthly dynamics are originally triggered by magnetic vibrations from the atmosphere, or outer space, from where the planets send forth their unseen waves. No living organism or mineral on Earth escapes these immense, if unseen, influences.

The geomagnetic field seems to affect life on Earth in certain observed ways, and these influences appear to correlate with planetary positions. It has been suggested that the fluctuations of the Earth's magnetic field are picked up by the nervous system of the in utero infant, which acts like an antenna, and these synchronise the internal biological clocks of the foetus which control the moment of birth. The foetal magnetic antenna therefore, is sensitive enough to sense these planetary vibrations and fields, and through a combination of inherited genetics and the positions of the planets at birth, they are imprinted with certain basic inherited and 'absorbed' personality characteristics.

Carl Jung, the Swiss psychiatrist and psychological theorist, suggested that the inherent disposition of the individual is present at birth, and is reflected in the patterns of his or her natal chart. Further, he theorised that there is a 'priori factor' in all human activities, namely the inborn, preconscious and unconscious individual structure of the psyche. The preconscious psyche, for example that of a newborn baby, is not simply an empty vessel into which practically anything can be poured, but rather it is this preconscious psyche that gives us the free will to become what we are instead of what others or our environment makes us. The child is not merely a receptacle for the psychic life of those around him or her, albeit sensitive and susceptible to the surrounding unconscious forces in childhood; for he/she also brings something of his own to his experience of them.

Further, Dr Harold S. Burr, who was a Professor of Anatomy at the Yale University School of Medicine, and author of *The Nature of Man and the Meaning of Existence* (1962), asserted that there is order in the Universe, unity in the organism and man is endowed with a soul. He stated that a complex magnetic field not only establishes the pattern of the human brain at birth, but continues to regulate and control it through life, and that the human central nervous system is a superb receptor of electro-magnetic energies, indeed the finest in nature. He contended that the electro-dynamic fields of all living things, which may be measured and mapped with standard voltmeters, mould and control each organism's development, health and mood, and named these fields 'fields of life'.

It can therefore be suggested that astrological and planetary influences endow us with the majority of our characteristics at birth, characteristics bestowed upon us according to our Sun sign and other planetary forces. Other parts of the chart are also highly significant and need to be integrated for a 'whole' picture to form, however the Sun sign is an excellent starting point.

The ancients taught that astrology was one of the keys to the many enigmas that plague humans in their unceasing quest to determine what the meaning of life is, and what their role and place in the Universe is - and this quest still persists today. Astrology, which dates back over 5,000 years, is indeed one such key to unlocking the many secrets of the Universe - and ultimately, the individual self.

"KNOW THYSELF"

"Man, know thyself.
All wisdom centres on this."
Carl Jung

Before the temple of the Oracle at Delphi, the ancient Greeks imparted a special piece of advice that was carved onto one of the portals: "Know Thyself." These two powerful words are easy enough to understand, but much more difficult to apply. Throughout life's inner and outer journey, astrology can provide us with an inner navigational system by which we can be guided towards our highest potential, and closer towards the eternal quest of 'knowing thyself'. It provides the hope that this higher spiritual plane exists and that if we can 'read' and therefore be guided by the unique inner blueprint that our individual birth chart has stamped upon us at the moment we take our very first breath, indeed we can reach this higher spiritual plane and realise our innate potential.

Always remember that astrology is not fatalistic. The stars may incline, but they do not compel. Astrology simply provides us with an inner guide, a blueprint, for our journey through life and the finding of our true selves - and what we do with the resulting knowledge is entirely up to us.

Good luck on your journey!

THE ZODIAC & YOUR PLACE IN THE SUN

The zodiac is a circle of 360 degrees, consisting of equal segments of 30 degrees each. These represent the twelve houses of the twelve astrological signs. This zodiac is how the early astrologers imagined the Solar system to be, a perfect circle with the Earth at its centre, around which the Sun, Moon and the planets revolved. Each sign of the zodiac corresponds to one of the twelve segments, following a chronological order and established according to the rhythm of the seasons and cycles of the Sun and the Moon. But the zodiac itself, or the band of constellations which comprise it, has shifted over the millennia, creating division between astronomical and astrological schools of thought. It has been said that due to this shift over time, one who once considered themselves as an Aquarian, is actually a Capricorn, the sign before it, and a Leo is actually a Cancerian, its preceding sign. This is the result of misunderstandings and differences in perspectives, and explanations around it are beyond the scope of this book, but can be researched further should you wish to delve a little deeper. From the astronomical point of view, it is true that the zodiac to which we refer today is not situated where it 'should' be, but indeed, nothing is fixed under the celestial vault. And so the starting point of the ancient zodiac does not correspond exactly to the one we can observe today. But for the purposes of increasing your power and luck, let's keep things simple and enjoy the ride; after all, astrology - while based upon many scientific theories, mysteries, scepticism, superstitions, facts, measurable patterns, ambiguities, correlations, paradoxes, contradictions, links, stigmatisms and observations that seek to support, refute, prove and disprove this ancient art time and again - is ultimately meant to be *fun* too!

THE SUN

Earth's Luminary ★ *Our Brightest Shining Star*

Our Centre, Core Self, Identity & Inner Guiding Light

"Perfect is what I have said of the work of the Sun."
Hermes Trismegistus, *The Emerald Tablet*

The Sun is our essence, centre, source, ego strength, power, life force, will, vitality, creative expression, purpose, life's direction, our sense of identity, and who we really *are*. Our brightest star is the core of our individuality, our inner guiding light. The Sun is externalising, and represents totality, infinity, eternity, the striving toward and ultimate reaching of one's personal destiny, and *completion* in all areas. It is the creative energising giver of life and the 'father' of the zodiac. It endows us with our inherent creative potential and personal identity - our urge to *create* and to *be*. The Sun is our core self, conscious purpose, our sense of creating something out of our own being. It is the integrated personality and represents the *present*, our greatest Gift. The Sun rules the heart and is thus symbolically the centre of self. Indeed, the Sun *is* the heart and the most commanding presence in our birth chart; the luminary Ruler who governs our essential self and wants to be noticed and appreciated, and above all, to *shine*.

★ KEY WORDS ★

Identity, core self, spirit, life force, power, essence, creativity, higher self, the Father, ego, vitality, pride, individuality, leadership, majesty, inner authority, will, expression, willpower, purpose, the journey, the path and the destiny.

THE SUN ★ THE ULTIMATE SOURCE OF LIFE ON EARTH

Throughout the ages, and indeed since life forms began, the electromagnetic waves generated by the Sun have kept planet Earth habitable for humans, animals, plants and minerals. The Sun is, in fact, the only true source of energy on planet Earth. It provides the perfect amount of energy for plants to synthesise all of the products required for growth and reproduction, which is then stored by plants and ingested by humans and animals who, through many complex processes, utilise these various forms of encapsulated Solar energy - and so the cycle continues. Wood, fuel and minerals (crystals included), too, are merely various forms of this encased Sun energy. In fact, all matter is essentially 'frozen' light. Human body cells are bundles of Sun energy; we couldn't conceive or process a single thought without the molecules of Solar-energised oxygen and glucose.

In essence, the Sun supports the growth of all species, including human beings and microscopic life forms, and without it life on Earth would simply not be possible. The mathematical and metaphysical complexity that stands behind a system of organisation and order so infinitely diverse and intricate as planetary life cannot be truly fathomed, but unerringly and miraculously, the Sun instinctively knows what each species, from a tree to a human, intrinsically needs in order to fulfil its evolutionary purpose and cycles.

Ultimately, the electromagnetic waves generated by the Sun come in a variety of lengths, which determine their specific course of action and responsibility. There are gamma rays, x-rays, cosmic rays, various kinds of ultraviolet rays, infrared, shortwave infrared, radio waves, electric waves, and of course the visible light spectrum, consisting of the seven colour rays.

Most of these energy waves are absorbed and used for various processes in the layers of atmosphere that encircle the Earth, and only a small portion of them - the electromagnetic spectrum - reach the surface of our planet. Although the human eye is only able to perceive about one percent of this spectrum, the waves exert a very strong influence upon us. The waves and rays which do affect us so profoundly, allow all life forms to undergo constant cycles of change necessary for growth and renewal. Physically, we can observe this, but on a deeper, more spiritual plane, we can even *feel* it and allow its radiance to permeate our very souls. Such is the might, force and power of that astonishing ball of fire in our sky: the brilliant, ever-shining Sun.

THE SUN ★ WHAT IT REPRESENTS IN THE HUMAN PSYCHE & NATAL CHART

☼

"The Sun is the most powerful of all the stellar bodies. It colours the personality so strongly that an amazingly accurate picture can be given of the individual who was born when it was exercising its power through the known and predicable influences of a certain astrological sign; these electromagnetic vibrations will continue to stamp that person with the characteristics of their Sun sign as they go through life."
Linda Goodman's Sun Signs, **Linda Goodman, Pan Books, 1968**

The Sun is our essence, our core self, conscious purpose and sense of identity, our creative potential, our spirit, the integrated personality that shines outward from within us. It is concerned with the present. It is our centre, source, power, life force, will, vitality, purpose, life's direction, what and who we *really* are.

The Sun represents our basic urge for self-expression. It is the 'Solar energy cell' in a person's character, the Lord and giver of life, and symbolises the way in which an individual will shine out to the world. Our Sun is our personal identity and aspects to it from other components in the chart show the ease or otherwise of assuredness and confidence with which one will project and express one's individuality. The Sun sign will also show how an individual bounces back from setbacks and disappointments, their resilience and their general outward expression of energy.

The Sun is the archetype of the Father and represents the primary masculine principle in the natal chart. It indicates how we express and experience our masculine side, or animus, our conscious self, how we express ourselves creatively, our personal potential, individuality, self-expression and personal power. It has to do with courage, power, generosity, creativity, vitality, self-confidence, nobility, self-worth, dignity and strength of will. It symbolises authority and purpose, the *ruler*, and its potential is the peak of constructive maturity. It signifies self-sufficiency and abundance, containing enough energy to radiate warmth and give life to everything around it.

The sign in which one's Sun is posited, and its placement in the birth chart, strongly indicates the level and type of vitality available to the personality (the sign), and in which area of life this may be most strongly directed (the house).

The Sun in a natal chart is a powerful symbol because everything is filtered, at a conscious level, through it. It tells us what we need to do to feel fully alive, the type of engine 'driving' us, what we need to do to be authentic and to be fully functioning. Listening to the special message of one's Sun sign can provide one with greater direction, and a more dynamic energy and life purpose.

The symbol for the Sun ☉ depicts a circle with a dot or 'seed' at its centre, from which the core self, power, creativity and the first sparks of life can spring. The circle around this 'seed' represents spirit, symbolising wholeness, eternity and the never-ending flow of energy.

While the Moon, the night sky's luminary, represents the *soul*, the Sun, the day sky's luminary, represents our *spirit*.

There is a reason your Sun sign is otherwise known as your Star Sign - it's because, quite simply, the Sun *is* a star; in fact, it's the largest, brightest, shiniest one in Earth's known visible Universe. This book is about your Sun sign and how you can become much larger, glow with far more brilliance, and shine brighter than you ever dreamed possible. I wish you all the magic in the galaxy for your dreams to come true and your deepest wishes to become reality, through tapping into the amazing power and inherent potential of your Sun sign. So get set for a galactical ride through the lucky stars of your constellation - and may a shooting star cross the path in front of you as you go!

PISCES THE FISH

★ Mutable Water, Negative, Feminine, Feeling ★

"The self is sacrificed in the waters of redemption"

Body & Health
Feet, lymphatic system, nervous digestion, immune system, liver, gastro-abdominal system

How Pisces Emanates its Life Force / Energy
Vaguely, passively, kindly, with sensitivity

Is concerned with
★ Compassion ★ Sympathy ★ Altruism ★ Love
★ Dreams ★ Psychic realm ★ Precognition, sixth sense
★ Illusions, magic, fantasy ★ Film ★ Make-believe ★ Art, drama, music, poetry, dance, prose
★ Memory ★ Intuition ★ Unusual talent
★ Sensitivity ★ Humour ★ Satire ★ Secrets ★

Spiritual Pisces

Your Archetypal Universal Qualities
The Compassionate One, Mystic, Dreamer, Psychic

What You Refuse
To stop dreaming or to face reality

What You Are an Authority On
Dreams, fantasy, empathy and psychic insights

The Main Senses Through Which You Experience Reality

Sleep, imagination, intuition, collectivity, forgiveness

Positive Characteristics

★ Loving, caring and compassionate ★ Shy ★
★ Mystical ★ Spiritual ★ Helpful ★ Trusting ★
★ Imaginative ★ Empathetic ★ Sympathetic ★
★ Creative ★ Romantic ★ Adaptable ★ Merging ★
★ Accepting ★ Gentle ★ Understanding of others' shortcomings ★

Negative Characteristics

★ Self-pitying ★ Easily led, impressionable ★
★ Gullible and over-trusting ★ Lacks confidence ★
★ Boundary-less ★ Dependent ★ Weak-willed ★
★ Undisciplined ★ Depressive and temperamental ★ ★ Sensationalist ★ Easily overwhelmed ★ Vague ★ ★ Unsure ★ Escapist ★ Can lose touch with reality ★ Gives up easily ★ Impractical ★ Guilt ★
★ Becomes entangled with others' problems ★
★ Tends to blame self for everything ★

To Bring out Your Best

Meditate, create a work of art, go on a spiritual retreat, swim, take a ghost tour, learn to read the Tarot, capitalise upon your psychic abilities, walk along a moonlit beach.

Spiritual Goals

To learn the meaning of sacrifice without loss of self. To learn boundaries and realise where you 'end' and another begins. To avoid your tendency to 'drift' and miss opportunities through aimlessness, you need to find a creative purpose and voice to express the beauty, pain and duality of your nature.

PISCES

19 February - 20 March

Mutable Water

Ruled by Neptune

"I BELIEVE"

Gemstones ◊ Amethyst, Turquoise, Aquamarine, Bloodstone

★ Understanding, sympathetic, impressionable, romantic, sensitive, imaginative, selfless, weak-willed, artistic, withdrawing, escapist, delusional, timid, introverted, saviour, psychic, insightful, sacrificing, mystical, trusting, poetic, vague, prone to addictions, deceptive, spiritual, gullible, indecisive, perceptive, compassionate, day-dreamer, charitable, unassuming, unreliable, helpless, vulnerable, impractical, idealistic, confused, disorganised ★

PISCES

♓

Romantic ★ Sentimental ★ Idealistic
Poetic ★ Spiritual ★ Sensitive
Intuitive ★ Impressionable

Pisces is the sign of the Fish, two fish swimming in opposite directions but still connected by a cord. Sympathetic, compassionate, caring, spiritual, gullible, impressionable, escapism, psychic, kind, dreamy, and artistic are Pisces' most notable traits. Being a sensitive and feeling water sign, this sign feels its way through life guided by its instincts and well-developed intuition, but being the chameleon of the zodiac, it will often merge into whatever situation it finds itself in. Gentle and impressionable, Pisces is easily swayed and its trusting and weak-willed nature can make it easy prey to undesirable circumstances. The Fish is a self-sacrificing sign who will always put others before itself, always offering a shoulder to cry on, and others often call upon its sympathetic and insightful nature. Escapism is a big thing for the withdrawing Fishes' spirit, and it will quickly retreat into a world of inner fantasy and delusion if the real world becomes too much to bear, making it prone to addictions and ultimately self-undoing. Pisces is poetic, mystical and spiritual, with a love of peaceful surroundings and pleasant company. A selfless and romantic lover, understanding friend and an imaginative artist, Pisces is the twelfth sign and the empathetic healer of the zodiac, swimming in whichever direction that life takes it and always managing to be too slippery to really hold on to, even sometimes to itself.

KEY CONCEPTS
★ Unselfish in all matters ★
★ Self-sacrificing, appeasing ★
★ Vivid imagination, hallucinatory ★
★ Intuitive mind ★
★ Seeks to manipulate or control through giving ★
★ A sensualist in all things ★
★ Slippery, elusive intellect ★
★ Poor sense of individuality ★
★ Universal in scope of expression ★
★ Escapist and delusional ★
★ Self-deceptive ★
★ Strong spiritual aspirations ★

SOME CORRESPONDENCES THAT ARE ASSOCIATED WITH PISCES

Alcohol, mist, mediums, television, fictitious names, spiritualism, mazes, privacy, actresses, swimmers, delusions, actors, imagination, sleep, fishing, photography, submarines, anaesthetics, hidden places, fish, impracticality, aquariums, psychics, footwear, sanitariums, bartenders, fog, petrol, boats, confusion, hospitals, fakes, clairvoyance, shipping, rivers, spirituality, ghosts, convents, coral, naval affairs, séances, poisons, mysteries, drugs, deception, dancers, divers, films, transcendentalism, the feet, fantasy, hidden things, hydraulics, mysticism, pretenders, falsehood, prisons and other places of confinement, retreats, hermitages, muddles, imitation, fountains, aliases, the sea, sensitivity, and dreams. Take your pick and enjoy the ride!

QUOTES BY PISCEANS

"Imagination is more important than knowledge" - Albert Einstein (14 March 1879)

"If it's not growing, it's going to die" - Michael Eisner (7 March 1942)

"I would rather be hated for who I am, than loved for who I am not" - Kurt Cobain (20 February 1967)

"There's something liberating about pretending. Dare to embarrass yourself. Risk." - Drew Barrymore (22 February 1975)

"You have brains in your head. You have feet in your shoes. You can steer yourself in any direction you choose. You're on your own and you know. And you're the one who'll decide where to go" - Dr Seuss (2 March 1904)

"Tonight I'll dust myself off, tonight I'll suck my gut in, I'll face the night and I'll pretend I got something to believe in" - Jon Bon Jovi (2 March 1962)

"There is nothing like a dream to create the future" - Victor Hugo (26 February 1802)

"Dreams have only one owner at a time. That's why dreamers are lonely" - Erma Bombeck (21 February 1927)

"The greatest danger for most of us lies not in setting our aim too high and falling short; but in setting our aim too low and reaching our mark" - Michelangelo (6 March 1475)

"Today you are you that is truer than true. There is no one alive that is youer than you!" - Dr Seuss

"Every day, in every way, I am getting better and better" - Emile Coue (26 February 1857)

"It has been my observation that parents kill more dreams than anybody" - Spike Lee (20 March 1957)

"The most beautiful thing we can experience is the mysterious. It is the source of all true art and science" - Albert Einstein

"What a grand thing, to be loved! What a grander thing still, to love!" - Victor Hugo

"Reality can destroy the dream; why shouldn't the dream destroy reality?" - George Moore (24 February 1852)

"When I read biographies, I'm only interested in the first few chapters. I'm not interested in when people become successful. I'm interested in what made them successful" - Michael Eisner

"Big girls need big diamonds" - Elizabeth Taylor (27 February 1932)

"The only way to do great work is to love what you do. If you haven't found it yet, keep looking. Don't settle. As with all matters of the heart, you'll know when you find it" - Steve Jobs (24 February 1955)

"Great spirits have always encountered violent opposition from mediocre minds" - Albert Einstein

"Some of my best leading men have been dogs and horses" - Elizabeth Taylor

"When a woman gets dressed up to go out at night, she wants to give 50 per cent away, and hold the rest back. If you're an open book, there's no allure" - Alexander McQueen (17 March 1969)

"Believe in love. Believe in magic. Hell, believe in Santa Claus. Believe in others. Believe in yourself. Believe in your dreams. If you don't, who will?" - Jon Bon Jovi

"The position of the artist is humble. He is essentially a channel" - Piet Mondrian (7 March 1872)

"I take pleasure in my transformations. I look quiet and consistent, but few know how many women there are inside me" - Anais Nin (21 February 1903)

"It has become appallingly obvious that our technology has exceeded our humanity" - Albert Einstein

"Love is the ultimate expression of the will to live" - Tom Wolfe (2 March 1931)

"I fell off my pink cloud with a thud" - Elizabeth Taylor

"If one changes internally, one should not continue to live with the same objects. They reflect one's mind and psyche of yesterday. I throw away what has no dynamic living use" - Anais Nin

"All the forces in the world are not so powerful as an idea whose time has come" - Victor Hugo

"And the day came when the risk to remain tight in a bud was more painful than the risk it took to blossom" - Anais Nin

"If you can't explain it simply, you don't understand it well enough" - Albert Einstein

"I'll give up this sort of touring madness certainly, but music - everything is based on music. No, I'll never stop my music" - George Harrison (25 February 1943)

THE PISCES CONSTELLATION

The signs of the zodiac are the twelve symbolic features that ancient people imagined while observing the heavens. They saw shapes, patterns, faces, and natural and supernatural beings in the stars, from which they established, over centuries, a kind of celestial hierarchy and system based upon their observations. Groupings of stars became constellations, and twelve of these constellations make up the zodiac, a Greek word meaning 'circle of animals', that we know today.

Star constellations are not really self-contained groups but are particularly bright stars that give the appearance of being close together and form distinctive patterns. These are the patterns that over the ages have been identified as animals, deities or mythological figures and heroes. The stars are the living past. We receive their light long after it has left the star itself and so they are a good focus for escaping from the parameters of time. Their stellar influence is analogous with the aura, the bio/psychic energy field surrounding humans, animals, plants, crystals and even places. These individual energy systems interact with the energy waves emanated by other people, and even the cosmic rays emitted by planetary bodies, for psychic energies are not limited by time or distance.

The cluster of stars we know as Pisces can only be seen in a very dark sky, and is an unremarkable and faint constellation. Two fish are supposedly represented in this group of stars, joined by a thick line of dim stars.

WISHING UPON YOUR STAR

The practice of wishing upon a star is familiar to most of us, and is a mystical superstition that is ingrained in many of us from childhood. As a night-time ritual, you can wish upon your own sign's constellation or that of the sign whose energies you wish to call forth; indeed, you can wish upon any constellation you feel an affinity with. If you can't see a particular constellation in your night sky, you can always meditate on it in your mind, or you can use the traditional technique of wishing upon the first star you see, while reciting the popular rhyme: *Star light, star bright, first star I see tonight, I wish I may, I wish I might, have the wish I make this night!* Any one of the three rituals will hold power for your own special wish. Good luck!

THE PISCEAN SYMBOL ♓

Astrology uses symbols or 'glyphs' to represent the planets and signs. The glyph is made up of shapes representing the energy and physical matter of which the Universe is composed, and how these shapes are used in each symbol provide hints as to the properties of the sign or planet it represents.

The ancient view was that there were five elements: Fire, Water, Air, Earth and Ether (or Spirit). Ether is invisible energy, while the four tangible elements are known as 'matter'. Ether, as pure energy, cannot be influenced by any of the physical/matter elements, although it surrounds them and indeed fuels them. The Greek philosopher and scientist Aristotle regarded this idea as a circle (Ether/Spirit) with a cross (matter) in the centre. This glyph is used in astrology as a symbol for Earth, and the cycle of life. All the symbols used in astrology represent the relationship between energy and the 'matter' elements.

Pisces is often regarded as the most misunderstood sign of the zodiac, and it certainly merits this appellation, for it embodies a great esoteric principle. The glyph, or symbol, for Pisces is composed of two semicircles, not unlike crescent Moons, with a straight line dissecting them through the centre horizontally. One of these arcs represents the finite consciousness of Man, while the other stands for the infinite consciousness of the Universe, or cosmic consciousness. The centre line is our Earth - said to be that point in the Grand Plan where the spiritual and the material realms unite. The two semicircles could also be interpreted as representing the two fish, one facing down towards deep waters and the other facing up towards the surface of the water.

This symbolism reflects the inherent dualism of the Fish: the urge to connect itself with the invisible forces of the Soul struggling with the desire to merge with and manipulate the material sphere of Man. On a personal level, these diverging currents reflect one of Pisces's greatest internal conflicts: the need to completely sacrifice her own desires for the sake of others, and the need to fulfil her own wishes. It represents that there is always a choice between two apparent opposites: whether to follow the high road or the low road, to go with the current or swim against it, or to express the negative charge or the more positive, Divine charge.

The simplistic symbol is drawn like a pair of parentheses, their backs to each other, with a line across the middle. This simplified glyph can be likened to the image of two fish, back to back, swimming in opposite directions to each other, but still essentially connected (by the cord in the imagery of Pisces, or by the line running through the centre in the symbol). This 'line of force' between the halves can symbolise the burdensome yoke of Karma or ignorance which binds our split or conflicting selves; the split between our spiritual nature and our physical selves, both from which we can never fully swim away from.

The glyph of Pisces indeed is said to represent the two halves of experience, evolutionary and involutionary, placed in opposition to each other but linked. In Pisces the missing link is to be found that will unravel the mystery of the apparently contradictory and irreconcilable character of these two halves. The two fishes that are the symbol of Pisces are creatures that are perfectly at home in the great sea of life, their natural element, and the two complementary phases of experience that they symbolise are, together with the symbolism of Virgo, all that is needed to feed the multitude, according to the parable.

As the part of the body under the influence of Pisces is the feet, this glyph is also believed to represent the two heels tied together, signifying both limitation of movements, and of paying one's dues, or Karma, to the Earth. The feet, being always in some kind of physical contact with the Earth, therefore absorb the vibrations of our Mother planet.

The fish itself which represents Pisces, is a positive symbol which is associated with freedom, abundance and sexuality in different cultures. Because fish are found in the ocean, following the ebb and flow of the tides, they often symbolise the Lunar gods, as well as ultimate freedom from worldly constraints. The fish, one of the oldest forms of life, springs from the very waters of creation. They have a long spine and an ultra-sensitive body. Their fins notice the smallest changes in rhythms and vibrations in the currents of the surrounding water. Sound is louder and travels faster underwater than in air, so the Fish can sense those sounds quicker than most other creatures on Earth. It could be further stated that this extreme sensitivity extends to the Human form - the Piscean person.

THE FISH ANIMAL

Fish have been regarded as powerful luck producers since the early Egyptians made figures of fish in gold and silver to bring luck to lovers. The Romans followed this Egyptian tradition that fish brought luck in courtship and marriage. In China, Japan and other parts of the Far East, and within Feng Shui principles, fish charms are said to bring wealth, luck, good fortune and happiness.

THE AGE OF PISCES ★ 0 - 2000 AD

The Age of Pisces spanned the last two millennia, encompassing the growth of civilisation, society-changing inventions, and industrialisation. This is perhaps the most remarkable period of human history. The beginning of the Age of Pisces coincided with the birth of Jesus Christ, who exemplifies the compassionate, kind, forgiving and self-sacrificing qualities that are typical Piscean traits. In general, the Piscean Age was one of phenomenal change, leading to extraordinary advances. But perhaps also typical of the sign of Pisces, much of this progress involved damage to the environment, peoples and a lack of foresight; too often Pisces is deluded and refuses to face reality. Hopefully any damage done can be repaired and equilibrium restored by the much more future-conscious vibe of the Age of Aquarius.

As we are still on the cusp of the Age of Aquarius, the era in which we are currently living is the Piscean Age. Opinions differ as to precisely when this Age began or when it will end, although almost everyone agrees that we are very close to the end of the cycle, and that its beginning lies somewhere near the onset of the Christian era. If Universal love and compassion encapsulate the main essence of Christ's message, then that message is in keeping with the sign of Pisces. The guilt that humanity has suffered due to its inability to heed the messages of global compassion and harmony until it was too late, has become a rather tragic by-product of the Piscean Age. Furthermore, far too many of us are yet to learn how to throw off the bad habits we contracted in an earlier and wetter age. It seems we are still lurking in Neptune's dark caves searching for illumination in the bottom of a wine bottle or the glowing end of the joint being passed around the circle of life. However, a mighty groundswell is gathering force as we enter into the final years of this era, and we are also beginning to use Neptune's energy in more positive ways.

Pisces and the Piscean Age has taught us that true merging with the collective unconscious involves a surrendering of the personal ego. It has been said that in this Piscean phase of the striving for Universal connection, the soul must face the unknown with simple faith. It is little wonder then, that more than half of the Age of Pisces was known as the Age of Faith. And absolute faith or trust in the Universe is the greatest challenge most Piscean individuals are forced to confront - but it is also your greatest strength.

THE RUNDOWN & LESSONS
SOME QUIRKS, ODDITIES, UNIQUE CHARACTERISTICS AND IDIOSYNCRASIES OF PISCES

"He is stronger than he thinks and wiser than he knows, but Neptune guards this secret until he discovers it for himself."
Linda Goodman

There are two types of thinkers: what I like to call 'right-brainers' and 'left-brainers'. The left hemisphere of the human brain deals with things such as control of speech, verbal functions, logic, reason, mathematics, linear concepts, details, sequences, the intellect and analysis; the right hemisphere is concerned with spatial, music, holistic, artistic concepts, as well as simultaneity and intuition. You could go on to say that the left brain is masculine or yang in quality, and the right brain is feminine or yin in quality. Based upon these very simplistic outlines, it can be further stated that Water sign Pisces dwells mainly in the right hemisphere, with a teensy bit of left thrown in for good measure.

The feeling, flowing nature of Water epitomises Pisces the Fish. Pisces is largely motivated by emotions, feelings and daydreams, all three of which this twelfth and final sign of the zodiac is an expert in. Negative, cool, moist, phlegmatic and slippery, a flexible (Mutable) feeling (Water) approach characterises the sign of Pisces.

Pisces is one of the earliest signs on record; the two fishes appear on an Egyptian coffin lid dated c.

2300 BC. Traditional astrological wisdom describes Pisceans as dreamy, artistic and mystical, and indeed all of these individuals are born with at least one toe dipped in the oceanic depths of the collective mind and Universal consciousness.

Pisces is the last of the Watery signs, is negative in magnetism, and is ruled by the mighty planets Jupiter (traditional) and Neptune (modern). People born under this sign are the softest, pliable and most feminine of the whole zodiac (alongside Cancer) and are therefore vulnerable, able to nurture people and animals, and generally lacking in overt aggression. Pisces is the sign of intense emotional sensitivity, the desire for togetherness and absolute, mystical or religious love. Pisceans can be idealistic and unable to face reality, which can sometimes lead to irrational or fear-based behaviours.

Pisces strives to move beyond personal sensitivity and into higher intuition, ultimately finding emotional security through discernment of spiritual realities based on some type of extra-sensory perception. Your attunement to higher dimensions can lead to brilliant creative expression, or to compassionate service for the greater good.

You are an imaginative, creative, thoughtful, compassionate and philanthropic sign, but your negative side is your tendency to be overly sensitive, changeable and too easily hurt. Sympathetic, dreamy, spiritual, gullible, withdrawn, escapist, psychic and artistic are Pisces' most notable traits. Being a sensitive and feeling water sign, your sign feels its way through life guided by instincts and well-developed intuition, but being the chameleon of the zodiac, you will often merge into whatever situation you find yourself in. Gentle and impressionable, Pisces is easily swayed, your trusting and weak-willed nature, making you easy prey to undesirable circumstances.

However often dismissed you are as weak, when the chips are down you soon prove to be stronger than others realise. Your survival skills are powerful, if for the most part untapped, and your instincts are remarkably sharp, enabling you to always somehow manage to slip out of life's tangled nets.

Inside anyone who has a strong Pisces influence in their natal chart, is someone who makes the most extreme choices of the zodiac. Pisces can accept the challenges of life and rise to the top, or become overwhelmed or engulfed by their emotions and give up completely, sinking to the bottom. This choice is symbolised by the two fishes facing in opposing directions. There is always a little confusion, guilt and sacrifice involved in every decision a Piscean makes, and you will usually take flight rather than fight; your tendency for escapism is very pronounced.

Possessing great and deep faith, the sign of the Fish possesses the endearing quality of unwavering belief in the invisible, psychic and spiritual side of the human experience. This side of things is as real to you as anything else, and sometimes you may ignore tangible realities in order to pursue and live within these 'unseen' forces. Pisceans believe in fairy dust, trolls under bridges and gnomes in gardens; you have belief in miracles, pixies and magic, no matter what 'proof' you are presented with that these things don't - or cannot possibly - exist.

Pisces has the zodiacal distinction of having the most highly developed intuitive and emotional faculties, and you only use your intellect if you need to rationalise what you already know instinctively. No matter what your personal religious beliefs happen to be, there is always a sense in you that life can hold a higher purpose and that finding that purpose is paramount.

You're an imaginative and serene individual with a strong wish to be allowed to live in a world where harsher realities fade into the background and the dreamier aspects can come into focus. You're a very talented individual, and it is indeed important for you to find a channel for your vast creative energies, otherwise you could find yourself slipping into a world of unreality and apathy. You may even find yourself drawn to the world of mind or mood-altering substances as a form of escape. You're the type of person who finds it is important to set aside time each day for meditation, quiet time or artistic pursuits. Quiet activities such as sitting on a beach or listening to soothing music may appeal, in fact any activity which suits your gentle nature. You invariably find yourself drawn to the mystical or spiritual side of life, in particular pastimes or studies which develop your intuition and understanding of the sacred side of life.

Your instinctive behaviour is sometimes stimulated and sometimes inhibited, by intense emotional turmoil. Your personality is inspired and you yearn for intimate and spiritual union with others, but you also tend to be elusive and need your solitude more so than most, or at least be afforded the space to daydream and drift wherever a whim may carry you.

Changeable and deeply feeling, Pisces is the most other-worldly of all the signs, drawing from all the experiences of the previous eleven zodiac signs. Pisces is also both an end and a beginning. The Twelfth House, over which your sign naturally rules, reveals our leftover karmic 'debts' from previous lives, and lessons from the other eleven signs that we haven't yet learned, or that we didn't learn properly the first time around.

Symbolised by two fish, Pisces is mistakenly thought to be a dual-natured sign which is as such torn by dual desires, but this is not the case, for duality belongs to Gemini, the Twins. The two fish swimming in opposite directions represent the choice given to every Pisces: to either swim to the top, or sink to the bottom. Sometimes the Piscean will be so undecided which direction she wishes to swim in, that she will just go with life's flow by default and never quite achieve anything in doing so. After all, the Fish, with eyes that see clearly on both sides, can all too often have difficulty seeing straight ahead.

Being so adaptable and chameleon-like, there is a little bit of everyone in your personality, and this is why you can so easily relate to and empathise with others. Your compassion and non-judgement of other people mark you out as a truly caring and sensitive individual. You are often generous to a fault with your time, money, charity or a listening ear, and you will rarely miss an opportunity to do good or to ease someone else's distress. As well as being generous, you are a romantic dreamer with a vast imagination and highly intuitive resources. You are not unrealistic, as you too often have an undeserving reputation for, in fact you have broad vision and the ability to see the bigger whole-forest picture in its fullest panoramic image in most situations, albeit tripping over the logs and undergrowth directly underfoot, while others struggle with the trees, leaves and other petty details. You don't only want to dream; you want to create a life as beautiful as that which you see in your dreams. This colourful imaginative faculty also makes you a good story-teller who is enchanted by poetry and moved by words, especially if they dance off the page; and you are sure to follow them off the page. Being such a good 'story-teller' can have its drawbacks however; others may accuse you of fabricating or indeed lying your way through life, but these aren't lies to the Piscean spirit; there's never any malicious or cowardly intent behind your tales. Plus, you actually *believe* them yourself, which renders them a kind of slippery truth.

Pisces is not a mentally oriented sign. What a Piscean does, does not stem from reason but from instinct, feeling and flow. For the Piscean there is no such thing as dogma; the Fish can slip through the nets of a rationally developed system of thought as easily as water seeps through a sieve. The Fish is often referred to as the sign of self-undoing, and it is easy to see why: Pisces refuses to be limited or confined by any thing, person or idea if she thinks the ensuing circumstances will inhibit any freedom of thought, movement or emotional self-expression, which can often work against the Piscean, as the very object of the opposition may turn out to be beneficial to her in the long run.

But the world is Pisces's ocean and you must feel that you are at liberty to explore, float, dive, splash and swim about as you choose. Real fish are the perfect metaphor for your tendency to glide through the infinite depths of feeling and fantasies; and while you long for pure water that sparkles and shimmers, you are often pulled down to the darker, murkier depths below. As a result of feeling caged in by a ruthlessly material world, Pisces becomes prone to self-destruction through the consumption of drugs or alcohol, as these at least afford you the freedom so often denied in the real world. This escapism can also often be your way of tuning into the higher thoughts that inspire you artistically and musically, for you are very gifted in these areas, and any current pulling you towards mundane everyday concerns, you will usually fight and thrash against.

Multitalented and able to adapt to a wide variety of situations, you have an other-worldly intelligence which allows you to trust your feelings and follow your heart, enriching your own life and the lives of those around you. Your first instinct is to help the vulnerable, but you too are vulnerable yourself; you may just feign indifference or hide your true spirit, to fool the world that you've got it all together, when the reality is that the Earthly world just isn't yet tuned into the finely-tuned, sensitive Piscean wavelength. Since the depth of your Neptunian waters run so deep and cause you to feel and absorb every pain and sorrow as if it were your own, it's little wonder many

Pisceans pretend they are travelling more lightly than they are.

Your emotional temperament is very up and down, anxious and vague, but being a Mutable sign means you can be unexpectedly resourceful and therefore very resilient. You have a great mental receptivity and innate gift to sense the qualms and feelings of others, to anticipate events or to make the most of pleasant situations. You have latent mystical aspirations, and these, coupled with your rich creative imagination, gives you a leaning towards anything that is poetic and lyrical. Able to rise above the level of material realities and become open to impressions, you may be left confused and bewildered, or else brilliant and inspired. Although you can rise to most challenges, you do have a tendency to experience irrational anxieties and fears and to sublimate your own feelings - leading to your famed escapism or repression - or all too often, both.

On a spiritual level, Pisces is a born medium, priest, clairvoyant, monk or nun, the more highly evolved among you naturally called to the mystic and religious life. In order to live in the material world, you need to learn how to balance the religious or occultist aspirations of your profound inner life with your outer experiences and various Earthly responsibilities. But this is never an easy challenge for Pisces to master.

Although you can be timid, you have a natural flair for theatrical endeavours, as you can hide easily behind an illusion - hence, a great deal many actors and actresses being born under this sign. Even if you never realise the acting inclinations that are so innate in the Fish, at least a part of you will desire it or dream about it at some point in your life. However, this 'ambition' materialises or manifests, to every Pisces, life itself is a huge stage; acting a part and hiding behind veils is your forte. Humour is your secret weapon, your smile can disguise inner tears, you wear laughter as a protective mask, and you are an expert master of satire.

The Piscean memory is legendary, especially memories of feelings and other-realm experiences, although paradoxically, you can often forget your own name. Despondency is always a threatening cloud in the Piscean sky, and you may have peculiar dreams and strange been-here-before nightmares which are often precognitive. When Pisces has even a slight inkling that something will happen, it usually does. You also possess a magnificent imagination and a sparkling elfin humour, and your Neptunian sense of beauty can give rise to the most delicate, ethereal prose and poetry. Indeed, the world would be a colourless and soulless place without your artistic contributions; it could even stop spinning. But you also need privacy and solitude to get on with your art, and in the noisy confusion and chaos of life, you can find this all too difficult. As a result, you may bury your personal dreams for a time. They will always resurface, however, as they are such a part of the fabric of your very being.

Your great Piscean virtues are your intuition and your natural understanding of people and sense of their needs. In fact, you can be so receptive to other people's feelings that you become tangled up in them and don't know which emotion belongs to you and which has been taken on board on behalf of somebody else. And although rarely tactless, you are capable of being hurtful if you feel threatened, however unintended.

You have a tendency also to be an elusive and evasive character, and you will rarely answer a question with a direct yes or no; with Pisces, it's always maybe. You can change as quickly as a flashing fish too, turning on tears one minute and sunny smiles the next. After all, everything is illusory with Pisces, and you often find it hard to discern the difference between light and dark. You are altruistic and filled with an inexhaustible, saint-like sympathetic love for every living being, however, when it is directed inwards it can manifest as self-pity and a 'what-about-me?' demeanour.

Furthermore, the Fish's spirit needs a healthy amount of attention and appreciation. You have to be noticed and encouraged because you are often so uncertain of your own abilities. You can feel like, and come across as, a square peg trying to fit into a round hole; often you will not slot into either, and in schools or workplaces you may have had a hard time trying. But underneath all this, is a person who wishes to conform but simply can't seem to; and the institutions and establishments of the world have yet to catch up with your rare brand of Neptunian wisdom.

You are clever, resourceful, artistic, always creative, and more capable than you are given credit for. However, your weakness is your lack of confidence and a tendency to be overwhelmed by stronger, pushier personalities. Although you are a fair target for bullies, you also have the uncanny ability to slide out of a situation if it doesn't suit you. And you can just as easily slip through nets if circumstances are undesirable or intolerable. But you always suffer a little first.

On a less positive note, being so sensitive and open, it's relatively easy for you to lose yourself in someone else's troubles or personality. Lacking confidence in yourself, you may take the easier option of living through someone else rather than taking on the enormous task of building self-esteem and believing in yourself enough to find your own unique and authentic potential. Because of this, most Pisceans profoundly benefit from someone in their life who encourages them to find and therefore express their *true* selves.

You also have a tendency to slip into self-pity or 'victim' mode, and your sensitivity can make you incredibly vulnerable to rejection and criticism, which can knock your confidence off course and lead you into temptation, addiction or escapism as a form of refuge. Given your broad, panoramic view on life, you can also be indecisive, and often find it so difficult to make choices that you end up doing nothing instead, which can make you appear weak-willed and idle. You can also be naïve and gullible, falling easily for tricks and charms, and winding up feeling lost and confused and back to square one. Taking the easy way out is an ever-present danger for those born under this impressionable sign, but this apparent 'laziness' hides a tumultuous undercurrent - a wasted life, losses through being taken advantage of, or worse.

A Piscean's home is her fairy tale castle. It may be a mansion or a tiny flat, but you feel strongly about it and you will usually try to live in pleasant, peaceful surroundings. You are not necessarily a homebody, nor are you an eternal adventurer, but you fit somewhere snugly in between. You like to be home and put your feet up while watching a romantic comedy or fantasy movie, glass of vino in hand of course, but you also like to be out and about on the social scene. You tend to flit between needing periods of socialising and times of withdrawal and solitude to recharge your easily depleted batteries.

Pisceans often spend quite long spells of their life in an atmosphere which may look attractive but which lacks emotional harmony. You like to be surrounded by friends, and make a gregarious and warm host, and are always glad to have visitors or to get out and visit others. You love conversation and make a wonderful friend, but your nerves are quite delicate and so it is important you try to avoid those who have too many problems, as you are apt to slip away if too many demands are placed upon you.

Most Fish are fond of food and drink and many make excellent cooks. You have a reputation for drinking too much on occasion, however, and you are inclined to go through phases of hitting the bottle, especially during times of stress, chaos or crisis when a form of escape is needed. Pisces is indeed a hard sign to categorise. Your well-known tendency to drink alcohol or to misuse substances arises from your need to run from the harsh realities of life, yet many of you find other forms of escape, such as artistic or dramatic outlets. Sex can also be an escape into another world for the Fish, and you are known to be strongly sexed and deeply sensual; indeed, tantric sex was probably invented by, and for, the Piscean spirit.

Pisceans generally have an easy charm and good nature, albeit are apt to be lazy and too easygoing at times. Most Fish simply ask that they be given the freedom to feel and dream their way through life, and not being a great warrior, you will normally take the path of least resistance. You will, however, fight for the underdog or those on the margins of society, just not in a mighty, triumphant or overt way. Your way of fighting for those less fortunate is to be their shoulder to cry on or to lend them the shirt off your back - and indeed, you never expect them to return it.

You were born to see the world - and indeed the entire Universe - through rose-coloured spectacles. You enjoy life most when the edges have been blurred. Although you know too well the harsher sides of life, you'd much prefer to live in your own dreamy, watery, pink-hued bubble, where everyone is beautiful, all actions come from a pure heart, and everyone gets along peacefully. When life dunks you under the waves and tosses you around like a tumble-dryer, you may not leap out of the murky danger but instead sink to the bottom and hope for the best. In your world at least, the water always returns to calm eventually.

You are sensitive and hurt easily, and if rejected, you are inclined to further deepen your idealistic nature and wallow in false hopes. You are a creature of denial, and Piscean artists are notorious for their indecisive procrastination, often tempted to feel make the corner of your local café your lounge room away from home, revelling in observing others and puffing on pipe dreams, daydreaming the hours away, while your *real* home wonders where you are, when it will be dusted and when the unpaid bills will be attended to.

Most Fish are interested in those matters which are outside the normal realms of daily life. Therefore, they become interested and involved in New Age subjects such as astrology, the Tarot, hypnotherapy, alternative therapies and unconventional philosophies of many varieties. Inherent within your sign is a strong need to understand those forces which cannot be experienced through the physical senses but of which you are deeply aware.

It's a rare Piscean who is found behind a teller's desk or in a mundane office job, for you are usually found in more spiritual or creative realms of occupation and pastime, fields which suit your imaginative and artistic nature and yearnings. The streams of life you like to swim in are often those in the arts or esoteric surroundings. In addition to this, you have very little worldly ambitions and if you do happen to accumulate money or status, it is usually through the company you keep or through an inheritance; rarely will it be through your own striving, for you strive for only one thing: to swim wherever, whenever and with whomever you please. A nine to five structure is as foreign and fatal to you as being, well, a fish out of water.

Pisceans make excellent mediums and spiritual healers, as you seem to represent some kind of thread which joins the world of spirit with the world of practical matters. It has been noted by this author and others anecdotally, that most people who work within the spiritual or New Age realm have either the Sun, Moon or Ascendant in Pisces, or an otherwise prominent Pisces in their birth chart.

Typically, you love children, especially if they are as creative and sensitive as you are. But you cannot cope with determinedly difficult children and may give up on them, leaving stronger members of the family to bring them up or take them over. Your lack of boundaries, dislike of responsibility and cold hard realities, and inability to effectively discipline both yourself and others, is also likely to prove troublesome when it comes to the job of parenting. On the whole, many Pisceans find animals easier to deal with than children.

The Piscean is more prone than most to 'madness', especially if you haven't passed the reality test of the Capricornian phase of the human experience, and can teeter precariously close to the boundary between reality and non-reality. You are the master of camouflage and adaptation, bringing forth the most suitable part of yourself in any situation. You feel the pain of humankind acutely, and one of your greatest challenges is to express empathy without falling into sympathy. Pisceans tend to feel affected or even tormented for a long while after a trauma, sad movie or experience, finding it hard to regain composure in the face of harshness. You are right-brained in nature, with an extreme sensitivity and vivid inner imagery. In fact, if Pisces is strong in the chart, such as the Sun in Pisces, imaginary friends are even likely.

The symbolism of the two fish, tied together by a cord but swimming in opposite directions, offers an apt metaphor for the confusion your sign so often feels. Pisceans are sensitive to the extent of having almost no boundaries, merging with the environment, psychically aware of other levels of existence in the watery depths, but vulnerable to the harsher aspects of Earthly realms. This gives the Piscean opportunity for extremes of spiritual and mystical experiences, but also makes you prone to hurt, confusion, deception and delusion. Escapism is often your easiest way out, and can be channelled into constructive and inspirational routes, such as music and art, but often Pisces can have a tendency to get caught in tangles. If, however, you put your spiritual enlightenment to good use and are tuned in to your inner visions, you are guided to produce the most magnetically hypnotising artistry and achievements known to humankind. Not all Pisceans, of course, are inspired to such heights by the cosmic ocean within; instead you may be easy prey to the addictions mentioned earlier, because you are 'lost at sea' or confusedly swimming in the wrong direction. Which current you choose to swim with will depend largely upon your sense of connection - with that within yourself, and with the Universal 'cord' which binds. You not only make the best alcoholics; you make the best mystics, psychics, 'readers', counsellors, musicians and world-servers.

Collective consciousness is the polar opposite of individual consciousness; in the Fish's character, therefore, the personal ego may be quite weak, while the cordial connection to the Universal wellspring may be exceptionally strong. Consequently, you may be easily influenced, and may come to believe, through listening to others, that your intuition is somehow inappropriate or just plain bent. Many Fish, having been given the gift of vision and prophecy, 'see' things that others are not capable of seeing, and although you perceive impending dangers, you often have no assistance or ability to avert them. You are instead left dangling between two worlds - the Earthly realm that appears to be correct according to everyone else, and the cosmic sphere, which most Fish are all too acutely aware of.

This dilemma is embodied in the symbol for Pisces, those two fish swimming in different directions, but bound together. However, these fish are not swimming in opposite directions as we have always believed. One fish swims upward, toward heaven, while the other fish swims downward, toward an entirely different plane. Therefore, we may conclude that one fish is seeking spiritual illumination while the other concerns itself with matters on the material plane. This constitutes the pressing conflict for the Piscean, who is all too aware of both directions but ever more comfortable in the heavenly realm than in the Earthly, physical one. There are, of course, exceptions to every rule, and some Fish have a love and even a greed for money. Such individuals, cut off from their creative and cosmic inheritance, are rendered spiritually bankrupt and are the ones to fall into the traps of destructive cycles, delusions and addictions.

The Piscean sympathy chord is easily evoked and self-sacrifice is second nature to you; you would think nothing of giving their last dollar or bread crust to someone going through hardship. But you are also gullible and impressionable and can easily be taken advantage of by manipulative others. As a Water sign, you tend to be submissive and usually haven't the slightest, even hidden, desire to control or dominate others. And since the Fish swims in both directions at once, you can adapt brilliantly and quietly to conflicting situations.

More than any other sign, Pisces has the most talents to work with to develop its character to its fullest potential - but more often than not you deceive, self-sabotage or deny yourself the amazing life you were born to live, somehow always holding the sparkling crystal waters a little out of handy reach.

Artistic and creative, you are able to work powerfully with pain and healing if boundaries between yourself and others can be set. Pisces yearns to merge with the collective, and doesn't want to be separate, yet also yearns to be 'invisible', unnoticed and illusory through the use of magic, fantasy, escape and even delusion. You are also the hardest sign to contain; water itself is changeable, adaptable and impressionable, taking on the shape of whatever container surrounds it. In fact, you are particularly vulnerable to suggestion, and this can lead to your self-undoing, which is inherent in all Fishy types.

One amazing quality you possess is that of your peculiar power to stand outside of yourself and see yesterday, tomorrow and today as one; this deep wisdom and knowing comes from another place, non-existent on a mundane, everyday level. But somehow, you know where it comes from - you may not be able to express it in words, but you sense its origins. This profound knowing comes simply from the combined knowledge of every area of human experience.

The Fish is a self-sacrificing sign who will always put others before itself, always offering a shoulder to cry on, and others often call upon your sympathetic and insightful nature.

But you are apt to suffer through victimisation by outside forces and seem to have no real power to rid yourself of such parasites. But despite all your softness and apparent helplessness, you do possess a strong sense of spiritual self and a surprising well of inner strength, which you can draw upon if you can untangle yourself from the seaweed which so often constricts you. Furthermore, being a Mutable sign, you can walk away from a situation or relationship which is no longer viable or spiritually nourishing and adapt to a new one surprisingly quickly and far more successfully and smoothly than other, supposedly stronger zodiacal types.

Symbolically, in this final stage of the astrological mandala, the soul longs only to return to its place of origin. Indeed, as a symbol of the void or cosmic ocean, Pisces is the last of the twelve signs, and is said to contain each of the twelve within it, and it could be said that Pisceans live inside a twelve-sided geometrical figure which encircles them with the multi-faceted dimensions of human experience. Indeed, when the Piscean stage is reached, one has passed through all the possible aspects of the full human cycle - and lived through the other eleven archetypal energies. All aspects, all systems of thought, all desires, all spiritual quests, are gathered in Pisces, and it is for this reason that the Piscean individual can so readily empathise with any situation or issue that arises. And through your whole life, all twelve windows must be considered whenever you take action. Your answers will always come not from a rational viewpoint, but from the heart within - sometimes even all twelve of them, for you have an insight into the collective memory of the whole human race and an ability to call forth a chord of any note.

Astrologers who use the term 'old soul', are referring to a soul which has gone through many lives, absorbing and retaining the wisdom of each. While Aries represents birth in the zodiac, Pisces represents death and eternity. The Fish is the Twelfth and final sign of the zodiacal wheel of life, a composite of all that has gone before, and this endows the Piscean with a blend of all the other signs and house experiences, which is quite a lot for one soul to carry and live out. Karmically, the Fish has learned the collective and individual soul lessons of the other eleven signs, plus its own; this gives the Piscean a profound wisdom and knowing quality that all the other zodiac signs do not possess, at least not in this incarnation. As a consequence, the life of a Piscean can be the most difficult obligation a soul can choose, or it can be seen as a chance to realise perfect spiritual and personal fulfilment, by drawing upon the wisdom from every other sign and area of human wisdom before it. With this in mind, another term for the Pisces experience could be *The Path of Ascension*.

Pisces is poetic, mystical and spiritual, with a

love of peaceful surroundings and pleasant company. A selfless and romantic lover, understanding friend and an imaginative artist, Pisces is the twelfth sign and the empathetic healer of the zodiac, swimming in whichever direction that life takes you.

Some planets in Pisces in the birth chart are more comfortable in these watery realms than others; the Sun is not so strong in the sign of the Fish. The Piscean personality is often so diluted by its merging with the world around it that the Fish's ego (or Solar energy) may feel like a tiny raft adrift in a vast, but ever shimmering, sea.

LESSONS TO BE LEARNED FOR GREATER POWER, ENLIGHTENMENT & LUCK

Piscean problems and ultimate undoing's arise through your inability to deal effectively with life's harsh elements, burying your head in the sand, denial, delusional thinking, your innate confusion and indecision, and escapism when things become too difficult. You can be manipulative, whether knowingly or not, finding it hard to distinguish truth from reality, and your habit of reneging on promises makes you unreliable. You often play the victim/saviour role too and sometimes sacrifice the self to help others. You may lack boundaries and not know when to stop giving or to simply say 'no'; guilt and confusion often ensues. You are also gullible, impressionable and easily swept away with the current, so you need to learn how to tap into your naturally intuitive side, and discern with a sharper mind to avoid the disappointments and setbacks, from which you find it so difficult to recover.

It is not hard to find 'watery' metaphors when it comes to speaking of Pisceans, for their characteristics are often those reminiscent of the sea, with its hidden depths, sudden storms, and strong and shifting currents. But these powerful emotional undercurrents can work for or against you, and many Pisceans will use their feelings as a fallback or an excuse to keep them from facing reality and the real truth about themselves, keeping them on the path of least resistance, but which can too easily lead to indolence, laziness and inactivity. Some of the world's most inspired artists have Pisces prominent in their birth charts, and have been able to put their emotions to constructive use through their art. But diffuseness and lack of purpose can all too easily consume the Fish's deeply feeling nature, and turn your emotions in on yourself - and all will be lost in the process. Chaos may also reign supreme when you let your emotions overcome you, and although you come across as soft, gentle, humble, unassuming and innocently charming, your friends - and even you - may not notice the turbulence swirling inside. To combat this, look to more practical others for support, and to help bring you back down to Earth occasionally. Even though you can use your feelings in positive ways to create delightful masterpieces in your field of choice, all too often you can slip under the surface and find it hard to resurface. Further, it is not easy for the Fish to conform; you cannot cope with discipline or routine, and will not run your life in anything that resembles a regimented or orderly existence. But you will find that if you slowly work a bit of routine in your life (in baby steps), over time you will become more comfortable with the idea, and even more satisfied with a more predictable and less disorganised existence. Pisceans need to challenge themselves, take bigger risks, be more assertive, develop extra applications for their compassion, and foster more courage - and once all your inner demons are confronted, you may not find it as hard to live in the real world as you've always suspected it might be.

Believing in the reality of your inner vision and listening to your secret heart can lead to your greatest strengths and your weaknesses. When you are grounded firmly in deep intuitive faith, your spiritual and moral qualities flourish as you draw inspiration, assurance, self-respect and understanding from that deep well. As you are not ambitious in the normal sense of the word, for you serve unmaterialistic ideals, your inward gaze can leave you drifting, floating, feeling guilty, and unable to say no; victimisation, addictions and self-deception can all follow on. Your higher motives and depth of understanding become powerful assets when they are channelled and focused with greater force and discipline.

You have the inborn ability to permeate, renounce, sacrifice yourself and receive impressions from all directions and sources. Versatile, sensitive, kind to others, you love to dream but find it difficult to be practical. You lack, and therefore need to cultivate, a greater practical outlook, willpower, more determination and persistence, the powers of focus and concentration, and the ability to say no to associations and substances which enable you to escape. Through incorporating more of these qualities and characteristics into your personality, you will evolve, grow, glow and simply flow - and may even be allowed to keep your rose-coloured glasses on as you go!

THE THREE DECANS OF PISCES

Decans are thirty-six groups of stars that rise in a particular order on the horizon throughout each Earth rotation. These decans were developed in Egypt thousands of years ago. The rising of each decan marked the beginning of a new 'decanal hour' of the night for these ancient people, and eventually three decans were assigned to each zodiac sign. Each decan covers ten degrees of the zodiac wheel, and is ruled by different planetary rulers that rule over the other two signs of the same element (and a traditional ruler, when only seven of the planetary bodies were known). Decans continued to be used throughout the Ages, in astrology and in magic, but many modern astrologers, for whatever reasons, tend to disregard them. Following are brief descriptions for each decan of Pisces. Which one do you belong to? Can you relate to the description and the energies of your decan's ruling planet?

FIRST DECAN PISCES ★ February 19 - 29

Ruler ★ Saturn (traditional *) / Neptune (modern)

Keyword ★ Perceptive

First Decan Pisceans' Three Special Tarot Cards
The Moon, Knight of Cups & Eight of Cups

Birthdays in this decan range from 19th to 29th February. This is the Pisces decan, ruled by Saturn * and Neptune. Saturn's lucidity and reason, coupled with Neptune's emotional receptivity, may make you intelligent and perceptive, but also anxious and misanthropic. Pisceans born during this decan tend to be visionary, largely impractical and have a powerful imagination, perceiving beauty and poetry in everyone and everything. This is the decan of spirituality, and those born under its influence are romantic, selfless and deeply intuitive. You can sense the moods and feelings of those around you, and are sensitive to atmosphere and emotional depths. You make a wonderful friend and a gifted healer, possessing good listening skills and a strong empathetic streak; you are glad to help others and to help carry their burdens as your own. Although you are a great empath, you take on others' pain as your own and this can lead you down a path of your own self-imposed pain, leading to the Piscean tendency toward self-medicating. You take a positive and optimistic view on life, but this can border on naiveté as you seldom see the bad in others, making you easily taken advantage of by devious or ruthless characters. This decan is the bohemian artist's dream come true, for you are able to play the inspiring muse for others' creativity in fields such as music, dance and the arts - and may even take on a lead role yourself.

SECOND DECAN PISCES ★ March 1 - 10

Ruler ★ Jupiter (traditional *) / Moon (modern)

Keyword ★ Open-minded

Second Decan Pisceans' Three Special Tarot Cards The Moon, Knight of Cups & Nine of Cups

Birthdays in this decan range from 1st March to 10th March. This is the Cancer decan, ruled by Jupiter * and the Moon. Pisceans born during this decan have a strong connection with the Moon, making you moody, withdrawn and dreamy. The double presence of Jupiter, as both this decan's traditional ruling planet and Pisces's secondary ruler, exalts the qualities of your Neptunian side. Therefore, generosity, self-sacrifice, nobility of spirit and spiritual concerns join together with an intense sensuality, extreme emotions, the ability to adapt, and a surprising gift for persuasion. Your decan's traditional association with Jupiter also makes you the most slippery fish of the three Pisces decans, making you elusive, mysterious, other-worldly and intriguing. However, your deep sensitivities, intuitive powers and impressionable nature can make you easy prey for the shadowy worlds of addictions, escapism and fantasies, and you can be quickly drawn into overindulgence of sex, drugs, alcohol or more powerful others who can exert a profound 'spell' over you; you are advised to steer clear of any such influences for they will all too easily consume you. You are likely to be changeable, versatile and enjoy delving into the deeper meanings of life, and are incredibly psychic and spiritually-oriented, *if* you are able to tap into these abilities and not swim away from them. As you are such a sensitive, deep-feeling soul, you sometimes experience mood swings and extremes of emotions, being elated one minute and dwelling in the pits of despair the next; these mood changes can mar your self-confidence and erode your self-esteem. But this influence also makes you imaginative, caring, sympathetic and supremely absorbent of your environment - which of course can work for or against you. Second decan Pisceans are characterised by a trusting, kind and giving nature, only seeing the best in others. You have the potential to be a great healer or miracle worker, as you are always one spiritual step ahead in the dance of life.

THIRD DECAN PISCES ★ March 11 - 20

Ruler ★ Mars (traditional *) / Pluto (modern)

Keyword ★ Receptive

Third Decan Pisceans' Three Special Tarot Cards The Moon, Queen of Wands & Ten of Cups

Birthdays in this decan range from 11th March to 20th March. This is the Scorpio decan, ruled by Mars * and Pluto. This is the most powerful personality of the decans for this sign. Pisceans born during this decan are characterised by experimentalism, a rich mental imagery, dynamism, charm and romanticism. Highly attuned to your intuitive and psychic connections, spirituality and soul-searching play big parts in your life. Jupiter and Neptune, rulers of Pisces, confer a great kindness on Mars, ruler of this decan, making you particularly receptive and attentive to others, and ensuring your actions are always sublimated. You are understanding, hyper-emotional, touchy, deeply sensuous, and passionate. You are a deep thinker who has the potential to produce moving and poignant poetry, music and performances. To anything you consider worthwhile, you unwaveringly and wholeheartedly devote your time, energy, heart and attention. A natural romantic, relationships and sensual pleasures also play big roles in your life, and you are endearing, charismatic and magnetising, attracting many admirers to you, but your changeable nature and your innate dreaminess and tendency to indecisiveness can prove a challenge to achieving sustained, intimate relationships. Third decan Pisceans are characterised by redemptive qualities, the ability to intuit others' feelings and motives, and powerfully intense psychic faculties, which can be used constructively or destructively. You possess mysticism, musical talent, and a strong imagination, which, when combined with your visionary ambitions, can help you rise to dizzying heights. You would make an excellent actor or magician, as you have a chameleon-like nature which can adapt subtly or dramatically, depending on the situation, to suit your surroundings. You aim high and imagine big, not stopping until your dreams materialise. You know no bounds and perceive no boundaries; the sky for you is indeed the limit.

* The decan's traditional ruler based on the Chaldean order of the planets

YOUR ELEMENT ★ WATER

According to the *Oxford English Dictionary*, the word *element* has a mysterious origin, and was first found in Greek texts meaning 'complex whole' or 'a single unit made up of many parts'. From the ancient up to medieval times, there were only four elements - Earth, Air, Fire and Water - and the occult-oriented also believed in a fifth: Spirit, or Ether. (Cornelius Agrippa called Spirit the 'quintessence'.)

Alchemy is a tradition of visions and dreams, and images can combine on different levels of reality. Alchemists have long used images in their illustrations to express the enigma and mystery of their art, and to include all dimensions of our experience. The traditional worlds of Earth, Water, Fire and Air symbolise these dimensions very well. Broadly speaking, and in human terms, Earth corresponds to the level of the body and the senses, Water to the flow of thoughts and feelings, Fire to inspiration and energy, and Air to the world of the higher mind and intellect. Each of these worlds has its own realm of imagery. Pisces belongs to the realm of the Water element.

★ The Emotional Group ★

The Path to SPIRITUALITY

Focused on Emotion and Feelings

Alchemical Associations ★ The Subconscious, Quicksilver and the Colour White

Key Attributes ★ Sensitivity, Flexibility, Intuition, Creativity, Feeling

Symbolism ★ Healing, Reflection and Cleansing

Governed by ★ The Soul and the Feelings

Water Characteristics ★ Subjective, Emotional, Intuitive, Sensitive, Imaginative, Receptive

★ THE MAGIC OF WATER ★

Water is the flow of emotions, the tide that carries you out to sea and will bring you back to a safe shore after your whimsical adventures. It can be placid or tempestuous, and without it life cannot flourish. It can cause your dreams to carry you away on the waves, without anchoring your aspirations. You can sink or swim in Water, having nothing to cling to for support, as it has no form, shaping itself into its surroundings. It needs a container to prevent your dreams being swept away; cups, goblets and bowls are often associated with water, and the term 'Holy Grail' describes your greatest desires.

The sage is like water.
Water is good, nourishes all things,
and does not compete with them.
It dwells in humble places that others disdain;
hence it is close to the Tao.
In his dwelling, the sage loves the Earth.
In his mind, he loves what is profound.

In his associations, he is kind and gentle.
In his speech, he is sincere.
In his ruling, he is just.
In business, he is proficient.
In his action, he is timely.
Because he does not compete,
he does not find fault in others.
Lao Tzu (604-517 BC)
***Tao Te Ching,* VIII**

★ KEYWORDS ★

Impressionable, compassionate, reflective, insightful, merging, fertile, receptive, absorbing, responsive, habitual, perceptive, secretive, submissive, possessive, nurturing, sensitive, clingy, dependent, instinctive, emotional, sympathetic, intriguing, protective, empathetic, psychic, mysterious *

* All these words don't necessarily describe all three Water signs. Pisces, for example, is not possessive, and Scorpio is not submissive.

Water is the most important element of all, for without it there would be no life on planet Earth. Without Water the land would not be fruitful or fertile, but dry and sterile. It has long been revered as the wellspring of life, enabling human civilisations to grow and flourish across the planet. The ancients understood the generative energy inherent in Water, and it has given rise to many myths, stories, superstitions and symbolism. For example, the chalice, a vessel for holding this element, is a legendary symbol of abundance and spiritual power. The Moon and its compelling influence on the seas and female reproductive cycles, is strongly linked with the Water element and its deeply feminine nature.

As the ultimate source of life and growth, Water is the most significant element in terms of regeneration and metamorphosis. Water follows a relatively unchanging cycle, going from a liquid state to a solid state, and according to scientific observations, reproduces itself around thirty-four times in the course of the terrestrial year. Under the combined influence of the movement of the Earth's rotation upon itself and of gravity, water shapes the Earth's surface. The perpetual motions and meandering courses of all the bodies of water on the surface of the globe, as well as the numerous currents, are caused by this terrestrial rotation, and also by the movements of the Moon around our planet. By the same token that water is the source of life - by drinking it or immersing yourself in it, you can regain your strength, satisfy a primary need, quench your thirst, be regenerated, and be washed and cleansed.

Water is the Universal Solvent, and the Universal Coagulant in the alchemical laboratory of nature. The Sun of Life, the Ego, passes through the waters of parturition in three definite stages symbolised by the Watery signs. They are the most primitive of all the animals depicted in the zodiac: the scorpion, the fish and the crab. The different astrological animal and human symbols, are said to represent the hierarchical instincts (e.g. aquatic, deep, dark) and the temperament of each creature or human type - our primal, instinctive and unconscious sides. Two of the Water signs - Scorpio and Cancer -

are symbolised by half land-half water creatures, amphibious and flexible, but the Fish that represents the sign of Pisces can't breathe air and must live eternally in the cool water, sometimes muddy, sometimes clear, but always flowing.

In Greek mythology, Poseidon (Neptune to the Romans) rules the oceanic and water domains. Symbols and images most associated with the Water element include mermaids, wells, reservoirs, swimming, fish, crabs, lakes, rivers, dolphins, whales, diving, water-skiing and boating.

Water has long been associated with the powers of birth and regeneration, representing the feelings and healing energy. Ancient people built their settlements close to the life-giving rivers, streams and springs that became the source of several magical traditions and beliefs. In most cultures, wells, lakes and ponds were worshipped and venerated. Offerings were dropped into the watery depths in return for blessings - a ritual that survives today in the form of a wishing well.

Pulled by the Moon, the tides of Water can help you attune to change. The unpredictable nature of the waves and tides can be overwhelming however, and it's for this reason that Water brings powerful emotions to the surface, where they can be purged. Working with Water in your daily magic rituals can restore your spirit, increase your sensitivity, awareness and receptivity, and gently renew your faith in the flow of the Universe.

Astrologically, Water is associated with the feeling principle and function, representing the emotional realm. Its primary motivating force is deep yearnings. It is characterised by emotional depths, compassion and perceptions. Water signs are sensitive, experiencing life through their feelings. Attuned to delicate nuances, they can be dependent and vulnerable, often misinterpreting signals through the bias of their own feelings. When the intuitive function is working well, Watery signs can access an inner level of knowing that goes beyond the five physical senses.

Water is a paradoxical element and represents integration, dependence, merging, blending and union. Cancer represents personal development, Scorpio represents interpersonal development, and Pisces represents transpersonal development. The Water signs, living in the fluid world of emotion and feeling, express themselves in these differing ways: Cancer, through a great nurturing compassion, especially in home and family affairs; Scorpio, through its enormous sexual intensity and capacity, and its fascination for, and immersion in, the ultimate forces of life and death; and Pisces, through its acute sensitivity to the environment and its strongly developed depth of subconscious Universal undercurrents. The Water signs are feminine in polarity, introverted in expression.

Water signs are empathetic, attuned to others' feelings, and reflect the world around them as a reaction to how they feel. They experience the world subjectively. Water knows no boundaries and locates itself in the past, giving it a strong sense of memory and past experience. Often vulnerable to and overwhelmed by their emotions, their most appropriate outlets are expressed spiritually and artistically, or alternatively, to withdraw, hide, protect, deny, escape or defend.

Water, symbolic of the 'Great Mother', is the fountain of life and the source of all things, associated with birth, transformation, purification and movement. Deep, purifying and cleansing, it can symbolise the unending cascade of spiritual energy. But this movement can have its downside: although on the surface Water signs may appear calm, docile and placid, underneath there can be restlessness and deeper motivations brewing, for like the ocean, Watery people have many cross-currents. They are fearful of any form of confinement, and can therefore be extremely secretive about their true intentions or emotional undercurrents, making them at once enigmatic and mysterious.

As the element suggests, Water is sometimes turbulent, sometimes flowing, sometimes deep and murky, merges with its surroundings, and almost always fluid. Psychic, penetrative and intuitive, Water signs rely on instincts rather than logic. Acutely aware of the pain, feelings, suffering and thoughts of others, they are extremely sympathetic and will often put others' needs ahead of their own. Indeed, Water signs have an immense insight into human nature, making it hard for others to 'hide' around them; they dig, probe and 'feel' around to get to secrets and hidden matters. Although inherently private, Water signs can always be counted on for emotional support, sound advice and a receptive ear. Given that their self-expression is quite subtle, truly knowing a Water sign often involves a long but worthwhile learning process. Whether a nurturing Cancerian, intense

Scorpio or an empathetic Piscean, Water signs are complex, deep, introspective and anything but frivolous. While Water types can be moody, changeable, over-sensitive and irritable, they can also be affectionate, playful, humorous and loyal.

The Water element is connection-seeking, fluid, and paradoxically powerful yet powerless, representing the strongest and weakest traits of the human experience, moves around obstacles, is chaotic by nature, has a sense of oneness, is life-giving and life-sustaining, purifying, rebirthing, feels 'in the moment', is wise and understanding on deeper levels, is boundless, aroused by empathy and passion, is never the same, feels others' feelings, can be a curse or a blessing, absorbs feelings and can lose itself in its response, can operate out of others' feelings, is generally unconditional, is creative, past-dwelling, nurturing, sensuous, surrendering and sacrificing, has depth of self, has emotional integrity, contains itself or allows its feelings to gush forth depending on the situation, can idealise suffering, shies from the mundane world, is relentless, eroding, nostalgic and sentimental, and has a great capacity for depth in union. Watery temperaments have an innate capacity for sympathy, protectiveness, romance, empathy, intuition, psychic insights and sensitivity, but can be subject to secrecy, and can suffer mysterious, unfathomable moods. They can also be hidden, escapist, evasive, dependent, manipulative, 'slippery' and elusive.

The Water element puts a strong emphasis on relationships and they are compassionate and responsive to others' needs, especially if Cancer or

Pisces predominate. Scorpio is a little less subtle than the other two, being ruled by Pluto and having a tendency towards more hidden, penetrative and occasionally explosive behaviour; passion and intensity are also Scorpio traits which the other two express much more gently.

Overall, Water is the cleansing, purifying element, necessary for all life. It is the major component of the human body and is associated with our lymph systems. In the form of rain, it nourishes the Earth, promoting and enabling fertility and growth. Water is formless and meandering, and it connects, enters and merges, while still retaining its own essence. It needs the freedom to flow and like the tides, it has its own behaviours and rhythms. Sensitive to stimuli, it is highly receptive, absorbing that which comes into contact with it, and often encompasses or envelopes those things. Self-contained and protective, Watery types are able to experience the contentment of simply being, continually replenishing themselves from their inner reservoirs. These types are flowing, and oriented towards forming connections and blending with their surroundings. Highly instinctive and feeling, they are attuned to unseen realms, and possess a psychic sensitivity which enables them to excel at nonverbal communication and to hear and receive unspoken emotions. They are also imaginative, dedicated to their ideals, introspective and creative. Although some Watery types may not consider themselves religious, they have a heightened sensitivity to spiritual disciplines and forces, and so are naturally drawn to these areas by their very natures.

Water is encouraged to experience emotions without repressing or being overwhelmed by them, achieve inner emotional security, and to handle intuitive and psychic sensitivities adeptly, that is, without becoming engulfed by them and through being both open and self-protective.

Positive Water Qualities ★ Empathic, feeling-oriented, flexible, compassionate, sensitive, responsive, deep, intuitive, receptive, nurturing, adaptable, caring, devoted, self-contained, retentive, protective, attuned to the unseen, imaginative, private, introspective, idealistic, flowing, understanding, resourceful, spiritual, psychically aware

Negative Water Qualities ★ Secretive, wallowing, evasive, closed, cynical, overly subjective, brooding, self-absorbed, oversensitive, disillusioned, elusive, overly emotional, passive, waterlogged, clingy to past, moody, gullible, self-pitying, overwhelmed, inaccessible, hidden, manipulative, resigned, withholding, timid, expect too much, irrational, muddled thinking, directionless, devitalised by fears which focus on negatives, takes everything personally, blaming, indecisive, insecure, vindictive, unrealistic, confused, dependent/co-dependent, symbiotic, compulsive, drifting, regressive, impressionable.

THE ARCHANGEL OF WATER ★ GABRIEL

An archangel is an angel of greater than ordinary rank. They possess a stronger, more powerful essence than the guardian angels, through overseeing and guiding the other angels who are said to be with us here on Earth. The word 'angel' derives from the

Greek word *angelos* meaning 'messenger'. To humans, angels are often seen as bringers as all sorts of messages. Angels in all their forms are believed to bring the message of 'spirit' into matter, carrying the blueprints of creation and the Source from the Divine into the manifest world. Angels are not and never have been human; they, like fairies and nature spirits, are part of a different evolutionary pattern – but they do appear to us in human form (usually with wings) because that is what we understand. An angel can be in many different places at once, and with the same intensity and concentration, and wish for us to be aware of them and benefit from them.

There are said to be three categories of angels in the cosmos, each with three subdivisions *. 'Angel' is the generic term and also relates specifically to those closest to the physical. Similarly, archangel may be taken to mean any of the higher orders, and indeed signifies the order just above ordinary 'angel'. Found in a number of religious traditions, the word 'archangel' itself is usually associated with the Abrahamic religions. The word archangel is of Greek origin, and means literally 'chief angel'. All archangels end with the 'el' suffix, 'el' meaning 'in God' and the first part of the name meaning what each individual Angel specialises in. The archangel who rules your sign will be the one with whom you most resonate. The astrological sign is an energy signature, a matrix of a specific stellar pattern that will subtly affect and influence you. Although there are many associations for the great archangels of the Universe, we must keep in mind there is great overlapping in their duties and guidance. For example, we may say that one is for healing and another for protection, but they can all perform the functions of the others, and each has only areas of greater focus and responsibilities. Four of the multitude of archangelic beings work intimately with the Earth. These are Raphael (Air), Michael (Fire), Gabriel (Water) and Uriel (Earth). Associated with each of these archangels are one of the four elements, specific colours, one of the four directions or quarters of the Earth, three signs of the zodiac, and a variety of other energies and powers. Understanding these associations and considering them in relation to our own paths, can help us determine with which of them we are more likely to resonate. Your sign, being of the Water element, vibrates to the essence of Gabriel.

* The first sphere, the *Heavenly Counsellors*, comprises Seraphim, Cherubim and Thrones. The second sphere, the *Heavenly Governors*, comprises Dominions, Virtues and Powers. The third sphere, the *Heavenly Messengers*, comprises Principalities, Archangels and Angels. Of course, all such classifications are a human construct, a way of placing order upon the unknowable and allowing us to perceive something about which we have no words to express. However, as long as we think of angelic hierarchies as a way of working with celestials, of remembering important attributes, and we are able to imagine and experience these beings, this order of angels will prove useful to those wishing to draw upon their messages and assistance.

★ ARCHANGEL GABRIEL'S ASSOCIATIONS ★

Element of Water
The Western quarter of the Earth
The winter season
The colours emerald, silver and sea green
The crystals opal, fluorite and moonstone
The astrological signs of Cancer, Scorpio and Pisces

Gabriel, meaning "Strength of God" or "The Divine is my strength," is known as the messenger and can help us to find our true soul's purpose. As archangel of the Moon and ruler of dreams, Gabriel is chief archangel of the night and the alter ego of Michael, the Sun archangel. Some consider Gabriel a feminine energy. The archangel of life, hope, truth, astral travel, unconscious wisdom, illumination and love, he inspires and motivates artists and communicators, and delivers important prophetic messages to people. He guards the sacred places of the world and the sacred waters of life. Gabriel provides intuitive teaching, guidance, mystical experiences, inspiration and enlightenment of spiritual duties, including awakening within us a greater understanding of dreams. He can be called upon when you are feeling alone, afraid or vulnerable. Gabriel is said to be the angel who chooses the souls to be born and cares for them in the womb. He is also an angel of death, but a gentle one, bringing release from sorrow and pain.

PISCES'S ZODIAC ARCHANGEL ★ TZAPHKIEL

Additionally, each sign is associated with a particular archangel. Such knowledge can help you to build up a relationship with these beings, based upon your strengths and needs. However, no link is rigid, and as you work with angels you will come to develop your own affinities. When invoking a specific archangel, a useful ritual to draw them closer is to light a candle in that angel's colour, burn some oil or incense of its scent, and hold the appropriate crystal while focusing on what you are needing guidance on.

YOUR ARCHANGEL ★ Tzaphkiel is understood as a feminine presence and is close to Sophia, the 'mind of God'. Tzaphkiel is a capable nurturer and encourages mystical states, altered consciousness and the blessings of an open heart. She reveals other realities and the mysteries of the Universe and Source. Tzaphkiel can help you release the thoughts, feelings or pressures that emanate from others, as well as releasing tension and bringing deep emotional healing.

SCENT/OIL ★ Clary sage

CANDLE COLOUR ★ Lilac

CRYSTAL ★ Labradorite or purple fluorite

THE DEVIC REALMS & WATER ★ WEST: REALM OF THE UNDINES

"Through magick we do conjure the Elements, evoking unto us the special properties of the Life-force for our learning and our coming-into-light. And yet are there secret paths of knowledge that have fallen from the minds of men ... For the way of Magick is a path to sacred knowledge, of reverence and humility - and the world is a wondrous place. Yet how many amongst us have fathomed these depths?"
***Merlin's Book of Magick and Enchantment*, Nevill Drury**

Deva is a Sanskrit word that means 'shining one'. Devas are the life force within nature, and there are four devic realms - Fire, Earth, Air and Water - which contain ethereal elemental spirits or sprites. Elementals are the building blocks of nature, and close to being true energy and consciousness. The four elements correspond to four different states of matter: energy/transmutation (Fire), gas (Air), liquid (Water) and solid (Earth), which are linked to the four human states of consciousness: inspiration, thought, feeling and practicality. There are four spirits, or elementals, which reside in the devic realms, associated with each element. People have been painting pictures, telling stories and writing about these devic realms for hundreds of years, albeit sometimes through disguised mediums such as fairy tales or children's fantasy stories like Tolkien's *Lord of the Rings*. The power of the natural world is easily observed and since ancient times primal forces have been ascribed to various spirit beings. Belief in nature spirits is of such ancient origin and is Universal; cultures everywhere have names or words to describe them. In the sixteenth century, a famous Swiss physician, alchemist and mystic called Paracelsus * defined these beings as 'Elementals', classifying them according to the element of nature they inhabit. There are four main levels of elemental beings: Gnomes (Earth), Undines (Water), Sylphs (Air), and Salamanders (Fire). The fifth element of Ether is the element from which came forth the other four, and Ether, or Spirit, has never been defined in any particular category, and encompasses the aspects and beings of all the other elements.

Elementals are usually benevolent guardian beings or spirits that look after nature's secrets and treasures in whatever part of the natural realm they occupy. They can only be seen or 'felt' by those possessing heightened psychic abilities, yet they can be summoned by those practising alchemy, spells and magic in order to harness the forces of nature for their own particular intentions. In our modern lives, it may seem as though this magic doesn't exist, but the truth is that most of us are simply less in touch with it than ever before. The consequence of this is that we are destroying vast areas of land, polluting waters, creating toxic landscapes, and disrespecting the laws of nature, which often whisper their messages softly. It is therefore important for us to look at the beauty that surrounds us with true appreciation and genuine regard, and to open ourselves up to the magic resides within it. The four devic realms can teach us much about nature; they act as custodians for the four elements, and learning to work with them is a way of attuning to all the energies and beings of nature. Elementals are four-dimensional, and have nothing to obstruct their movements. Therefore, they move as easily through matter as we do through air and space. They do require some contact with humans for their own evolution. Helping to direct them is an overseer, traditionally called the King of that element, and an archangel. Each of these elements is affiliated with one of the four directions and each elemental spirit embodies its own special energy. If you wish to re-connect and re-harmonise yourself by working with nature and its messages and lessons, you could begin by learning a little about your element's realm: Your element is Water, which is connected with the West direction and the realm of the Undines.

* Paracelsus is considered the most original medical thinker of the sixteenth century. His belief in supernatural beings, intuition and the invisible causes of illness helped him discover hydrogen and nitrogen. Paracelsus believed that "Elementals are unlike pure spirits for they are mortal, but they are not like man for they have no soul."

★ UNDINES ★

Undine is from the Latin *unda*, meaning 'wave', and therefore these spirits are said to control the waters of the Earth. Undines are perhaps the best known of the four elementals as they appear frequently in stories and legends. Usually female nymph-like beings, they are beautiful, eager to tempt, and enjoy associating with humans. They like to lure with their musical enchantments, creating sweet, intoxicating melodies with their harps, or singing pure, uplifting songs for those who are still and near enough to listen. Found wherever there is a natural source of water, the undines are responsible for the vitality within liquids and they also work with plants that grow underwater. All water upon our planet - rain, rivers, oceans, lakes, et cetera - has immense undine activity. Undines, like the gnomes, are subject to mortality, but they are more enduring. They are dependent upon humans for growth, and as we evolve, so do they.

One of the most famous of the Water elementals is the Lady of the Lake who features in the legends of King Arthur. This undine beauty rose from her lake to present Arthur with the sword Excalibur and captured the hearts of many of the Knights of the Round Table. The undines govern the realm of autumn and Water, the west, and the Cups in the Tarot deck. In many religions, water symbolises the initiation through baptism in the 'waters of life'. In ancient times all great rivers were considered holy and sacred, without which nothing could prosper; springs, wells, ponds, pools and fountains were regarded as holy places where great healing properties and energies could be found and prophecies foretold.

The Undines work to maintain the astral body of humans and to stimulate our feeling nature. This is associated with heightened psychic functions as well as emotional ones. Theirs is an energy of intuition, creation and birth. Undines guard and carry the secrets of the Dreamtime, inner visions, emotions, feelings and journeys.

Water is the springwell of life, and these beings are essential to our finding that springwell within. Essential to the gifts of healing, purification and empathy, they work with humans to help us discover both our inner and outer beauty. Human beings are made of around 75 per cent water, which acts as a channel or stream for all physical and chemical changes to occur; and the same percentage again is echoed by our planet's water composition - three quarters of the Earth's surface is covered by seas, rivers and oceans, which are governed by the Moon, which provides a natural rhythmical rulership over planetary phenomena. Folklore says that water gives to us what we give to it. The undines, who dwell in the Watery realms, will indeed do the same. The King of Water is Llyr or Niksa, its archangel is Gabriel, its magickal tool is the Cup (which calls down the spirits into form), and its sacred ceremonial stones are Amethyst, Moonstone and Pearl.

INVOKING THE WATER DEVAS

Water represents flow and change – in many myths crossing a stream signifies a shift in consciousness, all cultures regard water as the biggest life-giving source, and baptism is a rite of passage in some religions. Water is mysterious, moody and changeable. Water devas embody all of these attributes and most are hauntingly beautiful. Water can be a tricky medium to work with, but overall they help to connect you with the wellsprings of your feelings, bringing sympathy, empathy and the bonds of human love. If you are feeling raw, lonely, sad, uncared for or buffeted by life, ask the water devas for their help. Undines will give you blessings when you are going into any situation that requires deep emotional strength. They can be found in any body of water, the tides and rains, in mists and in fogs, and are purifying, healing and cleansing.

THE WEST DIRECTION'S CORRESPONDENCES

If you wish to work more with your particular element and direction, the following may help propel your wishes and magical journey:

Time of Day ★ Sunset
Polarity ★ Female, negative
Exhortation ★ To know
Musical Instruments ★ Strings, bells
Colours ★ Blue, green
Season ★ Autumn
Magical Instrument ★ Cup
Altar Symbol ★ Chalice
Communion Symbol ★ Wine, water
Archangel ★ Gabriel
Human Sense ★ Taste
Art Forms ★ Music, song
Animals ★ Fish, whales
Mythical Beast ★ Sea serpent
Magical Arts ★ Healing
Guide Forms ★ Moon, water goddess
Meditation ★ The ocean, rivers

Images & Themes ★ Lakes, pools, living underwater, healing, calm, the setting Sun

HOW YOU CAN GET IN TOUCH WITH YOUR WATER ENERGY

"Water flows on and on ... It does not shrink from any dangerous spot nor from any plunge, and nothing can make it lose its own essential nature. It remains true to itself under all conditions."
I Ching, hexagram 29, k'an/k'an

★ Use Water energy when making wishes around the following: Healing, spiritual and psychic development, relationship harmony, emotional issues, psychosomatic illnesses, dreams and trust

★ Spend time in and around water - oceans, rivers, streams, lakes, waterfalls

★ Install a water fountain in the space in which you spend the most time

★ Carry a small spray bottle of water with you and spritz yourself with it throughout the day

★ Float in the water - surrender to its unerring support and let it keep you afloat

★ Research, make and use gem (crystal) essences

★ Try to take a bath rather than a shower; you can linger for longer, and even meditate more effectively, in a still bath

★ Engage in water sports (not too extreme though, unless Scorpio is strong in your chart!), such as water skiing, swimming, kayaking, surfing, yachting, scuba diving, canoeing, sailing, or water volleyball.

★ Drink lots of water

★ Meditate on the Cups suit in the Tarot (the Cups suit represents the Water element)

★ Eat watery, water-based foods, such as brothy soups, watermelon and juicy fruits

★ Purify and cleanse your body occasionally, by undertaking a day-long fast / liquid diet

★ Sleep on a waterbed

★ Green-coloured crystals will activate your connection with the element of Water and enhance hope, healing, love and creativity.

★ Join an emotional support group - or facilitate one

★ Install a water fountain in your home, garden or office - water features, placed strategically, are believed in Feng Shui tradition, to attract certain desired things into your environment and experience

★ Wear and surround yourself with the colours blue, silver and green

★ Decorate your home or office with soothing watery images, such as scenic lakes, panoramic beach photographs, ocean-side postcards

★ Listen and meditate to ocean waves and bubbling brook sounds on an audio system

★ Walk in the rain, jump in puddles

★ Visit a spa regularly, and indulge in saunas and Jacuzzis - better still, install one in your home

★ Learn and practice graceful, flowing forms of movement, such as t'ai chi

★ Express your emotions fearlessly; try to use them as your ally

★ Nurture others and inspire them to nurture themselves

★ Express your feelings through art, poetry and drama

★ Cultivate a spiritual practice

★ Develop your counselling and listening skills so you can help others - and yourself!

★ Meditate regularly. Embrace your inner silence, peace and spiritual essence

★ When working with the Water element in magical practice, stand at the West quarter of your magical space, as the West is its domain, and invite its living essence into your 'circle'

★ Use chalices, bowls, crystals, blue or silver items, and cauldrons to represent your element. If you are fortunate enough to live near the ocean, its tides can be a great energising force that evokes dramatic magical transformations. When the tide goes out, visualise your worries being drawn away. High tide is an optimum time to focus on wish magic, and as the waves move in closer, imagine your dreams coming towards you. Spells cast on a riverbank or near a spring will also be empowered by the moving energy of Water

★ The best days on which to employ Water magic are Monday, ruled by the Moon, and Friday, ruled by the planet of love Venus

★ Water spirits are also known as sea nymphs, naiads, undines or sprites. They are responsible for the cleansing, refreshing and clearing of our spirits, so Water signs would be wise to adopt one (or all) as their very own spirit guide!

YOUR MODE ★ MUTABLE

Each sign belongs to one of the three quadruplicities, Cardinal, Fixed and Mutable. If we closely examine the Earth's yearly cycle, we can form a very accurate picture of the nature of these quadruplicities, for they correspond directly with the manifestation of the seasons. Each season has three months: the first month brings the new phase of the cycle, the second month brings a concentration of the season's energy to its fullest expression, and the third month represents the transition from the current season to the next one. The astrological quadruplicities represent the three basic qualities in all life: creation (Cardinal), perseverance (Fixed) and destruction (Mutable). Every thing that is born, from a period of time to a human being, experiences a life and then dies. In this context, death can be taken to mean that the form of the energy changes; but the energy itself can never be annihilated, for form is mortal, whereas essence is immortal.

The Mutable mode covers the signs Gemini, Virgo, Sagittarius and Pisces, and is the most flexible group of the three modes (the others being Cardinal and Fixed), able to shift and change to facilitate action. You instinctively know how to go with the flow and you adapt most easily to new situations and have diverse interests, but can lack perseverance and are prone to restlessness. Operating with flexibility and mobility, you are adaptable to change and have a circulating quality. Cooperative and friendly, you can fit in almost anywhere, put up with anything and turn any situation to your advantage. You can steer projects through periods of transition and can also bring them to a conclusion, but are conspicuously absent when hard work, long hours or persistent effort is necessary (with the exception of Virgo). Although gentle, generally easygoing and likeable, you can be childish, sulky and ruthless if threatened. And although you have a natural benevolent streak and love to help animals and people, you can also be paradoxically selfish. The natural versatility of the Mutable quadruplicity can develop into a willingness to change and compromise, which gives an enormous sense of resourcefulness to these signs. Being so versatile, you are constantly seeking ways you can make improvements to yourself and your life; Mutable signs can always be relied upon to think of new and ingenious ways of dealing with changing circumstances. However, without the proper focus, centralising force, direction or persistence, your energy can become easily scattered, flighty, wavering and disoriented - and thus ultimately ineffective. You often lack a fixity and determination of purpose, which are needed to concretise goals. Your essential energy is one of movement, flow, fluidity, adaptability, adjustability, harmony, and versatility. Your feelings can switch and shift easily and you can be moody, indecisive, inconsistent and unpredictable. And although resourceful and ingenious, you can often project nervousness and worry. You may act as the intermediate between the Cardinal and Fixed signs. Mutable also indicates the ending of seasons, which are times of change and transition, merging into new territories and changing conditions.

Being of the Water element, Pisces is the most flowing of the Mutable quadruplicity; you constantly trying to adapt itself to its ever-changing feelings and to the moods and whims of others, and easily blends and merges with its surroundings.

YOUR RULING PLANET ★ NEPTUNE

The Great Artist, Mystic & Dreamer

Planetary Meditation
I am my Earth (my body),
and my Sky (my transcendence)
I am my Sun (my spirit),
and my Moon (my soul)
I am my Venus (my pleasure),
and my Jupiter (my faith)
I am my Mars (my courage),
and my Saturn (my lessons)
I am my Mercury (my thoughts),
and my Uranus (my truth)
I am my Neptune (my dreams),
and my Pluto (my transformation)

Each planet has its own distinctive and original meaning which, according to its position in the zodiac, combines with the qualities that are inherent in each of the twelve astrological signs. If a planet is your sign's ruler, however, it exerts a significant influence upon your life, regardless of its birth chart or zodiacal position.

Transcendental ★ Associated with Fantasies, Dreams and Spirituality ★ 164 Year Cycle

★ KEY WORDS ★
Inspiration, Dreams, Mystical Longings, Sensitivity, Mysticism, Imagination, Higher or Psychic Functions, Other-worldliness, Escapism, Delusions, Artistry,

Enigmas, Compassion, Intrigues, Cloudiness, Unreality, Spirituality, Subtlety, Idealism, Deception, Creativity, the Subconscious, Illusions, Fantasies

★ KEY CONCEPTS ★
★ Dreams, ideals, illusions, fantasies ★
★ The drifter, the fantasiser, the psychic, the dreamer ★
★ The mystic, the spiritualist, the prophet ★
★ Dissolver of boundaries ★
★ The great deceiver ★
★ The artist, the musician, the dancer, the filmmaker ★
★ The self-sacrificer, the carer, the spiritualist ★
★ The embracer of Universal love and compassion ★
★ The force for the awakening of the higher spiritual consciousness ★
★ The bestower of Universal love ★
★ She who swims to the ebbs and flows of her own ocean ★

Numbers ★ 7 and 11

Basic Energy & Magic ★ Dreams, Fantasies, Magic

Colours ★ Lavender, Mauve, Aquamarine, Sea Green, Etheric Colours, Indigo, Violet

Metals ★ Neptunium, Platinum

Gems/Minerals ★ Coral, Aquamarine, Amethyst, Fluorite, Jade, Coral, Sugilite

Zodiacal Influences ★ Rules Pisces; Exalted in Leo; Detriment Virgo; Fall Aquarius

Neptune, the eighth planet of the Solar system, situated between Uranus and Pluto, was 'discovered' before it was actually seen. Neptune, a sphere which lies beyond the boundaries of Saturn, was in fact discovered in 1846 as a result of its gravitational effects on Uranus. Twelve years' prior, an amateur astronomer, the Rev. T. J. Hussey, had suggested that the erratic motion of Uranus might be caused by the pull of an unknown body. His theory was developed by two mathematicians: John Couch Adams in England, and Urbain Le Verrier in France, who both calculated the hypothetical position of another planet from observed discrepancies in the position of Uranus. Eventually Le Verrier's ephemeris and calculations were received by an astronomer named Johan Galle at the Berlin Observatory and Neptune, recognised at first as an eighth magnitude starlike object, was located. It was found that Neptune had been seen and thought to be a fixed star by previous observers.

Neptune's meaning baffled astrology for the best part of fifty years before it was decided that astronomy's name for this eighth planet was no accident, and that the Roman sea god must represent aqueous themes such as dissolution, formlessness, haziness and impressionability. Neptune's well-known associations with anaesthetics and mind- and body-altering drugs can be explained through the use of ether in surgery for the first time in the same year of its discovery. That year also belonged to an age where gas lighting illuminated foggy streets, alcohol binges abounded in gin palaces, consumptive poets downed laudanum and yearned for transcendence, spirituality was striven for, and occult sciences permeated and influenced everyday life. But it was also an era of a prevailing 'Age of Reason', which had pushed intuition to the background, and during which nothing was acceptable unless it could be explained scientifically.

Beyond 1846, a renewal of interest in spiritual and psychic subjects and a proliferation of new religions occurred. After all, faith is what Neptune is all about, but the fact that this was the first planet to be discovered solely through mathematics, suggests that faith can be something more definable than leaps of the imagination. But faith can be shaky too, which is demonstrated by Neptune's ability, like the sea, to clean neatly and dissolve, sweeping away anything not firmly rooted before it has a chance to protest or cling. And just like religion, it can either inspire or confuse us, depending on whichever way we choose to be.

Perhaps nothing is more Neptunian in nature than the medium of photography, which appeared in 1839, a few years before Neptune's discovery and which, appropriately enough, given Neptune's strong connection with state-altering substances, was derived from chemical processes. In fact, the word 'photography' was coined by Sir John Herschel, son of the astronomer William, who discovered Uranus. Sir John was, perhaps not surprisingly, a Piscean. Photography shows real life in a way that a painting never could convey, but is still prone to ambivalence and trickery. Cinema and the world of moving pictures and films, too, are ruled by Neptune, and all are simultaneously the ultimate illusion, an act of mass escapism and enchanting glamour.

The glyph (or symbol) for Neptune is a cross with an upturned semi-circle cutting through the upper arm of the cross, giving the appearance of the three-pronged trident that the sea god Neptune carries.

Originally Neptune was just a big fish in a small pond. Starting as a god of fresh water, it became identified, in around 390 B.C. with Poseidon, a grandson of Uranus. To Neptune fell power over all the waters on Earth, and it could seemingly invoke storms, cause shipwrecks, or send favourable winds to blow mariners safely back to shore. It could undermine the land with hidden rivers, dry up lakes and streams, or strike barren rock with its trident, and cause life-giving springs to gush forth. As the mood seized it, it could work itself into a frenzy or become as serene as a gurgling rivulet.

What fascinates us so much about this bluish disc is not so much the planet itself as its two satellites. Triton, the brighter one, was discovered only a few weeks after its parent body. It has a retrograde orbit inclined 40 degrees to Neptune's orbit and 20 degrees to the planet's equator, which astronomers regard as highly unusual. And Nereid, which was not spotted until 1949, is the most eccentrically orbiting satellite in the whole Solar system. And so it seems that we can pin down Neptune easily enough once we know how it works, but the planet itself seems to have some serious problems controlling its wayward satellite offspring.

The ocean has always been the symbolic keynote of Pisces, and we attribute the sign's rulership to Neptune, who was the god of the sea. Artists and mystics are able to reach into the deep ocean of images that this sign's symbolism evokes, connecting Pisces with psychics and dreamers, artistic types and idealists; after all it is precisely from these watery depths that they garner their visions, poetry and melodic symphonies. Neptune is the planet of altruism, dreams and deep faith, and as such engenders great compassion, insight and inspiration, as well as a profound sensitivity to beauty. Its trident symbol, Poseidon's pitchfork, symbolises the threefold parts to each person: body, mind and spirit, the greatest of these considered by many as being spirit.

Certainly, Neptune's placement in a birth chart can indicate the magician, the artist or the drunkard - or even all three - and how you will likely express these personas. It also tells you how you relate to your soul, and how you react to current thoughts, beliefs, emotions and feelings. In your horoscope, all of the above qualities have to be studied and handled with great care, for their expression in material life is very subtle, and sometimes inexpressible and remote from more rational and practical concerns. To foresee, to anticipate, to intuit, to understand the underlying meanings of circumstances, to have a clear awareness of passing time and of the cycles of metamorphosis, is to enter the realms of Neptune.

Before the discovery of the three outer planets which lay beyond the detection of the naked eye, the ruler of Pisces was Jupiter. Today, after the discovery of Neptune, Jupiter is regarded as Pisces's secondary or traditional ruler. Indeed, the Piscean temperament seems to encompass qualities of *both* these planets, but Neptune is regarded as more fitting for this dreamy, nebulous and watery sign.

Being prominent as your ruling planet, Neptune gives you a heightened sensitivity, misty nature, a strong imagination and powerful psychic potential. Being an outer planet, Neptune is an impersonal energy, and can be difficult to understand or even describe. It presides over artistry, music and illusion, the kinds created by lighting, film and photography, colour, clothing and conjuring. It is also linked with religious miracles and mysticism of the mediumistic and psychic varieties. Neptune dances somewhere on the mystical side of life, and is prone to fantasising, daydreaming and idealising. Seeing the world through rose-coloured glasses a lot of the time, it compels its subjects to believe in magic, dreams, fairy tales and happy endings. The typical Neptunian is otherworldly, her vision tuned to an inner reality which may create fantastical castles that delight, or which can lead her into a dark, swirling undercurrent of undesirable emotions.

Naturally, due to its distance from the Earth, few among us are capable at all of being affected by Neptune, save that it produces a chaotic state of mind when placed in difficult aspect. When placed in angles, and particularly in elevations near the Midheaven, it produces occultists and mystics of the highest stamp. It will manifest in a Piscean in much the same way, embodying two of its most noted attributes: its connection with the art of dance, and its link with alcoholic or narcotic intoxication. It is the highest string in the lyre of the soul and is therefore the least used and the one to get most easily out of tune. Astrologers are the most affected by it, as are stringed instrument musicians. The ecstasy and heightened expression which comes about as a result, is both the gift and the fatal flaw of the Neptunian individual. In no time in history is this better illustrated than during the 1960s. Astrologers refer to this decade as a decidedly Neptunian period - and indeed, the drugs, the peace-for-all, the love-ins, the seeds of the iconic song *Imagine*, the long-flowing hair, the acceptance of and pervading compassion for others, the idealism, and the colourful bohemian attire, all suggest a strong Neptune influence.

Neptune is all about imagination, hypersensitivity, spirituality, intuition, clairvoyance, and the subconscious, but above all, dreams and fantasies. Neptune's energy exudes the urge to dissolve boundaries, to experience oneness, to merge with others, to practice the spiritual, divinatory or occult arts, and the need for unity, mysticism, transcendence, illusion, idealism, utopian, sacrifice and devotion. It represents collective feeling, Universal love, imagining and inspiration. One of its primary functions is to remove barriers, not by tearing them down, like Pluto, but by gently dissolving them; in fact, Neptune would like everything rendered to a state of liquid suspension, to be formless, to be returned to the state of nebulousness that existed in the *beginning*.

Neptune's essence can be encapsulated by the metaphor of trying to capture running water in a painting or photograph - it is very difficult to do, for however skilful you are, the result is never quite a hundred per cent effective or successful. Similarly, we may find the character of Neptune hard to grasp.

As well as being a slippery fish, there is also a heady tang to Neptune, which comes across in a sparkle or a zest that can change the mood, play on our emotions, transform the moment, and lift the spirits like no other force in our Solar system.

Neptune, the God of the Oceans, was allocated these domains because they symbolised the boundlessness of space. It is therefore said to represent the ability to transcend boundaries, limitless expansion, sympathy, renunciation, glamour, illusion, self-sacrifice and manoeuvrability. Neptune (Poseidon) was not always a nice presence in mythology, and indeed excelled at throwing storm clouds and nets in the way of his intended victims, making them lose their way at sea for long periods of time, hence the concept of 'not being able to see where you're going' when you are under a strong Neptunian influence. Although this may be frightening, the vision ahead often comes to us more clearly when we are cut off from a purely physical sense of reality. Therefore, one of Neptune's functions may be to encouraging the opening of the third eye so that we can see the unseen, and develop trust and faith in, and reliance upon, a higher power that can only come to us when we are adrift on a vast ocean and no longer able to control our course.

In mundane astrology, while Pluto rules volcanic eruptions, Neptune governs earthquakes, hurricanes, tidal waves and oil spills, occurrences which, except for oil spills, are quite beyond our control and occur with little or no warning as to when or where they will strike. This correlates to the kind of fear, trepidation or out-of-control sense one may experience all too regularly when strongly influenced by Neptune.

Neptune is also associated with spontaneous kindness and charity, through looking after those who cannot care for themselves, and the desire to give hope to the hopeless. Further, it rules solitary, confined and 'hidden' places such as hospitals, orphanages, institutions, mental homes, hospices, and any form of imprisonment, real or imagined.

With so much tenderness and sensitivity, most Neptune-influenced individuals don't survive very well in the outside world. But in time they figure out that they are not of this world and, most importantly, that they don't have to be. Their challenge in life is to keep in touch with their inner spiritual centre while continuing to function on the material plane, a process similar to that represented by the two fish swimming in opposite directions. Both their strength and their weakness, Pisces and Neptune have the ability, beyond all other signs and planets, to absorb everything around them, therefore blessing them with a refreshing absence of ego, but at the same time cursing them with an oft troublesome lack of boundaries.

Neptune's energy is dreamy, mystical, fantastical, delusional and magical. This planet pulls the veil of dreams over our eyes but it can just as readily pull it away. Its influence often coincides with both mystical and romantic experiences. Its adverse side can cause carelessness, impracticality, foolish decisions, needless worrying, and the tendency to live in either a fantasy world or under the influence of substances.

Denial literally means 'to look away', and denial, as played out in our lives or in society, is based upon this principle - looking away from reality. When reality (Saturn) is resisted or ignored, Neptune can take over with dreams, fantasies, addictions, anxiety and escapism - which is what seems to plague our society in the last part of the Piscean age, on both an individual and a collective level. Blame is also a manifestation of denial, and cycles will keep repeating themselves in our lives until we finally open our eyes and really dare to see ourselves in the mirror as we really are. Of course, this process takes much courage and strength, and a clearing away of the denial or fantasies that have protected us for so long, and most people, particularly Pisceans, prefer the path of least resistance for this very reason. In examining the astrological position of Neptune in your natal chart, you are able to pinpoint the areas of your life most prone to denial or self-delusion, and how your self-deceptions may be expressed.

Concerned with states of altered consciousness, this planet is also connected with mental illness and disturbances, some which are not always diagnosable, alcohol and drugs, anaesthetics, gases and poisons. Strongly influenced Neptunian characters, such as Pisceans, are essentially artistic, highly sensitive and other-worldly. Neptune appears strongly in the horoscopes of idealists, musicians, dancers (*especially* dancers), painters, as well as among alcoholics, drug addicts, therapists, and those who follow a metaphysical or spiritual vocation, such as healers, astrologers, mediums and psychics.

Neptune's actions are to loosen, to dissolve, to etherealise, sensitise, idealise, make intangible, refine, expand, inflate and distort. It also falls within the sphere of chaos and dissolution. Neptune in its highest form brings the blessings of a creative imagination. The positive side of Neptune ultimately leads to inspiration - which manifests itself as truth, light and wisdom.

The Neptunian is typically attracted to relationships that have a saviour-victim quality to them, and this can be unhealthy, even destructive. It is only by concentrating the focus of a relationship on transcendence that the Piscean can heal and reconcile her inner longings and achieve maturity of soul. Indeed, it can exert a rather foggy influence upon its natives, making them prone to being indecisive, changeable, romantic, sensitive, and often lazy without much self-control, but blessed with an abundance of inspired gifts and insights. Neptune has trouble articulating its thoughts into words, making it often difficult to understand and indeed misunderstood.

Neptune is often regarded as the higher octave of Venus, and Venus is exalted in the sign Neptune rules, Pisces, suggesting that Neptune's highest function and manifestation is a Universal, transcendental, all-encompassing brand of love and compassion. Neptune indeed operates on a more interpersonal than individual scale and works in a diffused way, concerning itself with changes on the social level as well as in our personal spheres, but we're often unaware of these actions until they've happened.

Neptune's rulership over Pisces conjures such images as those found in the artistry and spiritual dimensions, combined with the dreaminess and 'floatiness' of the sea. But Neptune certainly has its dark side. Arguably no planet has been more maligned and misunderstood in astrology theories and writings than Neptune. Perhaps because this archetype rules the ocean, symbolising the collective unconscious, where rational and practical processes do not exist, one must look through different eyes to 'see' Neptune, if indeed it can be perceived with the 'senses' at all; Neptune is slippery and evasive, like its sign Pisces, and often eludes tangible perception and definition.

It can intoxicate us at times, so we connect this influence with alcohol, gases, hallucinogens, and the many experiences to which they give rise. With this Neptunian influence, there is a tendency towards addictions, experimentation with drugs, obsessions, lymphatic issues, feet problems, and nervous disorders. Money may be made in strange ways, but there is a likelihood of trusting others too much and so being exploited or defrauded, or of just frittering money away. Being so romantic and tender, there is also a tendency to fall in love easily, and to bring great romance and idealism into a marriage. This planet lends a raw boldness, a childlike innocence, and deep romance to love affairs, which may typically contain an element of the Knight in Shining Armour or Prince Charming ideal contained somewhere within them.

Neptune is associated with divination, clairvoyance, dampness, coffee, acting, double dealing, ambiguous, dreams, ecstasy, fairies, cigarettes, fakes, abstract, bays, films, clouds, fish, floods, debauchery, fluids, aliases, chloroform, delusions, fluorescent, artificial, fumes, gas, germicides, deceit, graft, harbours, haze, heroin, conspiracy, hidden, embezzlement, hospitals, hypnotism, hypochondria, beguiling, hypocrisy, idealism, cheats, illusion, imagination, enchantment, imitation, fantasy, inspiration, fogs, intangible, flying, confusion, intoxication, escape, chaos, intrigue, enigmas, intuition, kelp, docks, breweries, kerosene, leaks, secrets, liquid, liquor, LSD, asylums, cinemas, lubrication, magic, clandestine, mariners, seclusion, mazes, fictitious, mediums, disguise, mirages, fountains, alcohol, mist, morphine, phantoms, motion pictures, music, drains, baths, mysticism, narcotics, collusions, navy, confidential, nightmares, ocean, anaesthetic, fish canneries, omens, paradise, bewildering, perfumes, fascination, periscopes, feet, petroleum, aquariums, prediction, photography, comas, premonitions, bluffing, pretence, coral, prophecy, pseudonyms, psychic matters, puzzles, apparitions, quacks, bigamy, drugs, pilots, rainbows, riddles, gin, rubber, schemers, glass, sea, camouflage, séances, drunk, sleep, smuggling, drink, spies, impostors, counterfeit, spiritualism, sponges, distillers, steam, drowning, submarines, irrigation, subversion, yachts, divers, swamps, swimming, fables, synthetics, tea, bogus, telepathy, dissolve, mystery, tobacco, odours, trance, impersonation, transparent, ponds, treachery, veils, visions, water, whirlpools, wine, oil, fraud, bleach, yeast, poisons, cameras, yoga, showers, ESP and witches. I'm sure you get the idea!

Neptune, as one of the three outer or generational planets, as well as being the higher octave of Venus, is regarded, along with Uranus and Pluto, as being one of the three planets of a higher octave. These higher octave forces account for those moments of fantasy, inspiration, illusion, confusion, and spontaneous and sustained spirituality that we are occasionally confronted with, when we become especially aware of our life's purpose and step into a refreshingly different dimension.

Neptune shares the 'sub'-dimensions with Pluto; their two respective gods were relegated to the underwater and the underworld realms, and both reside in domains where it's easier to ignore or sweep undesirable elements of our lives under the magic carpet rather than to deal with them directly.

Whether you observe Neptune's rulership over drugs and alcohol, the oil industry or your addiction to the paths of spiritual transcendence, everybody seems to be taking some form of Neptunian medication these days.

Indeed, Neptune's bag of tricks is akin to being in a funhouse full of distorting mirrors. It works its magic by offering us a glimpse of ourselves in an infinitude of images which are all ourselves. Some are amusing, some disturbing, some flattering, some grotesque, some fantastical, some frightening, and dazzled by so many reflections we decide that some profound truth may be revealed to us. But all the distortions in the Universe can't add up to one true picture, and no serious person, Piscean or otherwise, would delude herself that drugging her mind with any form of hallucinogen or intoxicant will lead to sustained enlightenment. Should we be curious enough to enter Neptune's House of Mirrors, no one will stop us if we gladly and willingly pay the price of admission and accept the conditions of entry. But Neptune never reads the fine print, and inside, we usually discover nothing there but deceiving, distorted reflections of ourselves and any perceptions we've taken in along the trip. Upon emerging, we often come to the gradual realisation that the experience has cost us far more than the freak show was worth. If we insist on lingering, we learn to our detriment that the longer we remain inside, the higher the cost becomes. Even worse, we discover that what initially seemed amusing begins to scare us and then wind up confused by the maze, bewildered by the trickery, and unable to find our way out again.

We see a similar phenomenon when we look into regular mirrors - we cannot see our own faces because we're behind them, but once we look into a mirror, we only see a reversed image. In order to get a correct visualisation of ourselves, we have to stand between two mirrors and look at the reflection of the reflection. Confused? So is your reflection.

An ice cube provides a fine metaphor for Neptune's message. What our senses perceive as solid substance is in fact a temporary arrangement of moving energy particles, and by making the right sort of effort we can alter the arrangement to turn the substance into something more useful. We take the ice cube out of its tray and it is an ice cube, but soon it loses its identity by melting. The water re-emerges, only to be used again in one form or another: we may drink it, retain it for a while in our bodily tissues, then excrete it as sweat, respiration, or urine; or we may just pour it down the sink where it ends up somewhere only to evaporate into the atmosphere and contribute to cloud formations, which then rain it back down to turn dust to mud, nourish a plant, cleanse the terrain, or contribute to a river system. Whatever happens to the water, it does not cease to exist; it may go through any number of recirculation processes and undoubtedly take on different forms, but it is still there. We realise through this example, which we are working not with specific units of matter but with Universal, widespread - and sometimes intangible - forces.

Water's infinite capacity to dissolve other substances and assume new forms offers us a physical demonstration of Neptune as the Universal Solvent. We associate Neptune with clairvoyance, telepathy, behind-the-scenes activities and that which is hidden. Indeed, Neptune has the ability to see more than meets the eye, and the ability to forgive, washing clean the slate and gently suggesting we start anew by trying again. It is not the healer, but has the capability of opening our hearts and minds up to be healed. Wherever we find Neptune in our natal charts, it tells us where and what we need to change, perhaps some aspect of our life experience which we are viewing from a distorted angle. The house in which Neptune sits and the sign to which it is linked will indicate where the problem lies. It also teaches us where to look for beauty in our lives through the manifestation of those higher, creative urges of the artistic realms. Indeed, a work of art is an act of love. Neptune is both the inspiration and the expression of that love - both personally and universally.

To finish off, a good analogy upon which to base this ethereal blue sphere, can be gleaned from the ocean itself. Observing waves lapping gently to sure, in rhythmic, non-resistant flows, smoothing out sand patterns and gently frothing with each lunge, it is easy to forget the power and turbulence that lies just beneath the surface. An undertow can pull the unsuspecting out of their depth without warning, an earthquake can shift the sandy plates so violently that it results in an all-engulfing tsunami, or a swirling rip can suck you under with a silent, powerful force, but unless you have the courage to float wherever the water may take you, you may never truly know what interesting new shores and depths can be discovered. Indeed, for those who stand safely back, feet planted in the practical, tangible world, Neptune may seem remote, but anyone seeking a deeper understanding of life will have to get their feet wet.

This Neptunian energy and influence, throughout a Piscean's whole life experience, gives you the wondrous gifts of creativity, illumination, dreams, spirituality, visions, intuition, and the potential to be the Dream Manifester and the Great Bringer of the spiritualism, compassion and Universal love that the world so desperately needs. Too much of this Neptunian energy can leave one confused, intoxicated, vague, secretive, indecisive, a little bit mad, weak-willed, in denial, and unable to cope with the practicalities of life, to the point of succumbing to escapism and fantastical paths. But the Piscean always manages to intuit what's best for her own soul; after all, your motto is "I Believe," and deep down, you really do *believe*, even when all hope seems lost. You may lose your head before everyone else loses theirs, but the power of your belief is beyond measure, and will always ensure you find your way again eventually. After all, Neptune's force encapsulates the essence and role of the pure Piscean - that of the humble, selfless, saintly saviour. Sometimes though, you must remember to save yourself. How will *you* use your phenomenally powerful Neptunian influence?

★ A NOTE ON THE THREE OUTER OR DISTANT PLANETS ★
URANUS, NEPTUNE & PLUTO

It has been said that the distant planets are actually *more* powerful than the others as they take longer to orbit the Sun; they therefore affect whole generations of people rather than individuals. But as a result of their longer-spanning orbits, these slower moving planets (Uranus, Neptune and Pluto) dwell in the zodiac constellations for longer periods of time, allowing them to leave a deeper and more indelible experience on the human psyche and experience than the swifter moving planets. In other words, their effect is thought to be more lingering.

YOUR HOUSE IN THE HOROSCOPE ★ THE TWELFTH HOUSE

The Twelfth House is the realm of your subconscious, encompassing dreams, mysticism, self-sacrifice and intuition, as well as hidden enemies (such as yourself). Planets placed here can be both a hidden strength and a hidden weakness, depending largely on your appreciation of their effects.

A house is one of the twelve sections dividing the terrestrial globe, viewed from a precise time and geographical place, into sectors from the poles to the horizon. The horoscope, or birth chart, is divided into these twelve sections called houses. Each house governs a different area or 'department' of life, such as relationships, career, leisure and even karma. The reason for this division of the Earth into houses can be understood when we consider that the Sun's rays affect us differently in the morning, at noon and at night, and also in summer and winter, and if we study the cause, we will readily observe that it is the angle at which the ray strikes us or the Earth which produces that difference in effect. Similarly, with the stellar rays, astrologers have observed that a child born at or near midday, when the Sun's rays strike the birthplace from the Tenth House, has an improved chance of public or career advancement in life than one born after sunset. By similar observations and tabulations, it has been found that the other planetary rays affect the various departments of life when their ray is projected through the other houses, and therefore each house is said to 'rule' or govern certain departments of the human life experience.

The Twelfth House, ruled by Pisces, is the house of the subconscious mind, what is repressed, secrets, spirituality, the hidden self, deep-seated fears, mystical inclinations, withdrawal, transcendence, one's spiritual path, solitude, seclusion, isolation, escapism, faith, institutions, karma, the Divine and inner worlds, self-undoing, the shadow self, psychic abilities, intuition, self-undoing, addictions, healing, faith, how we 'escape', transcendence, confinement, unconscious impulses, and secret and hidden enemies. As the Twelfth House is connected with clandestine relationships and concealed enemies, it may also indicate those internal factors which can contribute to one's undoing. It reveals the expression of moral and spiritual strength, our behaviour when faced with obstacles, and our abilities - and tendencies - to withdraw, to change and evolve.

As a Water-ruled house, this is one of the three Houses of Soul or Endings. But where Cancer is concerned with soul or endings on a personal level and Scorpio on an interpersonal level, the Pisces-ruled Twelfth House is concerned with soul or endings on a transpersonal, or wider-reaching, level, embracing all facets and intricacies of these concepts.

The Twelfth House is about endings, karma and secrets, and reveals your hidden strengths and weaknesses. The situations described through a study of this domicile, uncover the circumstances an individual must overcome in order to be free of firm bindings and destructive restrictions as well as negative patterns of recurring situations, relationships and behaviours. Such institutions as hospitals, jails, asylums, monasteries, libraries, the armed services, and other forms of secluded places of residence or confinement are also associated with this house. Other exoteric and esoteric keywords include fears, unseen adversaries and adversities, the collective unconscious, reparation of past wrongs, family secrets, reconnection, mysteries, sacrifice, surrender, 'return', unredeemed karma, disintegration, deception, and selfless service to humanity.

This house reveals whether you have many or few adversaries or enemies, and under what kind of circumstances they lurk. The Twelfth House has many labels, some of which are The House of Buried Treasures, the Realm of Concealment, the House of Retreat, Solitude and Institutions, the House of Karma, the House of Self-Undoing, the House of Sustainment, and the House of Secret Enemies. This house has an ominous reputation but it is very revealing of our inner secrets, and can be very empowering if we know how to deal with these properly. It usually shows us that the worst secret enemy is actually the one within us, and that ultimately we are all the creators of our own misfortunes or undoing's. However, conversely, we are also our own greatest source of strength and self-sustainment. It shows us how we 'escape' the pressures of daily life and the planets therein describe the nature of our inner strengths that we can draw upon. Here we have to confront the fact that we need to reconnect and unite with something infinitely greater than ourselves.

The Twelfth House acknowledges that we have

been on a journey through the previous eleven realms of human experience, accepts a kind of 'pre-existence', and realises that, since life is cyclical, we must re-join it at the end of our cycle, that we must go back to where we first began. Because the karmic principle of astrology suggests that your soul chooses a time to be born, we effectively choose the planetary pattern for that moment that indicates an appropriate horoscope for us, one that has been 'earned' by the previous incarnation. Planets within, and the nature of the sign on the cusp of the Twelfth House, therefore, reveal what you are carrying in your astrological 'suitcase' that may assist or hinder you on your current journey.

It is chiefly concerned with the private inner self which is often difficult to understand, and the troubles which you bring upon yourself by being what you are. It governs solitude, secrecy and self-imposed restrictions, and ultimately, the acquiring of wisdom. It is also the House of betrayals, ambushes, ordeals, misfortune, confinement and illnesses, and not only can it warn you about opponents of all kinds, but also offer strategies around how to handle them. For example, if involved in a law suit, it will indicate whether or not you will win it. It indicates whether any sadness in your life is caused by yourself, or through your associations with others. Being the house of loss, disappointments and personal sacrifice, it may also reveal where we have imposed confinement upon ourselves, or had it imposed upon us, and shows any connections we may have with institutions, prisons and hospitals, and whether indeed we are the inmate, the patient, the redeemed, the newly released, or the worker in these settings.

The Twelfth House is like a secret diary in which we have written things we don't want other people to know about us; it reveals any secrets you might prefer to keep hidden. Perhaps too we don't want to realise them about ourselves but are still carrying them around like burdens. Those secrets we're so 'guilty' about ought to be brought out into the light and dusted off so that we can benefit from what they have to teach us. Because the Twelfth House is also related to self-sacrifice and selflessness, it is a House where we *give* and do not count the cost or expect anything in return. It is also known as the repository for the collective unconscious, and a storehouse for Universal potential. The Twelfth House relates to your latent talents and your subconscious mind, your fears, your confinement and your sorrows.

Although not directly related to one's hopes, wishes and ideals (a domain of the Eleventh House preceding it), this house shows your ability to *secure* the fulfilment of your hopes and wishes on many levels and in many different directions. Being the final house in the symbolic Wheel of Life, it represents your capacity for complete integration with life. To the degree in which you fail to do this, your wishes will remain pipe dreams, weaknesses not overcome will become your undoing's, misfortunes may or may not abound, or you may be led into antisocial or harmful behaviours. As it offers us the opportunity to connect with the whole, it can bring into the light of consciousness all that was previously obscured. It is where the task of reintegration is undertaken, the boundaries of individuality is relinquished, and the Self surrendered back into the collective, Universal whole, the last process being either voluntary or involuntary, depending on the individual.

The Twelfth House tells us much about our personal karma and our experience of the previous eleven spheres of the horoscope wheel of life. It symbolises our integration and ultimate (symbolic) death, and subsequent return as a 'newborn' in the First House. The Twelfth House acknowledges our 'pre-existence', and represents our acceptance that, since life is cyclical, at the end of the cycle, we are called to re-join it where it all started, we must *go home*. Whether one believes in life after death, or the concepts of karma or reincarnation or not, is a moot point, for in this House you are still accepting that the Universe is a continually evolving cycle of formation, dissolution and re-formation.

If the Twelfth House influence is strong in the birth chart, we will be inclined to choose forms of self-expression which involve our karmic interests, whether conscious or unconsciously. The Twelfth House ensures that we learn and apply the lessons of all the signs that have come before us, and all those other areas of human experience. It is here, standing within the walls of this House of Endings that paradoxically, we can re-emerge as transformed beings into our next birth - in the House of Beginnings. And so the cycle begins again. What powerful karmic influences, inner experiences and soul lessons have *you* gathered along your journey?

YOUR OPPOSITE SIGN ★ VIRGO
WHAT YOU CAN LEARN FROM THE VIRGIN

If we look at the zodiac, we can see that it can be broadly divided into two hemispheres, this division being based on the natural division of the year by the two equinoxes. Astrologers often refer to the first six signs, the hemisphere in which the day predominates (the days being longer in the spring and summer months), as the Personal Sphere of Experience, and the second six signs, the hemisphere in which nights are longer, as the Social Sphere of Experience. These two halves of the zodiac perfectly balance and complement each other, and each individual 'personal' zodiac sign has something to teach its directly opposite 'social' zodiac sign. To generalise, the signs of the personal sphere tend to experience life through a type of self-projection and self-interest which is often socially uncomplicated, unsophisticated or naïve. Their objective is to learn greater social awareness and thereby integrate themselves with the larger, more Universal human collective. On the other hand, the signs of the social sphere are prone to experience life through the use of their more developed social consciousness. In essence, the personal signs (Aries, Taurus, Gemini, Cancer, Leo, Virgo) usually provide stimulation and new energy to their environment, while the social, more Universal signs (Libra, Scorpio, Sagittarius, Capricorn, Aquarius, Pisces) provide experience, opportunities for wider expression, and give a more broad-minded approach and perspective to their surroundings.

Each sign in a pair seeks and is attracted to the qualities of its complementary opposing sign. Virgo seeks the complete selflessness of Pisces, while Pisces desires to be able to discriminate in its self-assertions. Virgo dwells within the realm of the distribution of *personal* services, while Pisces resides within the realm of the distribution of *social* services.

Although the word 'opposite' conjures up feelings of separateness and differences, the astrological polarities should not be seen as two signs in conflict with each other - their positive expression is to create a natural balance and equilibrium. Each sign has something to learn from its opposite, but also has a contribution to make towards the other sign's more evolved expression. The Sixth (Virgo) and Twelfth (Pisces) House polarity is concerned with daily 'seen' life versus spiritual 'unseen' life.

The work and service represented by the Sixth House is taken into deeper, wider and more complex areas by the affairs of the Twelfth House. The Sixth house shows work for its own sake, practical and useful, whereas the Twelfth House concentrates more on the concept of service for a collective or Universal good; the individual ego is allowed to retire to a more subordinate role.

Negative and Mutable, this is the polarity of service and sacrifice. It is between the server and the sacrificer, the practical helper and the spiritual helper, the sensible carer and the compassionate carer. Virgo represents meticulous, hard-working efficiency and Pisces demonstrates compassionate, generous self-sacrifice. Both have much to offer the world, but also much to teach the opposite sign. Virgo can reduce everything to statistical analysis, dissecting the whole and using each part wisely so as to achieve maximum effectiveness. The expression of Mercury needs the wider, more generous application of Jupiter or the sensitivity of Neptune. Pisces shows that hard work and service are enriched by humanitarian application and spiritual inspiration. But if the Piscean does not seek to learn from the Virgo, then ideals become merely pipe dreams and sense of purpose is diluted by indiscriminate compassion and sacrifice.

Although the word 'opposite' conjures up feelings of separateness and differences, the astrological polarities should not be seen as two signs in conflict with each other - their positive expression is to create a natural balance and equilibrium. Each sign has something to learn from its opposite, but also has a contribution to make towards the other sign's more evolved expression. The Sixth (Virgo) and the Twelfth (Pisces) House polarity is concerned with daily, Earthly life versus spiritual, 'otherworldly' life; the Virgin dwells firmly in the seen, what can be grasped, the tangible and the physical, while the Fish dwells in the unseen, that which cannot necessarily be held, the intangible and the ethereal.

Virgo is analytical, mentally-motivated, particular, concerned with details, exacting, critical, organised, orderly, systematic, efficient, industrious, anxious, a worrier, perfectionistic, concerned with everyday realities, practical, self-doubting, negative, dissatisfied, helping, serving, useful, modest, unassuming, health-conscious and often hypochondriacal. While Pisces is sometimes confused as to her role in the scheme of things and may experience anxiety as a result, the Fish's qualities are far removed from those of the Virgin. Virgos are critical, discriminating and discerning, while Pisces swims much more with the flow, often tripping over details and scurrying away with a fright at the slightest upset.

Here is the difference between the analyst and the synthesist, the discerner and the settler, the left-brained thinker and the right-brained thinker, the scientist and the artist, logic and that which transcends it, and the practical helper and the empathetic helper. With Pisces, there's a great desire to help the sick, weak and vulnerable, whether they be animal, mineral or vegetable. You may share compassion for the downtrodden with Virgo, but you take the extra step to try to really understand the hearts of the burdened, offering soup and a listening ear, while Virgo's assistance usually ends at the soup, or at least the practical help. The Fish will gently comfort the misfits, the hapless, the failures or the friendless, while the Virgin will regard them as somehow weak by choice, or otherwise undeserving. Your understanding overflows, along with whatever physical help you're able to offer. You sense every vice and virtue, and are profoundly aware of each pitfall - you *sense* it, Virgo *analyses* it, rarely investing the intensity of emotion in people and their reasons that you do.

In this opposition, the Piscean is plunged into the heart of daily realities and material life. You manage your time. You take care of yourself. Instead of being careless, you become care-*full*. You deal with the small details of everyday life. You act and react methodically. You take practical action. You feel more secure. You submit to rules, structures and routine. You economise your time and get organised. You do not escape into fantasy. You get on with the job at hand. You are self-disciplined.

Because the Piscean is the least material and the most spiritual of the zodiacal mandala, Virgo's lessons can be tough nuts for you to crack. While you may lose your senses at times, Virgo brings them back into order for you. In fact, she will even go one step further and steady the ship, to stop you from falling overboard. But first, you must *want* to be saved.

To become fulfilled, you need to integrate both sides of yourself, and welcome the lessons of limitation, logic, order and reason that Virgo can teach you. And although it is also quite perversely necessary to experience madness, transformative behaviours, self-delusions, fantasies, leaving Earthly life behind for periods of time, and intoxication in any of its forms, it is just as necessary to return to the middle road of temperance in order to regain your composure.

The Virgoan soul thrives on routine, schedules and order, while routine, schedules and order are the Piscean's natural enemies and you will do everything in your imagination to avoid them. Pisces relies on intuition, Virgo relies upon logic; Pisces feels its way through life, Virgo is guided by its Mercurial intellect. Pisces relates to spiritual growth, as well as loving yourself and others. It also relates to the over-development of an aversion to the practical side of life by floating purely within the realms of escapism, pixie dust and daydreams. Virgo can help bring this quality down to an Earthly, practical level and *apply* it.

The discriminating, self-disciplined, dutiful and refined individual, adept at craftsmanship and motivated by a quest for purity, perfection and self-improvement (Virgo) should seek the sympathy and compassion and feeling for the unity of life which will allow her to offer her services through love rather than through duty (Pisces). The compassionate, imaginative and understanding individual, sensitive to the needs of others and gifted with a flow of creative ideas (Pisces) seeks to develop the skill, discipline and discrimination which will allow her to offer service and help others in a practical and truly helpful way (Virgo).

Pisces's key traits are associated with idealism, sensitivity, romanticism, appreciation of arts and poetry, gentleness, kindness and a special brand of genuine sympathy and empathy with others. On the other hand, Virgo resides in the 'real world', and although the Virgin shares an enormous sense of care, gentleness and sympathy with Pisces, she can also stop short of any assistance beyond the practical, and can be downright harsh in her treatment of those less fortunate if the moment or situation warrants it. This Virgoan tendency has to do somewhat with her ruler, the quick-minded and intellectually-based Mercury, which swiftly makes an assessment, comes to a judgement, and out of the judgement arises a response, which can either leave the recipient cold or can lift them to wonderful heights in the hands of these extremely helpful, but also clever and discerning, souls. Pisces, meanwhile, will help anyone and will go along with almost any plan life throws at her, and even goes so far as to take that person's problems on as her own, something Virgo will not do; Virgo will offer the shoulder, but can just as easily give a cold shoulder if she feels taken advantage of. Pisces makes no such judgements or assessments; quite simply, if someone is requiring a bit of TLC, the Piscean soul is only too happy and willing to provide it, no questions asked. But the Piscean, being so indiscriminate and embracing of all, can easily lose her personal identity by over-emphasising the needs of others before herself, and must therefore look towards the much more down-to-Earth Virgin for support.

The essential task for Pisceans on this Earthly journey, is to learn how to focus her cosmic, understanding, Universal background into productive, applied detail and action, and once you have grasped this conceptual dynamic, confusion and ennui will leave your life for good. Virgo makes things intelligible, and has much to teach the Fish in this realm, and the Piscean soul is surprisingly receptive and strongly absorbing of this lesson. Spiritual wellbeing is paramount to the Fish, while the Virgin makes it her own priority to be physically healthful and vital; both are consequently drawn to the healing modalities. Pisces can incorporate Virgo's natural leanings towards the natural healings aspects of herbs, diet, massage, yoga and general lifestyle, into her own tendency towards the arts and the mind-body-spirit connection. Here, both can see how the other uses these two sides of the same coin, and both must eventually be able to observe how one cannot exist without the other, that *all* is connected (which is the Fish's lesson for the Virgoan). Although the Virgo will fail to see the forest for the trees, the Pisces can't see the trees for the forest - both these souls need to work together to ensure that all is seen and all is embraced, for you cannot have lots of trees without the forest as a background setting, and you cannot have a forest without the trees.

If you do not learn these lessons from Virgo, your primary impulse towards improvement and refinement may be pushed into the unconscious, resulting in your feeling tired, restless, drained and depressed, or worse, unable or unequipped to cope with the realities of the real world. Pisces are strongly programmed with memories of pain and suffering, and even drawn towards them, but within you also resides the knowledge of how to transcend this suffering; Virgo, while not drawn to the same inner sadness, will help put a practical slant on this transcendence, by offering sensible and workable advice that you can apply in order to heal your heart and, ultimately, your life. Further, Virgo knows of no such nonsense as the martyrdom and persecution Pisces often inflicts herself with, and chases the demons away before they can take root in the spirit, for the Virgin knows deep down that these result in vicious cycles of weakness, confusion and disempowerment. The solution is not to deny your intrinsic knowledge of life's interconnectedness, and your vastly loving nature, but to develop more strength and use that all-encompassing love and compassion constructively. Virgo will always be willing to throw you a rope to lift you out of the deep well you so often find yourself in, and will also stop you escaping into fantasy. The Virgin is your wise, practical helper along life's path, and has the potential to naturally awaken the wisdom you already possess, as well as accrue more. Because as you work towards more practical implementation of the Virgo's sage example, you will become of increasing benefit to the greater destiny of humanity - and your own Universe, which you are ever seeking to widen.

In essence, Virgo can teach you the value of making sensible decisions based on fact rather than fantasy or idealism, to live life less by default and more by choosing your path consciously, to be more decisive and critical when making choices, to be less careless, to focus more on the practical rather than that which exists only in unseen dimensions, and to develop a stronger sense of mind. She can also encourage you to channel your spiritual energies more effectively, and to develop a higher form of intellect, from which you can live in a more rational state of spirituality that aligns with not only yourself, but those around you. If you ever thought that spirituality and rationality could never co-exist (as many Pisceans do), a Virgo is the one to teach you that they indeed can.

Ultimately, you need to swim to the surface of the water occasionally from the murky depths, shake yourself off, take a deep breath and see the world around you in its normal hues, once you take your rose-coloured specs off, in true Virgo style! The colours are even more vivid than you'd ever dreamed of in *this* new world. And you can be guaranteed that as you come out from under that water and from behind those tinted glasses, someone standing ashore, most likely a Virgo, will be awaiting your arrival eagerly, with a strong rod and line to help reel you in. It is then that you may stand upon firm, solid Earth for the first time, and see the horizon clearly for the first time in perhaps your lifetime. That is, after all, Virgo's forte - practical, purposeful, grounded guidance when it's needed most.

WHAT THE VIRGIN CAN ULTIMATELY TEACH THE FISH

Release ★ Fantasies, delusions, illusions, pipe dreams, over-idealism, drifting aimlessly, fatalism, over-reliance on emotions and feelings, despair, irrational fears, despondency, hyperemotional behaviours, fears based on the unseen

Embrace ★ Organisation, selective choice, practicality, a down-to-Earth approach, a sense of the tangible, realism, discernment, decisive action, a sense of purpose, stoicism, a sense of detail and measure, precision, method, analytical mind

To be more grounded, to be more organised, to be more down-to-Earth and practical, how to be more shrewd and choosy, to be more focused and not just drift along aimlessly, logic, realistic thinking, critical analysis, discernment, discrimination, a more grounded sense of self, how to convey thoughts with clearer articulation, the value of study and hard work, how to help others practically, how to be more sensible, frugal and careful, to discriminate between those who are in genuine need of sympathy and those who can help themselves, to be more decisive, and how to live with more emphasis on the intellect than the heart.

MAGIC, DRAWING, ATTRACTION, SPELLS, RITUALS, WISHING & POWER

A Note on the Universe

Within each of us resides the merging of the Sun and the Moon, the dance of the constellations, the vibrations of the planets, and the vast microcosm and macrocosm of the entire *Universe*. Uni means 'one' and Verse means 'song'; therefore, the word Universe literally means 'One Song'. If you learn to tune yourself in, you can even hear it!

What is Magic?

Magic is a kind of special energy that is beyond description, and like most kinds of energy it has its own rules and ways of being manipulated. It remains an elusive term, and no definition has ever really found Universal acceptance. Attempts to separate it from superstition, religion and other-worldly phenomena on the one hand, and 'science' on the other, are ridden with difficulties. However slippery the term 'magic' might be, there is a general agreement that most of us wish for more of its presence in our lives and often fall short of achieving this wish.

Those performing spells, 'asking the Universe', wishing, praying, or undertaking rituals, are using this very special energy to draw things to them. Learning to manipulate energy in these ways is never hard (and shouldn't be), but it can be complex and does require knowledge, practice, creativity, patience and above all, imagination. Most of us use simple magic every day, whether by saying little prayers, making wishes, visualising, and exchanging - sending out and receiving - good, positive or hopeful vibes. When you understand that all the forces and magic you need are *within* you, and you learn to *believe* in that power, you are then able to make all manner of changes to your life and, most importantly, yourself.

Magic is an invisible force which connects and permeates everything. Every thought you have and every action you take, will affect the strength of this force, and can be influenced and directed towards a specific purpose by using certain means. The most important of these are your intentions, facing in the direction of your desired outcome, your will and your *belief* that it works. The more you want something to happen, and the clearer you can visualise the desired outcome, the stronger your will and feelings towards it will be, ensuring an avalanche of amazing people, events and circumstances will flow into your experiences, gathering speed, momentum and power as it nears your goal or dream.

The Universe (or whichever higher power you believe in) works for us and through us. Ideas are given to us but they must be carried out *through* us, in the form of asking or acting or performing a ritual or casting a specific spell. The Universe's abundance is your abundance, and it flows through your mind into manifestation. The Universe or Divine Being in which you believe, gives you the necessary ideas and clothes them with all that is needed to bring them into form when we ask *believing*.

Based on ancient human beliefs, systems and superstitions, declaring what you want and acting out your deepest desires can actually help to make things happen. Magical ideas include the notion that thought affects matter and that the trained imagination can alter the physical world, that all aspects of the Universe are interdependent and that we can discover connections and correspondences between everyday occurrences and cosmic, or Divine, energies. A miracle or a wish coming true can suggest something is going on that extends beyond the laws of nature, that something unseen has occurred; but just because we cannot see it or touch it, it doesn't mean it's not there. Magic exists, especially if you truly believe it does, but science is so far incapable of capturing its essence or the rationale behind it. Personally, I prefer to leave that task to the higher powers of the Universe.

To help your dreams come true and to use your inborn power to its full effect, you can employ boosters based on the special energies and qualities of your Sun sign. These 'boosters' are chosen to be in alignment with the purpose of a particular goal, and contain energies of their own which will enhance the strength of your spell, prayer, ritual or 'asking'. Specific magical energies can be invoked by carrying out a spell or ceremony using specific herbs or colours, or on a particular day of the week, according to either your Sun sign (to heighten the power of the asking), and/or that is in sympathy with that for which you are asking (I have included days of the week for other Sun signs and spell types).

Some materials and boosters you can use to increase the power, magic or energy in any area of your life include: candles, wish lists (written on an appropriate piece of paper written with a specially-chosen writing tool), symbols, affirmations, chants, incense, herbs and flowers, locations, colours, days of the week, elements, crystals and gemstones, animal symbols, charms, talismans, amulets, gods and goddesses, essential oils, planetary hours and your Solar totem animals. All are covered, some more briefly than others, for your very special Sun sign to radiate the energy to powerfully draw your wildest dreams towards you!

Overall, it pays to remember that the Universe (or whatever higher power/s or force/s you happen to believe in) creates *through* you that to which you give your attention. What you contemplate becomes the law of your being, and through your pure unwavering belief, is eventually brought through to manifestation on the material plane. What you think about is entirely up to you. But just be mindful that whatever you think about the most becomes your dominant thought, then your main point of attraction, and is ultimately magnified until it becomes your reality or your experience. So choose your thoughts with care. And to quote Ralph Waldo Emerson, "Be careful what you set your heart upon, for it will surely be yours." I carry a copy of this beautiful prophecy in my purse as its words resonate so strongly with me. In other words, be mindful about what you're wishing for, for you will most probably get it, whether it's good or bad - magic, after all, doesn't discriminate. Just make your dominant thoughts good ones, and you will attract everything you set your heart and intentions upon. Good luck!

ASTROLOGY & MAGIC

"Everyone practices magic, whether they realise it or not, for magic is the art of attracting particular influences, events and situations within human life. Magic is a natural phenomenon because the Universe is reflexive, responding to human thoughts, aspirations and desires …"
David Fideler, *Jesus Christ, Sun of God*

Astrology is the most sublime of the occult * sciences, while at the same time it is one of the most practical for everyday application, for it divines the human soul itself. The cosmos, particularly the patterns that formed across it at the exact moment we were born, indicates the road along which our mental and spiritual endowments are likely to impel us, therefore enabling us to prepare in advance for life's battles, pitfalls, milestones, celebrations and of course to make the utmost of opportunities. Such is the magic of the human mind, that it can 'see' into the future and relive the past without having to be physically present in either, and when combined with astrological *knowing*, particularly the knowing that springs from understanding some of the dynamics of our natal chart, however basic, our inner - and outer - magic can be lifted to phenomenal heights.

In ancient times, not only was astrology the ardent study of the most learned and powerful minds, but among the masses of ordinary people its authority and guidance was accepted and followed without question. How this powerful knowledge was used was - and still is - up to the individual, but all who used it applied it to their perceived advantage.

As primitive humans observed the skies, no doubt they gradually realised that certain stars upon which their fate depended accompanied the seasons, or certain times of the year. They may also have reasoned that if governed their fate, they also governed their bodies, and it is therefore conceivable that the skies were associated with Divine influence. Certain celestial influences were believed to emanate from the thirty-six decans of the signs, and the mysterious but apparent effect that they exercised upon humans were thought to be due to a subtle ether shed by the heavenly stars and spheres on the Earth, that affected not only people, but also other animals, plants and minerals. For the ancient mind, linking magic with astrology may have also provided a much needed sense of predictability and patterns.

Early astrologers named and made associations with the imaginary divisions of the twelve signs and the twelve houses, and people born under a certain sign were said to inherit to an extent, its properties and nature. They also believed that the influence of the planets and stars corresponded with the medicinal properties of certain plants and minerals. They therefore asserted that the influence of a star or planetary position would affect the type of medicine or healing they would offer a subject to attain the most beneficial outcome. Throughout the writings of early philosophers and theorists, there is constant reference to this unmistakable mystic connection between the seven known planets and Earthly affairs and ailments. The seven metals were connected with the seven planets, to which the seven colours and the seven transformations were added. So the alchemist came to share the astrological doctrine that each planet ruled some mineral: The Sun ruled gold, the Moon silver, Mars iron, Venus copper, Saturn lead, Jupiter tin, and Mercury quicksilver. Consequently, in alchemical symbolism the same sign came to represent the metal and its corresponding planet.

In subsequent years, astrology became closely related to alchemical knowledge and development, and the alchemist came to be regarded as an authority not only on the transmutation of metals, but also on astrology and magic. This goes some of the way to explaining how magic and divination, which had always been inseparably bound up with astrology, came to be associated with alchemy. In all the occult sciences, the supreme power was believed to be in the stars above, and from their mysterious emanations all the metals, crystals, minerals, plants and herbs derived their special properties over time. Further, as alchemy became ever more spiritual and concerned with more abstract and philosophical concepts, eventually it was considered that the transmutation of lead into gold was simply a metaphor for the transformation of base matter, in this case the human soul, into a much purer and higher state of wisdom and being.

The Sun and Moon were believed to have greater influence over the human body than all the other heavenly bodies, and to exert their influence in various ways whenever they entered a certain sign of the zodiac. And although the Moon was traditionally regarded as the most important factor of a horoscope, the Sun has come into its own in later centuries, with the result that almost everyone knows their Sun sign but only those who have delved deeper are aware of the sign their natal Moon falls in. For this reason, I have chosen to focus this book series on the twelve Sun signs, as this is what the majority of people are most familiar with.

The following pages contain methods, energies, materials and objects which may be used to increase the magic and power of your Sun sign's influence upon you. Precious stones, flowers, colours and so on, are regarded as having a potent effect upon good fortune by attuning your mind to receive harmonious vibrations from the astral forces that surround you.

Finally, a basic working knowledge of basic astronomy and astrology is an asset when working with luck, abundance, wealth and personal power. You can attract more of these things when you align yourself with the workings of the wider Universe, the movement of the Sun, stars, Moon and planets and become aware of the correlations between the outer cycles of the skies and the inner cycles within yourself. Also, for those who are knowledgeable about Moon phases, equinoxes and solstices, a world of lucky possibilities can also magically open up to you. You don't need to know about astrology's deepest complexities to understand how everything interrelates; just learning the basics will give you an edge - and hopefully the following lucky tips will provide you with at least a small glimpse into the insights gleaned from your Sun sign, which I am certain will endow upon you the potential for amazing results to manifest in your life - and maybe even a step up one further rung towards the heavens!

* The word 'occult' comes from the Latin *occultus*, which literally means 'knowledge of the hidden'.

USING COLOURS, CRYSTALS, DEITIES, PLANTS, FOODS & MATERIAL SUBSTANCES FOR INCREASING POWER & MAGNETISING MAGIC

Alchemist, reformer and mystic Henry Cornelius Agrippa, born in 1486, in his principal work, *On Occult Philosophy*, expressed his belief in the doctrines of astrology and in the theory that the spirit of the world exists in the body of the world, just as the human spirit exists in the body of man. He contended that this spirit also abounds in the celestial bodies and descends in the rays of stars, so that the things influenced by their rays become conformable to them. By this spirit every occult property is conveyed into metals, stones, herbs and animals, through the Sun, Moon and planets, and even through the stars beyond and higher than the planets. A firm believer in the efficacy of charms, he stated that they may "be worn on the body bound to any part of it or hung around the neck, changing sickness into health or health into sickness." I believe the same effect could be applied to wishing and the thinking of positive thoughts, to mean, "Changing thoughts and dreams into manifest reality." He also recommended that these charms be worn in the form of finger rings (that have been created using the materials in agreement and harmony with your Sun Sign's magical energy).

Material substances are connected with abstract purposes by a complex but highly usable and accessible system of correspondences. Use these time-honoured connections in your own spells and wishes to magnetise your desires to you. The following pages will give you some materials, energies, forces and ideas you can summon the power of in order to enhance your magic and luck.

PLANETS

The planetary influence of the day is important when 'asking' for something. If you are wishing for luck, for example, try working with your Sun sign's inherent energies combined with the perfect day of the week for it. So a Piscean might try using her natural psychic and inbuilt intuitive expression, to ask for more romance on a Friday, which is Venus's Day and Venus is renowned for being a planet which deals with matters of love and sensuality, or better still, ask for romance on a Thursday, which is Jupiter's Day, traditional planetary ruler of Pisces, at the time of day when Venus's influence is at its most powerful (information about planetary hours for each day of the week can be found on the Internet or in books on the subject, and can be complex and detailed. It is an art to memorise the correct times, days and energies for the correct spells. If you are determined enough to achieve your dream or goal however, you will be determined enough to put in the research to do it properly!) Here is a very simplified list of the days of the week and their meanings:

DAYS OF THE WEEK & THEIR POWERS

MONDAY ★ Moon
Cancer

The Divine feminine, changes, intuition, emotions, secrets, dealing with women, purity, goodness, perfection, unity, psychic ability, magic, spirituality, invoking a goddess's or angel's guidance, anything that fluctuates, contracts, increases or decreases.

TUESDAY ★ Mars
Aries & Scorpio

Enthusiasm, competition, passion, energy, courage, protection, victory, anything requiring assertiveness, standing up for yourself, or a 'fighting spirit', determination, vitality, sexuality, self-confidence, men's power, men's mysteries, drive, ambition, achievement, triumph, masculinity.

WEDNESDAY ★ Mercury
Gemini & Virgo

Education, travel, exams, study, communication, making connections, thinking, dealing with siblings, writing and speaking, knowledge, learning, adaptability, charm, youth, absorbing information.

THURSDAY ★ Jupiter
Sagittarius & Pisces

Increase and expansion of anything (remember to be careful what you wish for), luck, growth, influence, worldly power, accomplishment, fulfilment, gambling, philosophy, higher education, abundance, optimism.

FRIDAY ★ Venus
Taurus & Libra

Love, luxury, the arts, indulgence, beauty, marriage, money, prosperity, fertility, women's power, women's mysteries, grace, charm, appeal, hope, pleasure, decorating, self-worth, self-esteem, personal values, business partnerships, romance, creativity, sharing, bonding.

SATURDAY ★ Saturn
Capricorn & Aquarius

Long-term goals, career, institutions, establishments, security, investments, karma, reversal, structure, protection, solitude, privacy, determination, ending, blocking, renewing, transforming, anything to do with the public.

SUNDAY ★ Sun
Leo

All-purpose, success, wishes, generosity, happiness, optimism, spirit/essence, recognition, health, vitality, material wealth, invoking a god's aid or guidance, personal empowerment, spirituality, the Divine masculine.

YOUR NATAL MOON PHASE

Although this book is aimed at enhancing your life through the energy of your Sun sign, a bit of Lunar help can give your wishing a boost! As well as using the planetary days and hours system to add a bit of zest to your wish fulfilment, try combining your Sun sign's power periods with your natal Moon phase (your natal Moon phase can be calculated using a number of sources on the internet, or through an astrologer), or even studying which constellation the Moon is situated in at certain times, to increase the power of your spells and asking rituals. For example, you might like to 'ask' for a promotion at work during a New/Waxing Moon period, particularly if the Moon happens to fall under an auspicious sign for career advancement, such as Capricorn. Your natal Moon phase can also be used to similar effect, by researching when your Moon phase will coincide with a certain Lunar constellation position.

In most astrological interpretations the Sun is regarded as the most important, central feature of a natal chart. But to many the Moon is equally, if not more, important than the Sun sign. Many ancient cultures considered the Moon sign to be more significant. The Moon passes through the 12 signs about every 2.5 days, usually covering the whole zodiac in around 27.3 days. The Moon symbolises our inner world, the world of feeling, emotions, habitual responses, instincts, intuition, security and the subconscious. It describes our nurturing style and needs, our emotional response to life, our attitudes and likely reactions to others, our instinctive and habitual responses, the receptive feminine side of ourselves, our experience of our mother or mother figure, and our childhood experience. It represents the soul. In relationships it symbolises how we like to be nurtured and cared for, and the potential depth of our involvement on personal intimate levels.

For many centuries, people across the world have recognised that the Moon influences the affairs of all living things on planet Earth. The waxing Moon appears to have a drawing, increasing and enhancing effect, whereas the waning Moon has a decreasing, receding and withdrawing effect. All things that come into being are stamped with the qualities of the prevailing Moon stage. It seems that people born during certain Lunar phases tend to share specific attributes with other people born during this same phase. In turn, their attributes will be subtly different from those of individuals born during any of the other stages in the Moon cycle. Knowing exactly which phase of the Moon you were born under gives you all kinds of extraordinarily valuable insights into your character, emotions, behaviour and motivations in life. It can make you aware of your deepest underlying drives, the fundamental purpose that you are drawn towards in life and the contribution you can make to others and society during the course of your lifetime. This knowledge may enable you to intuit and make the most of your own personal cyclical pattern that you go through each month, and allow you to know when the most auspicious periods of time are for you and your affairs, nurture yourself and channel your energies in the most positive directions.

Because this Lunar pattern repeats itself every month, you will find that you can even pace yourself on a long-term basis. This will enable you to effectively target your efforts and goals on periods of time that you know will be potentially fortunate for you. You may in fact find that your birth phase corresponds with the days of the month when you have abundant energy, feel inspired and can generate new ideas with ease. During this period, you should work towards the fruition of your efforts, bring your dreams into light and reach for the stars!

The Lunar Phases Are:
★ New Moon
★ First/Waxing Crescent
★ First Quarter
★ Waxing Gibbous Moon
★ Full Moon
★ Waning Gibbous / Disseminating Moon
★ Last Quarter
★ Waning Crescent / Balsamic Moon
★ Back to the New Moon

SPELLS, MAGIC & WISHING WITH MOON PHASES

Though the Moon has eight astronomical phases, it is the three phases corresponding to maiden, mother and crone that are the most significant in spells, ritual, wish magic and psychic work. By tuning into the physical Moon we can understand and harness these distinct energy phases in our daily lives and magical worlds. The four primary Lunar phases are the New Moon, First Quarter, Full Moon and the Last Quarter. Depending on what sort of spell you wish to perform, your spell should take place during one of these cycles or time periods. Each phase of the Moon is good for some types of magic, but not so much for others.

NEW MOON, WAXING & FIRST QUARTER

In astronomical terms, the New Moon occurs when the Moon rises and sets at the same time as the Sun. Both bodies are found in the same position compared with the Earth. Therefore, a Solar eclipse can only ever occur at the New Moon, when the two luminaries are found, for a short time, in a perfect line relative to the Earth, with the Moon positioned between the Sun and the Earth. The New Moon's sunlit face is hidden from the Earth.

In astrological terms, the New Moon occurs at a time when the Sun and the Moon are found in the same degree of the zodiac and therefore occupy the same zodiac sign, forming a conjunction, or a 'fusing' of energies.

In astronomical terms, the First Quarter occurs seven days after the New Moon. Seen from the Earth, this phase makes the Moon like a crescent, forming the shape of a capital D.

In astrological terms, it occurs when the Sun and the Moon form a ninety-degree angle, or the square aspect, inside the zodiac, the Moon always preceding the Sun.

As the New Moon marks the beginning of a new cycle, it symbolises fresh starts. This is an exceptional time to work magic and make wishes for new beginnings, and for the conception and initiation of new projects. Use this Moon phase for improving health, the gradual increase of prosperity, attracting good luck, fertility magic, finding new love, friendship or romance, job hunting, making plans for the future and increasing your general spiritual or psychic awareness.

Overall, the Waxing Crescent and First Quarter Moon phases are appropriate for spells, rituals and workings that involve growth, healing and increase. This is a period of time lasting approximately two weeks, to draw things toward you and increase things, such as love, prosperity and new opportunities. During this period is the time to bless new projects, anything that requires energy to grow, such as gardens, business ventures, new homes, or educational pursuits. Personal growth and healing are accented, as is 'attraction magic' - drawing something to you such as love, abundance, health, success or a new path - and if done well, you can expect results by the next Full Moon. Magical workings for gain, increase or bringing things to you should be initiated when the Moon is waxing (or New, going from Dark to Full). A time for divination of all kinds, spells of spiritual intention, and for any creative project you wish to see birthed, with magical and fruitful results.

While making a wish within the first forty-eight hours after the New Moon is a powerful way of helping it come to fruition, the most potent time for making wishes is actually within the first eight hours of the exact time of its position. Write down your wish list within this first eight hours on a piece of appropriately coloured paper with a special writing tool, and be sure to capture the essence of your wish by wording it in a way that charges your emotions and simply feels 'right'. Make a maximum of ten wishes (less is perfectly fine too), as making too many wishes might disperse their energy too much to be effective. After writing down your list and releasing your wishes to the Universe in whichever form you feel happy with, keep your list and check on it in a few days', weeks' or months' time to assess whether anything has shifted in the direction of your listed dreams, desires or goals. I'll bet it has - or at the very least, something even better has arrived in its place!

Although the first forty-eight hours after the New Moon is the most potent time to make a special wish, you can begin Waxing Moon magic when you can see the crescent in the sky and continue until the day before the Full Moon. The closer to the Full Moon, the more intense the energies. In fact, a personally devised ritual using any special Lunar-associated materials over three days up to and including the Full Moon is excellent for something you require urgently or within a short timeframe.

In some cultures, people turn over silver coins or jewellery three times when the crescent Moon appears in the sky and make a wish. As the Moon grows, it is believed that prosperity and good fortune will grow too.

While the New Moon is not known as a time for 'banishing' or releasing things we no longer want in our lives, I feel that if we are to ask and wish for things, we need to make room to receive them. Making room means that the Universe can slot it right into our lives where we have cleared our paths for it. Clutter, unwanted things, unhappy relationships, possessions that no longer serve us, are all things we can banish. So, to help what you are asking for come into your life quicker, the New Moon is a particularly opportune time to throw a few things out so you can make way for the new and clear up some space for that which you are wishing for. What are you waiting for? Start creating a space for your wishes today!

FULL MOON

In astronomical terms, the Full Moon occurs 14 days after the New Moon, on the day when the Moon sets at the same time the Sun rises, or conversely. The two luminaries are effectively facing each other, with the Earth in between, the Sun shining its light onto the reflective Moon, giving it the fully lit up appearance of a giant, bright, perfectly round sphere. Indeed, its entire face is bathed in sunlight. A Lunar eclipse can only occur at the Full Moon, when the Sun, Moon and Earth are all in line, and the Earth hides the lit side of the Moon to us.

In astrological terms, a Full Moon occurs at the time when the Sun and Moon are 180 degrees apart inside the zodiac, and therefore positioned in opposite signs, forming an opposition aspect.

The highest energy occurs at the Full Moon, making this is a powerful time for all manner of magical workings. Use the Full Moon phase for any immediate need, a sudden boost of power or courage, psychic protection, a change of career or location, travel, healing acute health conditions, the consummation of love or a commitment, justice, ambition and promotion of all kinds. This phase lasts approximately 3 days - 24 hours before the exact Full Moon, the day of, and 24 hours after it, according to many sources - giving us 3 full days to perform our spells. However, we are not strictly limited to a three-day period; the power of this phase can actually be accessed for seven days - three days prior to, the night of, and the three days after the Full Moon. The Full Moon period is when the Moon is at her most powerful, being the most luminous and radiant part of the cycle. Known as the 'high tide' of psychic power, the Full Moon represents culmination, climax, fulfilment and abundance. The Full Moon governs all kinds of magic, including manifestation, banishing, and is particularly good for calling forth protection and heightening your intuitive abilities. The Full Moon contains magic that calls forth personal power, fertility, spiritual development, and psychic awareness. Cleansing of ritual tools, crystals, wish lists, Tarot decks, and the like can be done during this phase. Magic worked during the Full Moon often takes one complete cycle to come to fruition. Try also reaffirming your desires during the New Moon to give them an added nudge in the right direction.

LAST QUARTER OR WANING MOON

In astronomical terms, the Last Quarter, or Waning Moon, occurs twenty-one days after the New Moon. The time difference between the rising and setting of the two luminaries is reduced to what it was at the First Quarter. Viewed from the Earth, the Moon resembles a crescent whose lit up area is decreasing in size, forming the shape of a capital C.

In astrological terms, the Waning Moon occurs when the Sun and Moon are positioned at ninety degree angles of each other in the zodiac, forming the square aspect again. However, during this phase, the Sun is instead *ahead* of the Moon.

The Waning Moon represents the Lunar cycle from Full to Dark. Any spells and magic performed during this period is based purely around banishing and releasing. It could involve releasing things which no longer serve you (such as behaviours, material things, relationships and attitudes), banishing negative energies, and removing obstacles which are standing in the way of achieving your goals or dreams. The Waning Moon is the best time for cleansing, gently releasing, eliminating, expelling and completion. It is of great assistance when you are wanting to let go of something, or someone, gradually. The Dark of the Moon, the period when the Moon is no longer visible to the naked eye, until the New Moon, is the most useful time for divination of all kinds.

★ What is your natal Moon phase type? Can you think of ways you can combine it with the power of your Sun sign to effect change and bring about wonderful happenings?
★

HARNESSING YOUR PERSONAL MOON MAGIC ★ MOON IN PISCES

When the Moon is in your sign of Pisces, it is a great time for working magic around: Personal spirituality, meditation, mysticism, connection to the Divine, inspiration, Psychism, compassion, creativity, devotion and Universal peace. Suggested operations could be around rituals and spells for improving your imagination, visualisation techniques, astral projection, dreaming, telepathy, communicating with the 'other side', and divination of all kinds. Invoke Lunar Pisces's energies to increase your sensitivity, intuition, and empathy and sympathy with others (and theirs with you). It is also an opportune time to undertake something which involves a degree of self-sacrifice in order to help someone else in need. With the Moon in Pisces, you can call forth the ability to expand your vision rather than getting caught up in the petty details of a situation.

THE MOON ★
WHAT IT REPRESENTS
IN THE HUMAN PSYCHE &
NATAL CHART

The Moon in the sky shines with the reflected light of the Sun. Although not a planet, the Moon is our nearest celestial neighbour and exerts a great influence upon us. The gravitational pull of the Moon affects our body fluids, which contribute to about 90 per cent of our biological make-up. It moves at approximately half a degree per hour and takes an average of 27.3 days to pass through all twelve zodiac signs, staying in each for around 2.5 days.

In astrology the Moon corresponds with the way in which we reflect and respond to what is going on around us. It has to do with our feelings, emotions and instincts and, in the same way the Moon influences the tides on planet Earth, it symbolises the ebb and flow of our emotional nature, our moods, fluctuations and changeability. The Moon is the archetype of the Mother, which is within us all, and represents the primary feminine principle in the natal chart. It is through the Moon that we express our parental instincts - caring, nurturing, protecting, and sensitivity. The Moon has links with the past and the subconscious and it is from this almost primitive source that our natural instinctual forces flow.

The Moon is essentially a feminine principle and associates with the inner personality, receptivity, passivity and inward-oriented feelings. It can act as an inner guide to the deeper self, the unconscious self, figures half-shrouded in mystery, linking the hidden personal world of the subconscious to the clearer world of personal awareness.

The Moon is the innermost core of our being, private feelings, habitual reactions and subconscious habits. It is the caring, nurturing sustainer of life, the 'mother' of the zodiac. It tells us about how we seek security, our urge to nurture, our nurturing style, our responses and feelings and moods. The innermost core of our being, private feelings, subconscious habits. It is concerned with habits, mothering, habitual/instinctive responses and personality. It is our karma, our soul, our past.

The Moon represents our mother or mother figure, our feminine side, maternal instinct, our nurturing style and needs, our unconscious self, our emotional reactions, the subconscious, our feelings, instincts, intuition, receptivity, habits, what we need to feel secure, fluctuations, cycles, moods, and our childhood. Its position in the birth chart is very significant, because as well as revealing feminine qualities and the potential gentleness and tenderness of a being, the Moon also reveals important information about the experiences and expression of the five senses.

The Moon is essentially receptive and passive; it reflects the life experience rather than initiating it. Fluctuating and cyclical, the Moon is the planet (although technically a satellite) of the childhood experience, and instinctual reactions. It represents the mother (a child's experience and expectations of their mother), maternal instincts and the feminine principle, indicating how strongly these manifest in an individual, male or female.

As it represents what our childhood experience is likely to be, and childhood is essentially a time where our consciousness has not yet fully developed, our Moon sign traits seem to be more apparent in our younger years. We will usually show our Moon sign traits more so than our Sun sign traits during the developing period of infancy and early childhood, until we have the presence of mind to more consciously develop our ego and true core self (the Sun).

The symbol for the Moon ☽ is a representation of its crescent in its waxing phase from new to full, but it can also be seen as two half circles - these form a bowl shape, a receptacle, a feminine container that 'receives' and 'holds' anything put into it. The half circle, unlike the full circle of the Sun, is finite and incomplete, almost as if striving for wholeness.

The Moon represents our *soul*.

YOUR MOON SIGN

The Sun / Moon Polarity
Conscious & Unconscious, Night & Day, Yin & Yang

"Man does, woman is."
Edward Edinger

Your Moon Sign, representing your soul, and your Sun sign, representing your spirit, work together to form the foundation of your basic personality, expression and nature. If you know what your Moon sign is, look it up below and read how it works with your Piscean Sun to blend your mind, soul and spirit.

♈ **With the Moon in ARIES**, Sun in Pisces, you are likely to be ★ Devoted to truth, understanding, romantic, quarrelsome, innocently childlike, independent, loyal, prophetic, affectionate, robustly sensual, emotionally edgy and reckless, frustrated, respectful of others' feelings, humble but self-centred, artistic, touchy, pioneering, original, impetuous, emotionally fluctuating, forward-looking, sensitive, off-the-wall, adventurous, vividly imaginative, wilful, moody, a quick thinker, a saviour, nervous, quietly charismatic, warmth and optimistic, spirited, fun-loving, resilient, adaptable, big-hearted, and always battling the paradox between romantic vulnerability and forthright assertiveness.

Sun/Moon Harmony Rating ★ *6 out of 10*

♉ **With the Moon in TAURUS**, Sun in Pisces, you are likely to be ★ Calm, sensitive to beauty, level-headed, harmonious, charming, easygoing, gentle, infinitely patient, able to transform your imaginative ideas in tangible outcomes, feminine, fair-minded, a practical romantic, slow-paced, able to manifest dreams on the material plane, practically idealistic, subjective and emotional, able to manoeuvre situations to suit your security and lifestyle needs, helpful, emotionally placid, devoted to people, animals and causes, emotionally demonstrative, loving of simple pleasures and delights, sensual, manipulative, artistic, musical faithful, friendly, resourceful, peace-loving but strong-willed, able to bring your romantic nature down to Earth, old-fashioned, strongly seductive, shrewd and philanthropic with money, caring, idealistic but down-to-Earth, thoughtful, compassionate, moody, sociable, warm, needy, security-striving, both a dreamer and a realist, and dedicated to grounding your inspiration, spirituality and idealism.

Sun/Moon Harmony Rating ★ *7.5 out of 10*

♊ **With the Moon in GEMINI,** Sun in Pisces, you are likely to be ★ Fanciful, a free spirit, childlike, humorous, imaginative, changeable, friendly, breezy, emotionally versatile, lacking in confidence, open, alternating between timidity and sociability, philosophical but flippant, perceptive, inspiring, charming and stimulating, like a leaf blowing in the wind, sociable, impressionable, flexible, curious, emotionally restless, fickle, non-committal, creative, aware of others' feelings, careless, easily influenced by others, sentimental, temperamental, emotionally naïve, forgiving, gifted, a sparkling friend, whimsical, popular, poetic, good with words, funny, sometimes reticent and sometimes talkative, intuitive, easily swept away by ideas and concepts, open towards and perceptive of new ideas, self-doubting, self-pitying, idealistic, eternally youthful, wordy and expressive, dependent on others, able to mimic with sharp precision, intelligently creative, emotionally and socially intelligent, squandering of your natural talents, diplomatic, appreciative of a wide variety of people, fluent and originally self-expressive, fun-loving, reluctant to face the darker aspects of life, too busy and dreamy to deal with feelings, and ruled by both your head and your heart.

Sun/Moon Harmony Rating ★ *6.5 out of 10*

♋ **With the Moon in CANCER,** Sun in Pisces, you are likely to be ★ Ultra-sensitive, intuitive, romantic, emotional, kind-hearted, sympathetic, shy, emotionally reticent, retiring, ruled by matters of the heart, hidden, private, thoughtful and caring, a bit of a hermit, peaceful, imaginative, poetic, creative, deeply kind, devoted to feelings and easing others' pain, a deep sense of the human spirit, helpful, companionable, old-fashioned, nurturing, introspective, colourfully imaginative, timid, a healer, good-humoured, able to express personal insights with close loved ones, self-protective, likely to take in 'lame ducks', involved, defensive, devious, fearful, overly sensitive, offended at the slightest provocation, easily overcome by more extroverted and 'powerful' personalities, moody, unreasonable, quiet, genuinely compassionate, and instinctively understanding of the human heart and psyche. **

Sun/Moon Harmony Rating ★ *8.5 out of 10*

♌ **With the Moon in LEO,** Sun in Pisces, you are likely to be ★ Proud, individualistic, charming on the surface with a gentle strength within, dramatic, sensitive, prone to dramatise your weaknesses in order to manipulate others' sympathy, in possession of a rich inner world, apparently sure of self but insecure inside, artistic, wise and generous in helping others, visionary, passionate, sociable, radiantly caring, receptive, enthusiastic, innocent, trusting, a dynamic healer, richly spiritual, romantically imaginative and creative, open, a tragic romantic, charismatic, quietly passionate, unstable, warm, inclined to get carried away by romance and idealism, theatrical, intuitively insightful, fluctuating in inspiration, huffy, emotionally volatile, sometimes mysterious, vain, glamorising of others and failing to see their true colours, friendly, generous and giving, emotionally demonstrative and expressive, creative, emotionally radiating warmth, emotionally idealistic, luxury-loving, helpful, affectionate, seductive, attractive, moody, and unwaveringly loyal and devoted to loved ones.

Sun/Moon Harmony Rating ★ *7 out of 10*

♍ **With the Moon in VIRGO,** Sun in Pisces, you are likely to be ★ Emotionally intelligent, perceptive, intellectually intuitive, both head and heart-oriented, an emotional perfectionist, well-liked, broad in mind and outlook, willing to look at things from all angles, divided between logic and intuition, a devoted spiritualist, a good healer, helpful, considerate, kind-hearted, unassuming, modest, caring, adaptable, reserved, altruistic, genuinely kind, a quiet thinker, dry-witted, self-sacrificing, nervous and fretful, polite, discerning but forgiving, an artist-scientist, interested in holistic health and healing, appreciative, a logical metaphysician, courteous, self-pitying, dedicated to ideals, understated, respectful of others, refined in tastes, and a devoted servant.

Sun/Moon Harmony Rating ★ 6 out of 10

♎ **With the Moon in LIBRA,** Sun in Pisces, you are likely to be ★ Emotionally intelligent, cultured, sensitive, whimsical, gifted with insights, gullible, eloquent, intuitive, diplomatic, emotionally refined, graceful, gentle, peaceable, romantic, generally well-balanced and moderate, easygoing, a hider of feelings, artistic, charming, approachable, tolerant, sharing, gracious, blessed with the ability to inspire others through your graceful self-expression, unrealistic, sociable, imaginative, cooperative, gregarious, cagey, approval-seeking, compliant, agreeable, hedonistic, indecisive, romantically idealistic, endearing, delightful company, artistically sensitive, trusting, tasteful, inspiring, creative, attracted to beautiful things, emotionally naïve, and conflicted between rational and emotional thought.

Sun/Moon Harmony Rating ★ *9 out of 10*

♏ **With the Moon in SCORPIO**, Sun in Pisces, you are likely to be ★ Intense, powerfully sensitive, insightful, investigative, intensely dedicated to ideals, self-protective, complex, feelings-based, richly imaginative, strong in adversity, resourceful, helpful, manipulative, sometimes extreme and sometimes gentle, understanding of the human spirit, compassionate to others' crises and tragedies, courageous and timid at the same time, drawn to sensationalism, resilient, irrationally suspicious of others' motives, devoted to ideals, embracing of the comic and the tragic together, psychologically penetrative, self-pitying, evasive, secretive, hidden, loyal, emotional, perceptive, emotionally powerful, torn between self-sacrifice versus self-reliance and control, and constantly experiencing pulls towards agony or ecstasy. ★★

Sun/Moon Harmony Rating ★ *8.5 out of 10*

♐ **With the Moon in SAGITTARIUS,** Sun in Pisces, you are likely to be ★ Eager, endearingly naïve, adventurous, friendly, a traveller of body and mind, big-hearted, trusting, believing, generous, warm, impatient with petty details and restrictions of daily life, prone to exaggeration, inquisitive, one who sees the best in everyone, an adventurer, affectionate, charismatic, able to see the 'big picture', idealistic, widely imaginative, lacking in focus, wanting to be all things to all people, exuberant, deeply spiritual and/or religious, emotionalising of moral issues, emotionally reckless and careless, a free spirit, faithful to social causes, devious, non-committal, a good teacher, in possession of a zany sense of humour, far-sighted, optimistic, a lover of learning, inspiring, able to make others laugh, procrastinating, morally confused, self-deceiving, aspiring, enlightening, a seeker of truth, gregarious, socially concerned, broad-minded, expansive, emotionally philosophical, freedom-seeking, and guided by both reason and emotion.

Sun/Moon Harmony Rating ★ *7.5 out of 10*

♑ **With the Moon in CAPRICORN,** Sun in Pisces, you are likely to be ★ Committed to causes, driven to help others, ambitious to make others' lives better in some way, perceptive, cautious, reserved, withdrawn, cool, wise, pragmatic and resourceful in the use of your imagination, unassuming, introverted, understanding of the practical applications of wisdom, prone to pessimism and worry, secretive and defensive, moralistic and judgemental in human relations, discreetly ambitious, a practical dreamer, a realist and an idealist at the same time, personally honourable, uptight, creatively down-to-Earth, a pillar of strength, aware of human character, sardonically humorous, charitable, serious and self-reflective, devoted, quietly adaptable, abiding, circumspect, a reserved romantic, strategic, dutiful, dependable, and able to pin down the elusive.

Sun/Moon Harmony Rating ★ *6 out of 10*

♒ **With the Moon in AQUARIUS,** Sun in Pisces, you are likely to be ★ Friendly and tolerant, idealistic, eccentric, 'different', unconventional, aloof, paradoxical, interested in science fiction and fantasy, imaginative, sympathetic, original, forward-flowing, highly observant, acutely aware of the human condition, living an unusual lifestyle in some way, well-meaning, a missionary, a servant of Universal concerns, open to the unusual, emotionally naïve, drawn to unusual art and beauty, over-identifying with causes, sociable, freedom-loving, unorthodox, impractical, loyal, humanitarian, easily influenced, globally aware, easygoing, aware of the human condition, able to use both the left and right sides of the brain, accepting of the whole gamut of society, morally trustworthy, genuinely desiring to make the world a better place, charitable, emotionally gullible, easily overwhelmed by the woes and causes of the world, devoted to your ideals, and in possession of an eternal sense of hope and belief in the triumph of the human spirit.

Sun/Moon Harmony Rating ★ *7.5 out of 10*

♓ **With the Moon in PISCES,** Sun in Pisces, you are likely to be ★ Highly imaginative, overly sensitive, intuitive, mystical, over-idealistic, a chaser of spiritual rainbows, good-natured, unworldly, shy, gentle, intriguing, kindly, friendly, emotional, easily moved, intensely subjective, passive, self-sabotaging, apt to go into flights of fancy and fantasy, an escapist, deeply sentimental, accepting, impressionable, adrift at sea, understanding, vulnerable, an artist and a poet, altruistic, self-sacrificing, unsure, able to identify with the whole spectrum of human joys and sorrows, hopelessly romantic, in possession of a Universal outlook, generous, receptive, creative, forgiving, mysterious, selfless, concerned with the welfare of others, empathetic, prone to drifting and wasting time in daydreams, easily swayed, gullible, impractical, evasive, psychic, adaptable, and aware of the feelings of others.

Sun/Moon Harmony Rating ★ 8 out of 10

** If your Moon is in Cancer or Scorpio, your Sun and Moon will form what is known in astrology as a trine aspect. This aspect is the easiest, most flowing and harmonious astrological aspect, ensuring that your Sun and Moon, or spirit and soul, are well integrated. With both luminaries in Water signs, this gives them the best possible degree of complementary energy - a blending of the elements suggests a balanced expression of personality. One drawback of the trine aspect lies in the fact that its easy flow can be *too* harmonious; if our path is too smooth and difficulties don't arise to challenge us from time to time, we can often become lazy and complacent, stunting our growth and spiritual evolution. As Water signs, you share the art of sensitivity, creativity, intrigue, compassion, a nurturing instinct, poetry, understanding, spirituality, a deep need for connection and merging with others, but may be overly sensitive, illogical, clingy, impractical, too emotional, irrational, dependent, manipulative and elusive.

YOUR BODY & HEALTH

"A physician without a knowledge of astrology has no right to call himself a physician."
Hippocrates (born c. 460 BC)

Hippocrates, the fifth century BC Greek physician and 'father of medicine' and supposed author of the Hippocratic Oath, maintained that no one should be allowed to practise medicine who had not first studied astrology. Another Greek physician, Claudius Galen, brought together a huge range of knowledge and ideas in the second century AD which dominated medical practice until the 17th century. Among his teachings was a diagnostic technique which assumed that illnesses and their treatments were affected by and governed by the phases of the Moon. For centuries, astrology was a compulsory component of medical training (and still is in some natural medicine degrees), albeit only one aspect of diagnosis and treatment.

Medical or health astrology concerns particular ways of determining and interpreting an individual's horoscope with particular reference to health issues - diagnosis of current dis-eases, identification of areas of bodily weaknesses, and the prescription of natural cures and remedies. In ancient times, and still even today, the movement of the stars and planets was believed to affect bodily functions, and to cause ailments, or cure them.

During the Middle Ages, many drawings of the 'zodiac man' were made, which showed which signs of the zodiac were related to each part of the body, providing information as to the best times of the year to undertake cures for ailments affecting the corresponding body parts.

Health astrology persists today in many forms and among astrologers themselves, from whom clients seek counsel on health-related issues, and while it certainly cannot be used diagnose a condition or dis-ease, one's Sun sign, along with other factors of the natal chart, can definitely indicate potential problem areas of weakness or possible troubles. This branch of astrology has been found to be surprisingly accurate in most cases. While mostly accurate, none of the following information should ever be used as a substitute for professional medical advice should you be personally concerned about any of the conditions or afflictions listed for your Sun sign.

PISCEAN HEALTH

Pisces is associated with the Feet, Toes, Lymphatic System, Immune System, Clotting Mechanisms, Blood Circulation, Veins, Body Fluids, Synovia, Nervous Digestion, Liver, Pineal Gland, Peritoneum, Appendix, Allergies, and the Gastro-Abdominal System. Pisceans are healthy people as long as they feel loved and have an outlet for their dreamy natures. Unhappy or despondent Pisceans are prone to problems arising from their escapist tendencies, such as indulging in alcohol, drugs or even developing eating disorders as a way of coping with emotions that may feel unbearable. Having such a delicate and impressionable constitution, intoxicants and narcotics should be avoided. You are more susceptible than most to addiction-related physical and mental health problems should you choose to indulge in substance misuse. Being easily led and rather weak-willed, an addiction or a compulsion of some kind will likely be an issue for you at some stage in your life. Pisceans are also vulnerable to depression and distress, a manifestation of constantly having to struggle to swim against the current to avoid being pulled under or overwhelmed.

Pisces represents the energy of diffusion. Your nature is cold, watery and receptive. Principal rulerships, as already mentioned, include the feet and toes, diffusion/movement of fluids and gases, immune and lymphatic functions, cerebral spinal fluid and the spinal canal.

Finding comfortable shoes can be a problem for you, as Pisces rules the feet. Also, troubles with or deformities of the feet and toes, hands or hips, may afflict Pisceans, and you may suffer such conditions such as bunions, chilblains, gout, corns, boils and foot deformities which make finding proper-fitting shoes even harder to find. Vein and circulation problems, incurable dis-eases, the lymphatic system and the spleen in its lymphatic role, and strange conditions that are difficult to diagnose or treat can also afflict the Fish. Flus, colds and pneumonia are common ailments too, which you may find hard to shake off. A typical Pisces may become more forgetful than usual when an illness is about to strike.

The sensitive psyche of the Piscean can suffer greatly in times of stress, and has little to draw on in terms of physical resources. You have a hidden inner resistance to many ills, however, and one of your challenges is to discover your latent strengths and call upon them. On top of this, you have an uncanny ability of being able to hypnotise yourself into or out of anything you choose, so choosing your thoughts with care is paramount to your health - both physical and mental.

Overall your health prospects are fairly good, if you can avoid becoming too receptive to the people and conditions around you, as you are prone to attracting similar conditions to those in your immediate environment, and as such are more vulnerable than most to infectious diseases. You easily pick up vibrations in the atmosphere around you so can be physical affected by such things as an unkind word, an argument or even depressing weather. This sensitivity can disturb the Piscean constitution and afflict you with emotionally-based health conditions.

Pisces should also beware of overindulgence in food, of which they are very fond. Poor eating habits can bring troubles with intestinal functions and digestive issues; sluggishness of the liver may also be a problem. Your metabolism is weaker and less dynamic than that of the other signs, and you seem to have a slow metabolism, which is why you may often wake up sleepy-eyed and listless. You also run out of energy quite quickly.

You are the most suggestible sign of the zodiac, so respond very well to optimistic and encouraging doctors; if you are assured you are making progress by someone in authority or one whose opinion you respect, you invariably show immediate improvement. Easily convinced and impressionable, you can even hypnotise yourself.

Sometimes you dreamily tend to think you can live forever, and you often act as though you believe this zealously. Feeling so invincible, you are notorious for typically not taking the best care of yourself. Your health being rarely robust to begin with, is then further depleted by other people's troubles and burdens, which can be a serious drain on your health and energy levels. Because of this, more than any other zodiac sign, you must conserve your energy and refrain from succumbing to stimulants, sedatives, fatigue, other people's woes, and vicious cycles.

Your ruling planet Neptune is connected with weakness, slackness, suggestibility, psychosomatic illnesses, delusions, obsessions, a tendency to allergies, viruses and infections, sleep disorders, habits, poisons, hypochondria, alcoholism and drug abuse, parasites, food sensitivities, and misdiagnoses. Neptune governs the Lymphatic System, Spleen, Pineal Gland, Immune System, White Blood Cells, Seminal Fluid, Fallopian Tubes, Intrauterine Fluid, Fluid in Flesh, and those parts of the nervous system which are receptive to psychic impressions. It is also influential in the functioning of the chakras (the psychic centres of bodily energy) and the human aura. Its governance extends to the Thalamus, a brain structure which affects the transmission of stimuli between the sensory organs.

Your dreamy nature can lead you to forget to eat or drink. Be diligent with your nutrition, hydration and sleeping regime or your immune system will suffer. When unwell, you need quiet, peaceful surroundings as near as possible to water, be it the ocean, a lake, or a spa bath. Music, fresh air, sunshine and regular grounding activities will help you to rebalance.

Keeping yourself in excellent health overall, with a special awareness of Pisces's vulnerable areas, is key to achieving optimal health and vitality, and getting the most out of your life!

THE CELL SALTS ★ ASTROLOGICAL TONICS

Homeopathy and astrology have colluded to provide a wonderful list of astrological tonics, one particularly suited to each of the twelve signs. These are called 'homeopathic cell salts', 'tissue salts' or 'biochemic cell salts', and are available in most health food stores, are inexpensive and easy to take. They are considered to be gentle, effective and safe, even for children, people in fragile health states, and the elderly. Although the full picture, drawn from a full natal horoscope, gives a fuller, more accurate idea of an individual's unique constitution, even simply working with one's date of birth can be enough for the medical astrologer to suggest the use of a cell salt based upon the correlation with an individual's Sun sign. As well as the cell salts having a significant effect upon physical ailments, they can also profoundly influence the subtle energy bodies, including the mental, emotional, etheric and spiritual. Although the most common use of these salts is based upon each salt's correspondence with a Sun sign, use of the cell salt related to one's Moon sign can assist with addressing deeper underlying emotional issues, such as anxiety, depression, panic and fear. Use of the cell salt relating to your Moon sign will therefore help to restore your sense of safety, balance, security and emotional resilience. In the first seven years of life, when the Moon is the most influential sphere in our lives, Lunar cell salts are the most appropriate choice as a remedy or tonic.

For specific health problems, take both the salt of your Sun or Moon sign, *and* the salt that pertains to the specific condition. The same principle applies to the Ascendant sign, as the First House represents one's physical health, and especially if the Sun or Moon is a rising planet, which means rulership of the whole chart. For the purposes of this book, however, the cell salt that correlates with your Sun sign only is outlined.

TISSUE SALT FOR PISCES ★ FERRUM PHOS.

Ferrum Phosphoricum, or Ferr Phos. (Iron phosphate), which is a mineral compound of iron and phosphorous, is the cell salt for Pisces. Both iron and phosphorous occur in the body independently; phosphorous contributes to bone and muscle health, and iron aids the exchange of oxygen in the blood. Ferrum Phos. is the only common metal salt among the twelve cell salts, and is vital in its function of making all of the other salts more effective. Ferrum Phos. has an affinity with oxygen which is carried into the circulation and diffused throughout the body by the chemical force of this cell salt; it is required for health red blood cells, a lack of which can cause anaemia. Homeopathic practitioners regard this tissue salt as being beneficial for those suffering ailments relating to fatigue and anaemia; indeed, it is a natural source of iron for anaemia. Lack of this cell salt can lead to low blood pressure, inflammations, low energy, glandular problems and heart irregularities, among other ailments. Ferrous Phos. is mostly used in the beginning stages of acute illnesses, and for all acute phases of disease.

Pisces rules the lymphatic system and the feet. Just as the feet are the foundation of the whole body, iron is the foundation of the blood. Ferr Phos. delivers oxygen to all organs and tissues, and is indicated in all cases of inflammation and fever. It enables the blood and the lymphatic system to carry waste and toxins away from affected tissues, and is especially recommended for people who are nervous and sensitive, or who are vulnerable to every transient cold, flu or other virus. Iron is known as a magnetic compound and on a spiritual level, this magnetism is made possible by a deep intuitive knowledge, of both the interlocking bodily cycles and the rotations of cosmic activity.

WATER SIGN PISCES & THE PHLEGMATIC HUMOUR

Greek physician Hippocrates (460 - 370 BC) theorised that certain human behaviours were caused by body fluids, called 'humours'. Later, Galen of Pergamon (AD 131 - 200), a Greek physician, developed the first typology of temperaments to encompass many facets of the human psyche and physiology. These also related to the classical elements of Fire, Earth, Air and Water - as choleric, melancholic, sanguine and phlegmatic respectively. According to the Greeks who developed the temperament theory (the word stems from the Latin word *temperamentum*, meaning mixture), temperament is the 'mixture' of qualities that combine to form elements in physics and humours in medicine. The Greeks sought equilibrium in the four qualities of hot, cold, wet (moist), and dry, the elements of Earth, Air, Fire and Water, and the four humours of choler or yellow bile, melancholer or black bile, blood and phlegm. If balance was achieved, the person was said to be well- or even-tempered, and the importance of determining the temperament allowed for imbalances to be treated.

In ancient times, each of the four types of humours corresponded to a different personality type, which were associated with a domination of various biological functions. It was suggested that the temperaments came to clearest manifestation in childhood, between around the ages of six and fourteen of age, after which they become subordinate, but still influential, factors in our personality. It is important to note that your temperament is not your personality. However, your personality can incorporate parts of the temperament in its expression. Personality is shaped by both external and internal factors, whereas the temperament is innate, an inborn, inherent part of each individual.

For Water, the humour is phlegmatic, and it is characterised by a longer response-delay, but short-lived response. Generally low in drive and motivation, phlegmatic natives seek to preserve low energy stores. Phlegmatic types usually give the impression of being calm, naïve and simple, longing for peace in the soul.

Generally inward, people with this temperament tend to be private, reasonable, patient, caring, thoughtful, passive, sluggish, content, tolerant, have a rich inner life, and seek quiet, peaceful environments. Being impressionable, phlegmatic types are often 'awakened' by others' interests in a subject. Steadfast, placid, controlled, reliable, even-tempered, consistent in their habits, they make steady and loyal friends. Your speech may be slow or hesitant, and you may appear clumsy or ponderous. On a physical level, the home of this humour is in the veins and lymphatics, and this humour nourishes the body on a deep and fundamental level.

A phlegmatic disposition represents a slow, even temperament. Its taste is sweet, its nature alkaline, its indication phlegm. The phlegmatic humour is connected with the *liquid* ^ body, and is traditionally associated with cold and wet conditions.

^ A couple of thousand years ago, the Mesopotamians, Chinese and Egyptians, and more recently the Arabs, practised a medicine called 'of three bodies'. According to the doctors of the ancient world (who often practised as astrologers as well), a human being had three bodies: the physical body, the ethereal (or vital) body and the astral body, imparting a holistic approach to health. In modern medicine, usually only the physical body is focused upon fully. According to tradition, this physical body comprises three principles or states corresponding to three primordial elements: *solid* (Earth), *liquid* (Water) and *gas* (Air). This is the material body, the physical outer cover of muscles, nerves and organs held together by the skeleton. The Fire element corresponds with the *astral* body, which sits outside the physical body in one's auric field.

.

MONEY ATTRIBUTES

Colour for Increased Earning Power ★ Purple

The following plants can be used by all zodiac signs to assist in attracting money ★ Ginger, Allspice, Clover, Orange, Marjoram, Cinnamon, Sassafras, Woodruff, Bergamot, Tonka Beans, Heliotrope, Alfalfa, Coltsfoot, Thyme, Mace, Irish Moss, Clove, Almond, Corn, Honeysuckle, Sesame, Nutmeg, Vetiver, Poppy, Jasmine, Dill and Elder Flower. To attract luck and success, try using any of the above, combined with any of the following: Alfalfa Seeds, Basil, Mustard Seeds, Vervain Leaves, Poppy Seeds, Rosemary, Lemon, Anise and Holly.

Striving for financial gain and abundance with a healthy inner moral compass is, in my view, one of the most noble goals we can set for ourselves. When we have more money, we are better placed to help ourselves and of course others; after all, as Abraham Maslow's Hierarchy of Needs model (1943) attests, once our primary and base survival needs have been satisfied, we can then advance higher towards loftier achievements, such as self-confidence, creativity and self-actualisation. Prosperity allows us to turn our attention to these more transcendental matters - to strive for lives not just of material comfort and luxuries, but of meaning, generosity, balance, harmony, fulfilment and joy. Our Sun sign can offer clues as to how we go about acquiring, earning, saving, maintaining, and allowing the overall flow of giving and receiving money. What's *your* money style?

"If someone's dumb enough to offer me a million dollars to make a picture, I'm certainly not dumb enough to turn it down," quipped actress Elizabeth Taylor, encapsulating the Piscean attitude to money: that is, that Pisceans may not seek money out necessarily, but will definitely take it should it be offered to them, and the less hard they need to work for it, the better; this leaves them with ample time to pursue the more spiritual endeavours they are naturally drawn to. Doing good, feeling good, peace of mind, and helping others are the things that matter most to Pisceans.

Money is generally not important to the Fish. Of course you need as much as anyone else, and many of you attain great wealth, but financial gain is not generally your primary objective.

Being impractical and not particularly future-oriented, money tends to flow in and then out for you. You overlook details, rarely check bank statements and you are not inclined to budget, which can mean financial disaster potentially looms around every corner. You tend to be careless with money and would be wise to seek the professional counsel of a financial advisor to stop you spending your money on meaningless investments or purchases. You can let money slip through your fingers easily and without care when you are young, but as you grow older you tend to learn from your financial mistakes, mostly the hard way.

Although you have an uncanny ability to marry into or inherit money, or to have it fall into your lap, you're more aware than most of its temporal qualities. The typical Piscean heart is free from greed. You seem to possess a lack of intensity, almost a carelessness, about tomorrow, coupled with a gentle acceptance of yesterday and an intuitive knowing of today. This attitude spills over into the realm of finances too: you care little for where your next dollar may come from, because your spiritual 'base' is of far greater urgency and concern for your soul.

Pisces tends to earn money intuitively and instinctively, and you follow your hunches rather than apply logic. You can be generous and overly charitable, and almost any kind of misfortune is enough to move you to give. Although your giving nature is one of your many virtues, you can be easily taken advantage of, so be wary who you give or lend your money to. As a naturally generous and trusting sign, you fall easily for woeful tales, finding yourself prey to financial deception, frauds and scams, getting tricked out of large amounts of money.

Pisceans care the least about money of all the signs, preferring to live your dream life in fantasyland in your head, where money issues are not so harsh. The biggest stumbling block for you is your passivity, your tendency to go with the flow of life rather than making things happen to create your own healthy financial circumstances. Developing greater tenacity and focus will help you achieve your wildest fantasies and dreams, and will guard against missing out on money-making opportunities, which you are often too vague to notice.

COLOURS

Chromatomancy, or divination by colour, is a form of energy therapy that has been used for thousands of years by many different cultures. It works on the principle that we make either instinctive and rational choices or preferences based on circumstances which are already present in ourselves; colour also has an effect on the energy in an environment, and we in turn respond consciously or subconsciously to our surroundings. If we look at the causes, and try to understand the reasons, as to why we are so receptive to one particular colour over another, we will see that there is a subtle link between certain hues and our emotional and instinctive individual reactions. The colour which we give to things results from a combination of three elements:

1. The light or the vibration of a body;

2. The context in which it is found and the interaction between its own light and that of its environment;

3. The sensitivity of the eye's retina which sees the body in question. Because of this, a colour can vary, depending on the individual's perceptions, namely, his sensitivity, his mood, and his view of reality. For a long time, people have understood that their vision of reality depends a lot on their moods, feelings and emotions.

Chromatotherapy, or colour healing, stems from this body of evidence, and its main application is the use of colours for healing purposes. Colours are generally associated with characteristics, feelings, stones, metals, plants and flowers, planets and even the zodiac signs. In varying cultures, they play a significant role in ceremonies and regalia.

We vibrate to the frequency of colour, shown through its continual movement and change in our aura ^. One of the most beautiful examples of colour is the rainbow. This architect of colour is caused by the refraction and internal reflection of light in raindrops. Colour can be perceived as either a pigment, or as illumination. The colour spectrum can be divided into eight main colours: red, orange, yellow, green, turquoise, blue, violet and magenta. Each colour has a wavelength and frequency that carry different therapeutic qualities which have indirect effects upon our health and bodily systems, and because of this, coupled with the fact that we as living energy centres emanate colour, colour can be a great medium in healing, calming, energising, increasing and attracting.

Aristotle, in the fourth century BCE, considered blue and yellow to be the true primary colours and related them to life's polarities: Sun and Moon, male and female, stimulation and sedation, in and out, expansion and contraction. He also associated colours with the four elements of Fire, Earth, Air and Water. Hippocrates, the father of medicine, used colour extensively in medicinal healing and recognised that the therapeutic effects of a white violet differed from those of a purple one. In the fifteenth century, Paracelsus placed particular importance on the role of colour in healing.

Each Sun sign and planetary body has a specific colour or colours which when used in combination with wishing rituals, can enhance their power immensely. Coloured candles can be used to good effect, as the fire energy of the flame/s increases the power of any wish, and flames are also a useful aid to meditating on, focusing upon or clarifying what you want. Coloured candles help to focus the energy for whatever purpose the colour is in sympathy with (e.g. green for money, pink for romance, orange for joy, etc.)

With all this in mind, wearing or using your Sun sign or ruling planet's magical colour/s on a regular basis will undoubtedly bring great benefits.

^ The aura is defined as an energy field, which interpenetrates with, and radiates beyond, the physical body. Clairvoyantly seen, the aura is full of light, colour and shade. The trained healer or seer sees or senses indications within the aura as to the spiritual, physical and emotional state of the individual. Much of the auric colour and energy emanates from the chakras.

YOUR LUCKY COLOURS

For Pisces ★ Sea Green, Purple, Violet, Silver, Deep Blue, Magenta, Pure White, Aqua, Indigo and Mauve

For Neptune ★ Azure blue *, Jacaranda, Lilac, Lavender, Violet, Mauve, and opalescent, iridescent and translucent colours. Also any colours which have a quality of being faint, indefinite, ethereal, misty, shadowy or 'ghostly'

* 'Azure' is from the Arabic for Lapis Lazuli, the amazingly brilliant blue gemstone. It is used to describe the colour blue, particularly when it symbolises royalty. This was particularly so with heraldry, where blue is also represented by the planet Jupiter, your secondary ruler.

Pisces, being a chameleon, carries in it traits of all the other signs. You are the original dreamer and are comfortable in most colour, but tend towards serene colours such as sea green and pale, shimmery shades.

Each of the eight colours of the rainbow spectrum also has a complementary colour to which it is matched. Red is complementary to turquoise, orange to blue, yellow to violet, and green to magenta. If these colour pairs enhance each other's most spellbinding qualities and energies, perhaps you could try wearing your Sun sign's lucky colour with its matching complementary colour in order to produce extra magical results! Your lucky Piscean colours are (sea) green and magenta, which complement each other, violet, which complements yellow, and silver and purple. Now you know your colours, you can dress for success!

FEATURE COLOURS ★ SEA GREEN, MAGENTA, VIOLET, SILVER & PURPLE

★ (SEA) GREEN ★

Planetary Associations ★ Saturn, Venus

Complementary Colour ★ Magenta

Healing Qualities ★ Balancing, Harmonising, Calming, Comforting, Relaxing, Soothing, Wellbeing, Freshness, Generosity

Keywords ★ Prosperity, Growth, Money, Springtime, the Emerald City, Abundance, Fertility, Good Luck, Harmony

Sea green is a medium, moderate green or bluish green, sometimes with a yellowish tinge. The colour green, of which sea green is a variant, is a colour of balance and harmony; from a psychological perspective, it is a great balancer of the feelings and the emotions, creating an equilibrium between the head and the heart. The most restful colour on the eye, it is the middle colour of the rainbow - a bridge between the colours of physicality and spirituality. Green is the colour of Venus and of the element of Earth. It shares the Heart chakra, Anahata, with pink and when the hues of this energy centre are in balance you feel an abundance of love and happiness. Its healing powers come from its alignment with the natural forces and rhythms of the Earth. It is the colour of nature, which can reconnect us to planet Earth, and we instinctively lean towards this colour when in need of peace or harmony. Green is also connected with spring, and the abundance of baby animals and seeds sprouting at this time, make it a youthful and playful colour. Being the colour of balance and sympathy, it has the power to bring the negative and positive energies of a person into balance. Likewise, it has the strength to integrate the right and left hemispheres of the brain, the right hemisphere being intuitive and the left being intellectual. It is also the colour of spring, of growth, of rebirth and renewal. Green, being such a pervasive colour in the natural world, is regarded as a symbol of peace and ecology. It can be used in healing to promote fertility and beauty. In Feng Shui and other spiritual disciplines, it is said to attract money through its vibrational energy.

As mentioned earlier, Green is the colour of the Heart chakra and bridges the gap between the physical and the spiritual worlds. Opening the Heart chakra allows one to love more, feel compassion and empathise with others. Meditating with a green crystal held over the Heart chakra can help to balance emotions. However, green can also evoke feelings of jealousy and envy when out of balance, hence the terms 'green with envy' and the 'green-eyed monster'. Darker shades of green can also symbolise wealth, avarice and greed. Despite some less desirable connections, this colour works to make your mood more like it: caring, contented, accepting, loving, nurturing and joyful. Green can also balance the three aspects of a person's being, namely the body, mind and spirit, creating a sense of wholeness and integration. Green is the midpoint colour of the rainbow spectrum, being neither at the hot nor the cold end. It occupies more space in the spectrum visible to the human eye than most colours. Positioned right in the middle of the rainbow spectrum, it gets along well with other colours and can be used alongside them to complement their effects and enhance and brighten duller hues such as grey or brown, rather than overpowering them. Coupled with blue, green is a great stress-reliever and natural tranquilliser. It is not always regarded as a gentle colour; for some, it can signify illness, such as when one's skin turns green if sick, and for others, it has connections with ghoulish monsters, aliens, zombies, vampires and dragons.

Also strongly associated with the fairy world, it is linked with elves, sprites, dryads and leprechauns - who can all be very helpful to humankind, but can also be 'impish', mischievous, spiteful and malicious. But despite some negative associations, overall, there is no better colour if you are looking for new ideas or a fresh start, as green is the colour that symbolises and supports growth and natural change - great for the Piscean tendency to merge with and get lost in their surroundings or better still, themselves! Sea green - as are all shades of green - is a wonderful all-round soother, balancer and harmoniser, and a beneficial tonic for the mind, body, spirit and heart.

★ MAGENTA ★

Healing Qualities ★ Uplifting, Compassion, Spirituality, Kindness, Prayer, Sensitivity

Complementary Colour ★ Green

A strong, cheerful and inspiring colour, magenta is the result of mixing red and violet, and is a colour which enables us to release and 'let go'. As a combination of red and violet, magenta encapsulates the passion, power and energy of red, calmed down by the introspection and quiet energy of violet. Magenta uplifts the spirits and can alleviate despondency and frustration. It can help lift us out of a stagnant, rigid or static mindset which is no longer serving us or helping us to grow and evolve, and allows us to let go of limiting ideas and thought patterns; in essence, it enables us to move forward. It can strengthen our intuitive and psychic faculties, and is an instrument of change and transformation. On an emotional level, magenta signifies the releasing of irrelevant feelings and situations we may have outgrown but are still clinging on to for fear of change.

A colour of Universal harmony and emotional balance, it helps to create harmony and balance in every aspect of life: mentally, spiritually, physically and emotionally. A colour for the non-conformist and free spirit, it can encourage you to take responsibility for your own life path and increases dream activity, while assisting you to turn your desires and wishes into reality. Used in excess, it can almost be too relaxing, so use with care if you have an introverted nature or tend towards depression. Overall, magenta represents Universal love and compassion at its highest level.

★ VIOLET ★

Planetary Association ★ The Moon, Neptune

Complementary Colour ★ Yellow

Violet is the most spiritual colour in the spectrum, the one most likely to trigger mental relaxation and meditation, and so is well suited to sensitive, deep-thinking, meditative and introspective types, or those who wish to incorporate these qualities into their character. Its healing powers are believed to benefit the entire nervous and cerebral systems. Although it is very calming, working with it may leave you feeling ungrounded and 'spaced out', so balancing this out with the grounding energies of red, black or brown energy might help. The colour of violet pertains to spirituality, dignity, insight, inspiration and self-respect. Violet is a wonderful tonic for those who don't trust their own thoughts or who are unable to love themselves. Various shades of violet have been associated with mystery, magic and the occult. It is a colour which can lift the receptive person into a higher state of consciousness, and can lead one into a realm of spiritual awareness where a gateway awaits, that passes through into a garden of being united with one's true self and Divine inner being. Violet (and all shades of purple in general) is regarded as a highly spiritual colour and is the colour for those seeking Divine fulfilment and nourishment. Violet represents the future, the imagination and dreams, and inspires and enhances psychic enlightenment and abilities. It teaches us to trust our inner flow, and also our intuitive and creative expressions. It is associated with the Crown chakra, linking it with higher wisdom, helping to connect us with greater cosmic awareness and sacred consciousness. Interestingly, this colour is found at the end of the spectrum, and when it extends a bit further it becomes ultra-violet, disappearing into the wide, unknowable ether.

★ SILVER ★

Planetary Association ★ The Moon

Healing Qualities ★ Happiness, Prosperity, Prestige, Opulence, Wisdom, Purging Negativity, Luck, Femininity

Keywords ★ Channelling, Clairvoyance, Astral Energies, Moon, Silver Birch, Amulets, Wisdom

The colour of the Moon, silver can be used for astral or dream work, practising scrying (crystal ball gazing or divination) and for wish magic. Because of its associations with the Moon, silver is also connected with femininity and feminine power. Silver has been revered as a mystical metal since the dawn of civilisation. Ancient alchemists regarded it to be especially valuable and attempted to transmute other metals to produce it *. They used the symbol of the Moon to represent this metal (identified in the Periodic Table of Elements as 'Ag'), which they named 'luna'. Silver, being linked with the Third Eye chakra, is useful for channelling energy, both of a psychic nature and, in more practical terms, of electricity and heat. Silver has also come to represent quality, class and style, as the expressions 'silver service' and 'born with a silver spoon in mouth' exemplify. It also embodies the wisdom gained by learning through experience and optimism, through questing for a 'silver lining' in the face of life's adversities. Mirrors are flat silver-coloured surfaces that reflect all light. Since medieval times, mirrors have been used by clairvoyants and other diviners to make contact with mystical spirits and foretell the future, back then leading to the belief that parallel worlds were hidden behind mirrors, something which Lewis Carroll's literary Alice explores in her *Through the Looking Glass* adventures.

When people and some animals grow older, their hair loses its original colour and turns silver. Someone who is older is more likely to have more knowledge, which is why the colour silver also relates to wisdom. Chinese Feng Shui is based on the principles of the five elements. Silver is a strong metallic element and as such has powerful Chi qualities. According to theory, it can be used to support the Water element, but destroys Wood. Another potent silver association is that in heraldry, metallic silver paint is called argent. The word 'argent' inspired the country name Argentina, because the first European explorers reported seeing a huge silver mountain there. Silver overall corresponds with that which is of material value, versatility, liveliness and higher levels of consciousness.

* Alchemists believed that mercury was the substance used in creation. They thought that this element was a particular type of silver which is why they called mercury 'quicksilver'.

★ PURPLE ★

"When I am an old woman I shall wear purple."
Jenny Joseph

Planetary Associations ★ Uranus, Jupiter, the Moon

Healing Qualities ★ Powerful, Psychic, Beautiful, Awareness, Inspiring, High Ideals, Wisdom, Protective, Spiritual Awareness, Creativity

Keywords ★ Problem-solving, Intuitive, Psychic Realm, Resurrection, Royalty (red + blue), Spiritual Power, Dignity, Piety, Creativity, Uranus, the Moon, Truth, the Cosmos

The colour of Uranus and of the element of ether or spirit, purple may also be used to represent the Moon's power in healings. It is the last visible colour before ultraviolet, so it is often associated with time, space and the Universe itself. Purple is an intriguing colour because it combines and balances the diametrically opposed attributes of two colours: the fire and passion of red, and the coolness and calm of blue. This quality makes purple both an exciting and thought-provoking colour that elicits mixed reactions, able to imply either greater wisdom or underlying confusion. Despite this conflict, it has been said that more than three quarters of children prefer this shade to any other. It can enhance ambition, astral work, compassion, psychic abilities, spirituality, and improve luck and spiritual love. A colour of transformation at a deep level, purple denotes spiritual peace and awareness. Purple crystals such as amethyst and purple jade, are associated with realisation and illumination, and as such are perfect stones for those wishing to succeed; purple gems can be used to attract good fortune into your life.

Lighter shades of purple, such as lilac and lavender, evoke gentle feelings of romance, comfort and nostalgia, and the warmth of pale purple is less striking than that of other bright shades such as pink and orange, because it is tempered with the coolness of blue. Striking a balance between the two, purple can therefore be soft and atmospheric, suggesting distance and aloofness, or whimsical and full of fancy, the colour of first love and of devotion. The blue and red elements within purple also symbolise powerful fusion of the celestial and the Earthly. Pale purples are connected to spiritual enlightenment, to the Third Eye and to contacting the spirit world. You can use purples to provide protective energy and enhance your strength and psychic abilities. It is associated with the Crown chakra, the link between yourself and Nirvana, or complete enlightenment and, when balanced, will render you happy, contented and fulfilled. Purple in Feng Shui is associated with the Fire element and is linked with the south and with determination, joy and inner Fire. As the colour of the south, it is connected with the desire for fame, status and recognition. Purple is the colour of mystery and nobility, merging the tranquillity of blue with the heat and boldness of red. Because it combines the energy and vitality of red with the stability of blue, it is the perfect colour to stimulate the mind while keeping stress at bay; shades of purple have been shown to help calm people with nervous or mental imbalances. A very spiritual and relaxing colour, its connections with opulence, nobility, dignity, power and wealth stretch back to ancient times, when it was believed to have been Cleopatra's favourite colour; and in Ancient Rome, a crimson substance was first extracted from molluscs and then used to create a purple dye that coloured the ornate garments of the emperors. It can stimulate your imagination, or inspire you and improve your creativity. People who are drawn to this colour often have an interest in spiritual growth.

During the sixties, the colour purple was considered unconventional and rebellious, and came to symbolise the decade's search for freedom and a more Universal concept of love. Overall, purple is a common colour in magic; a purple candle represents Uranus, Jupiter and the power of the Moon; it can be used to enhance luck or telepathy, while a purple 'spell' bag can be used for protection and healing. The herb and colour lavender is also an essential ingredient in any ritual or magical work, being used to make wishes, attract your soul mate or for healing spells. Purple magic is, in essence, potent, mystical and unique.

Sea green and magenta, complementing each other in the rainbow spectrum, as well as silver and purple, are Pisces's special LUCKY colours! These can be worn or otherwise used together to dazzling and mesmerising effect.

PISCES' CHAKRA CORRESPONDENCE ★ THE THIRD EYE

The word 'chakra' comes from the Sanskrit and means 'wheel', disc' or 'circle'. Chakras are vitally important to your physical health, emotional wellbeing and spiritual growth, and are regarded as a complete integrated system that works holistically. The chakras are funnel-shaped spinning energy vortexes of multicoloured light. These swirling vortexes of energy absorb and distribute life-force, the subtle energy known as *prana*. The seven master chakras - Root, Sacral, Solar Plexus, Heart, Throat, Third Eye and Crown - lie in the centre line of the body, with the first five embedded within the spinal column. Each chakra vibrates at a different vibrational frequency and on a different note, and responds to specific life issues or 'thought forms'.

The lower body chakras deal with physical issues. As we move up the body, the chakras correspond to increasingly spiritual concerns. As a consequence, each chakra's energy vibrates at a different rate, depending on whether they govern earthbound or ethereal issues. The lower chakras have slower and denser vibrations, while the higher chakras spin at faster speeds with higher vibrations.

Because the chakras have no physical manifestation and cannot be located using any scientific instrument, they have tended to be viewed with scepticism by many Western medical professionals, a distinction they share with energy points in acupuncture and the notion of meridians. Instead, they are believed to have been sensed intuitively by many people over many centuries, and indeed people in yoga positions and in deep meditation have reported experiencing the sensation of a surge of energy rising from the base of the spine and emerging through the top of the head. Some people have even said they have seen points of blue light when their *kundalini* energy has risen from the lowest chakra to the highest, as well as experiencing a profound sense of happiness and ecstasy.

In summary, the Universal Life Force enters the body through the Crown chakra at the top of the head. As it works its way through the body, it flows through the other centres. As it spreads to the Base chakra, it is said to arouse the kundalini energy, which yogis believe sleeps in a coiled serpentine form.

The chakra associated with Pisces is the sixth, or Third Eye chakra, which governs spiritual sight, Divine connections, wisdom, intuition, vision and clairvoyance.

THIRD EYE CHAKRA

Location ★ Between the Physical Eyes
Colour ★ Dark Blue/Indigo
Concerned with ★ Clairvoyance, Wisdom, Intuition & Vision
Gland ★ Pineal
Essential Oils ★ Basil, Angelica Seed, Carrot Seed, Clove Bud, Clary Sage, Ginger, Melissa, Peppermint, Black Pepper
Animal ★ Owl
Shape ★ Downward Triangle
Element ★ Light, Avyakta
Planets ★ Jupiter, Neptune

Zodiac Signs ★ Sagittarius, Pisces
Flower ★ Two-petalled Lotus
Energy State ★ Imagery
Mantra ★ OM

Positive Expression ★ Spiritually wise, intuitive, personal awareness of the Divine

Negative Expression (Blockage) ★ Too self-sufficient, lack of imagination, vision or concentration, clouded intuition, inability to see the bigger picture, delusional, distorted imagination or intuition, over-reliance on logic and intellect

The Third Eye chakra is located between and just above the physical eyes. Its Sanskrit name is *Anja*, and its symbol is two large white lotus petals on each side of a white circle, within which is a downward-pointing triangle. Balance in this chakra is expressed as developed and sound senses of intuition, clairvoyance, clairaudience and clairsentience. It corresponds to the pituitary gland and the carotid nerve plexus. Crystals that can be used to cleanse and balance this chakra are mostly indigo, deep blue and purple stones such as: Lapis Lazuli, Amethyst, Azurite, Charoite, Lepidolite, Sugilite, Azeztulite, Turquoise, Iolite, Larimar, Blue Calcite, Moldavite, Angelite, Phenacite, Tanzanite and Purple Fluorite.

LUCKY CAREER TIPS & PATHS THAT WILL MAKE YOUR BANK BALANCE & SPIRITUAL SELF SOAR

The branch of astrology known as 'vocational astrology' encompasses the areas of one's calling, career path, or ideal profession. Careers, jobs, professions and occupations can all mean different things to different people, but to simplify the definition, I refer to a vocation as one's true calling, one's authentic path, and a dynamic way of life which pays an income in some form and leads to a deep fulfilment of personal and spiritual needs. An ideal vocation will provide self-fulfilment, ego satisfaction, and feed one's inner drive to achieve what they ultimately wish to achieve, whether that be to gain recognition, wealth or approval, to travel, to learn and fulfil an inner need for knowledge, an urge to serve others in some way, or an urge to improve personal, societal or Universal conditions.

In order to gain ultimate fulfilment and self-esteem, we all need a purpose in life. Many people gain this through their work, providing the job or career they choose suits their temperament, talents and aspirations. If our professional life is unsatisfactory or disharmonious in any way, frustration, unhappiness and even despair can result. Although your whole horoscope would need to be drawn up and interpreted in order to gain more substantial, deeper insights into your ideal career and purpose, you can begin by being guided by your Sun sign, which can give you many pointers to a suitable, and therefore successful, career path. You just never know, something in the following might jump out at you and make your soul dance immediately - and hopefully all the way to the bank!

With your Sun in Pisces, you are spiritually gifted and are best suited to professions in which you can help, counsel or care for others in some way, and your impeccable empathy, perceptiveness and intuition gives you exceptional healing capacities - combining these two elements of your character, you would make a great spiritual healer.

Pisces intuitively knows that the only permanent factor in life is the never-ending flow of life itself, and it is to this stream that you direct your aspirations. While many Pisceans aspire to spiritual or healing quests or vocations, the majority have adapted themselves to and even wish to be a part of the material plane. In this respect, the multifaceted imagination and creative power of the Fish may prompt you to embrace the world of theatre, dance, film, and the arts in general. In these fields, the real and the unreal, the actual and the imaginary, the literal and the fantastical, can merge and intermingle, and you will feel at home.

Having such a deep imagination and a highly evolved affinity with fantasy, combined with your vision and inner wells of inspiration, you will likely excel in most types of careers which involve idealism, mysteries, creativity and romanticism. Your inherent talents will also flourish in the fields of clothing, dance, fabrics, furnishings, the film industry, garden art, gifts, jewellery, literature, painting, perfumes and oils, cosmetics, anaesthetics, drugs and alcohol (including the smuggling of illicit substances across bodies of water), pets, puzzles, souvenirs, stage and costume design, and anything to do with the ocean, such as the shipping, sailing, oil and fishing industries.

It's a rare Piscean who is found behind a teller's desk or in a mundane office job, for you are usually found in more spiritual or creative realms of occupation and pastime, fields which suit your imaginative and artistic nature and yearnings. The streams of life you like to swim in are often those in esoteric surroundings. In addition to this, you have very little worldly ambitions and if you do happen to accumulate money or status, it is usually through the company you keep or through an inheritance; rarely will it be through your own striving, for you strive for only one thing: to swim wherever, whenever and with whomever you please. A nine to five structure is as fatal to you as being, well, a fish out of water.

Pisceans make excellent mediums and spiritual healers, as you seem to represent some kind of thread which joins the world of spirit with the world of practical matters. It has been noted by this author and others anecdotally, that most people who work within the spiritual or New Age realm have either the Sun, Moon, Tenth House or Ascendant in Pisces, or an otherwise prominent Pisces in their birth chart.

The Piscean can also do well in the business and political world, often making a powerful, albeit idealistic, executive and administrator. You are perfectly capable of occupying positions of control, for you can naturally feel the vibrations of the thought waves around you and your brilliant intuition keeps you on the corporate ball. However, because you are so committed to living and working by your intuitive faculties, other people who are more materially, technically or scientifically inclined may find your methods and style difficult to understand. Consciously or unconsciously, you are always seeking union with the spiritual world and will try to maintain a close relationship to it.

Most Fishy types prefers to work clandestinely, as you do not seek praise or recognition, but concern yourself rather more with manipulating and moulding conditions. Indeed, you work comfortably and effectively behind the scenes.

Your natural urge to explore emotions, provide a listening ear or warm shoulder, and heal, is strong. And as you are the sign of Universal love and compassion, you will often be found working with, or at least drawn in some way to, the underprivileged, the marginalised, the emotionally disturbed, and the physically disabled. Generally, Pisceans are very altruistic and usually ready to take on the burdens of those around it, but there is another type of Fish who wishes to have no responsibilities whatsoever.

You may also be drawn to working in secluded or hidden places which deal with confinement (such as mental health facilities, detention centres or prisons), but no matter what your individual style and tastes, all Pisceans will feel occasionally compelled to seek out their own seclusion and solitude from others - and their profession must allow them this liberty, or Pisces will end up dissatisfied, disillusioned or worse, burnt out from taking on the problems of far too many people (co-workers included). In fact, Pisceans are so susceptible to taking on the feelings of others, and absorbing the vibrations around them, that they need regular periods of alone time to rebuild their strength and restore their spirit. This cycle is essential for Pisces, and in no other area of life is it more important, than their work. Without regular 'cleansings', your waters easily become polluted by others' negativity; Pisces is a psychic sponge, and for this reason you should exercise careful discrimination in your choice of profession, career path, colleagues and working environment.

Some Pisceans are excellent teachers while others may work in the fields of health or counselling, but you do need variety and the headspace to daydream and use your imagination in your work. Pisceans can be astute business people whose intuition helps them make gains and avoid pitfalls. Despite your unworldly reputation, you like money and may manage to make quite a lot of it, or at least attract the opportunities to do so, generally through artistic avenues. But problems may arise if you lose interest in what you are doing or if things start to go pear-shaped, as you lack the determination and discrimination which would otherwise keep you going through times of trouble. Piscean confidence can also easily evaporate, leaving you unable to cope or rendering you helpless and vulnerable to danger, bullying and deceit. You need a practical, supportive, motivating and encouraging partner at work (as well as in your private life) if you are to be successful.

As Pisces has a reputation for being unworldly, if you are to realise your full career and professional potential you need to travel more, educate yourself more and learn more about the real world, rather than day-dreaming and imagining.

To most typical Pisceans, the following fields and professions are ideal and may hold appeal: Spiritual Retreat Operator, Nursing, Cinematography, Special-Effects Artist, Oil Worker, Deep Sea Fisher, Photography, Creative Arts, Counsellor, Actor, Storyteller, Designer, Magician, Poet, Illusionist, New Age Healer, Foot/Shoe Specialist, Cartoonist, Virtual-Reality Producer, Spiritual Worker, Faith Healer, Anaesthetist, Social Worker, Priest, Costume Designer, Prop Designer, Composer, Yoga or Meditation Teacher, Writer, Artist, Hypnotist, Animator, Metaphysical Speaker or Workshop Facilitator, or Religious Leader. Many of these professions reflect the fact that Pisceans work well with spiritual ways of thinking and assuming different identities.

You also have the enviable ability to adapt to almost any situation, and will therefore be found in all walks of life and in every type of occupation. Overall though, you need to work in an atmosphere which is conducive to peace, harmony and cooperation and which gives you a large degree of soul satisfaction.

Of course this does not account for everyone born under the sign of the Fish, but for those of you who are strongly in tune with your ruling planet Neptune, there is certainly an element of the 'creative artist/actor' in your nature and you can slip into any role asked of you. Essentially, Neptune rules the creative arts, anything to do with acting and dancing, spiritualists, religion, healers, and the spiritual and occult sciences in general. Its influence is most pronounced in all aspects of role-playing and creativity, and concepts in trickery, camouflage or the illusionary arts, such as magic. Some purely Neptunian types will be more than happy to stay behind the scenes, and certainly do not expect accolades or recognition, but through their amazingly adaptable and highly creative work, will certainly attract much credit for their efforts anyway!

LUCKY PLACES WHERE YOUR ENERGY IS HEIGHTENED

As the Water element and phlegmatic humour correspond with cold and wet conditions, cool, rainy, damp or 'watery' places suit your constitution, disposition and temperament. The following nations, countries and cities are also places whose vibrations are closely allied with the sign of Pisces: The Maldives, Guadeloupe, North Africa, the Sahara and Gobi deserts, Samoa, Albania, Ivory Coast, Ivory Coast, Gambia, Ghana, French Guyana, Santo Domingo, Mediterranean islands, St Lucia, Martinique, Scandinavia, France (Normandy), Reunion, Portugal (Lisbon), Spain (Galicia and Seville), Poland (Warsaw), Morocco, Jerusalem, Santiago de Compostella, Taiwan, Tunisia, Bulgaria, Mauritius, Upper Egypt (Nubia), North America (Vermont, Hollywood), South Surin Island (Thailand)*, Calabria, Alexandria, Ratisbon, Germany (Worms), Lancaster, Compostela, watery and aquatic places of all kinds, and old hermitages. An organised tour through North America, and particularly a visit to the acting and movie capital of the world, Hollywood, California, or a leisurely trip through scenic and romantic Europe, with a couple of spooky ghost tours, gothic architecture-spotting, and abandoned mental asylums or old-style convent visits thrown in for good measure, could be very well be your ticket to Piscean heaven!

* South Surin Island (Kho Surin Tai) is home to the Moken people, who live in houseboats or in thatched huts

on stilts, diving and fishing for sustenance and livelihood. The most interesting thing about the Moken people is their unique and remarkable ability to see underwater. They maintain a nomadic, sea-based culture, and believe that the sea has a spirit; in fact, they believe that all things have spirits. They have a complex series of rituals, centred around totem poles, to communicate with these spirits. They survive against all the odds their capitalist 'concrete jungle' neighbours in neighbouring Thailand are faced with, because they are prepared to follow messages delivered in ways other than totem poles. When the tide suddenly changes and rapidly recedes a long way out, they interpret this as a message to "run for the higher grounds of the hills," for since the 2004 Boxing Day Tsunami, the ocean has become a "people eating sea." Indeed, while the 26 December 2004 tsunami killed well over 200,000 others, even though it struck the South Surin Island, it claimed just one member of the Moken people, a weak elderly man who was too slow to flee and forgotten in the rush for safety. Today there are two to three thousand 'water people' living in the region, and Pisces might well relate to these people's close connections to spirits and the sea.

GEMS & CRYSTALS

"People love stones, and apparently stones love people. Like the angels they may be, they seem endlessly willing to serve the wellbeing of humans and to help us achieve our desires …Unlike people of the ancient past, we now have access to virtually the entire mineral kingdom. We have the opportunity to work like modern alchemists, combining and arranging the stones and their currents, looking for combinations and patterns that can help us enhance our inner and outer lives."
Robert Simmons, *Stones of the New Consciousness*

Each crystal and mineral of the Earth embodies different qualities, patterns or potential expressions of the Divine language, the silent whispers of the Universe. If we can accept the fact that the human body is a sophisticated, multi-faceted antenna system comprised of a crystalline matrix that is constantly transmitting and receiving all manner of energies, it could then be assumed that energy and body workers who use quartz, shells and stones, which are also crystalline materials, have the power to promote resonant interactions with the liquid 'crystal' structures found in human tissues. It could even be said that we are all made of essentially the same substances and structures, and that crystals and gemstones vibrate at varying energetic levels which can connect with our own in order to 'buzz' and dance together to make a harmonious Uni-verse both within and without.

All crystals work through vibrational balancing and by channelling energy. The magic of crystals is in their colour, which is determined by the rate at which their atoms vibrate; these vibrations can be matched to the energy given by your own body's aura. And just as light can be focused and refracted through gemstones, so too can all kinds of psychic energy, from healing energies to Divine communications.

Gemstones can help us attune to higher vibrations and bring them into our own experience and being. This theory of crystal resonance suggests that the characteristic energy patterns emanated by any stone can be transferred into the 'liquid crystal medium' of our bodies through resonance. Our bodies, being composed of these tuneable liquids, can mimic and mirror any consistent vibrational pattern with which we come into contact; we can therefore resonate with the healthful qualities of various crystals and minerals.

Crystals and precious stones have been valued throughout world cultures over many centuries for their healing virtues and capacities to imbue courage, strength, invulnerability, clairvoyance, love and numerous other qualities. Wearing gemstones is one of the simplest and most effective self-healing practices you can undertake, and wearing or carrying those stones whose vibrations correspond with the qualities you wish to embody brings their energetic currents into engagement with your body.

Over time the phenomenon of energetic integration, may be felt tangibly and your own vibrational field may internalise the stone's currents and adjust to them and effectively 'store' them, making them, eventually, a part of your own vibrational make-up. And we seem to know from the resonances we feel within our bodies when in contact with these gemstones, that crystals emanate tangible, if oft immeasurable, currents.

Crystals act as transmitters and amplifiers of your will or intentions - as long as your will or intentions are in sympathy with the crystal's energy. The mineral kingdom refers to stones, minerals and crystals and the associations and vibrations they carry. When working with stones, we are working with several different layers of spiritual energies, and although they can be regarded as inanimate 'psychic batteries', they are actually moving, vibrating masses of energy which transmit potential and power into our lives. Some crystals and stones even have receptive powers, which means they can absorb energy and retain it within until cleansed or re-programmed.

Although it is untrue that the only stones you can usefully wear are the ones astrologically matched with your Sun sign or ruling planet, those which align with your Sun sign or ruling planet are your most fortuitous and therefore strongest 'attractors' and 'amplifiers'.

Twelve oracular gemstones were described in the Bible, as the author of *Exodus* (28-15 and 17-21) knew them. Yahweh spoke to Moses about the breastplate he would have to wear to train for priesthood, and described it to him in these words: "And thou shalt make the breastplate of judgement with cunning work; ... And thou shalt set in it settings of stones, even four rows of stones; the first row shall be a sardius, a topaz, and a carbuncle. And the second row shall be an emerald, a sapphire and a diamond. And the third row an opal, an agate and an amethyst. And the fourth row a beryl, and an onyx, and a jasper; they shall be set in hold in their inclosings. And the stones shall be with the children … (all) twelve (of them)." Given that the compilers of the Bible lived during a time when astrological belief was prevalent in Babylon, it seems valid to assert that these previously named gemstones would have some astrological basis. Further, since these ancient people supposedly made correlations between each of the twelve precious stones, and one of the twelve zodiac signs, there are seven crystalline systems set down in crystallography (or the science of the laws which influence the formation, structure and geometric, physical and chemical properties of crystallised matter) as analogous with the seven traditional ruling planets of the zodiac.

However, nobody is under the rule of one planet alone. We are all in essence a complex mixture of every planet, many elements and varying aspects, depending on their positions, placements and prominence in our birth chart. Everything that goes on in the skies above us affects what is going on here on Earth, and also *within* us. Your lucky stones are to assist you to tune into your Sun sign's energy and planetary influences, but you are by no means limited to the ones listed for your sign alone. Above all, let your stones, whichever ones you are drawn to, work for you and allow them to transport your very own unique and magical energy and intentions into the wider Universe.

> "Beautiful and strong is the material of stones, but more beautiful and much more powerful is the mystery that emanates from them."

Chinese Poet & Alchemist, Li Po, 8th Century A.D.

★ CLEAR QUARTZ ★

The Master Healer ★ *For All Zodiac Signs*

A common, well-known and popular gem, clear quartz (sometimes known as rock crystal) is an all-purpose 'jack-of-all-trades' stone. It amplifies the magic of any work you do or wishes you make. It is connected with all the chakras and increases the power of all other crystals. Clear quartz is a deep soul cleanser, which unblocks and regulates energy and emotions on all levels. It is balancing and harmonising. In various cultures, quartz crystal is reputed to be the most powerful crystal, the 'grandfather crystal', and the 'chief of the Stone People'. Clear quartz is also considered to be the only gemstone that is modifiable to suit your needs *, as other crystals automatically contain and retain their own specific resonance or natural signature. In essence, clear quartz is the most easily programmable and the most overall healing and readily accessible crystals of the mineral kingdom, holding a unique importance in the Universe of gems. And because of its all-encompassing nature and wide-ranging healing abilities, it has zodiacal affinities with all the signs.

* To program your clear quartz crystal, simply hold it on your Third Eye chakra (between and just above the physical eyes) and concentrate on the purpose for which you wish to use it. Be positive and receptive while you allow your crystal to fill with this energy. If you wish, you could also state the intention of the programming out loud, for example, 'I program this crystal for love / healing / meditation / abundance / protection or (insert your own word here)'. You could also run your clear quartz crystal under running water, allow it to dry naturally, then hold the stone with both hands, bring it up to your mouth and blow into it sharply three times in order to impregnate it with your own breath. Then, hold it firmly in one hand and silently invite and welcome it into your life as a friend, helper and guide.

PISCEAN & NEPTUNIAN LUCKY CRYSTALS, STONES & GEMS

Pisces birth stones ★ Amethyst, Turquoise, Aquamarine

February birth stones ★ Amethyst, Hyacinth

March birth stones ★ Jasper, Bloodstone, Aquamarine

Amethyst, Turquoise, Aquamarine (your three primary birthstones), Jasper, Hyacinth, Bloodstone (February and March birthstones), and Yellow Sapphire (Jupiter) are your luckiest stones, and one or more of these gems should be worn about your person to ensure good luck and increase your overall magnetism. Coral, Mother of Pearl and Emerald are also particularly auspicious gemstones for Pisces. Moonstone, Clear Quartz, Labradorite, Fire Agate, Beryl, Staurolite, Chrysoprase, Pumice, Chrysolite, Sugilite, Sand, Blue Lace Agate, Tibetan Quartz, Green Grossular Garnet, Sodalite, Citrine, Titanium Quartz, Chevron Amethyst, Diaspore, Sunstone, Calcite, Tourmaline, Smithsonite, Spessartine, Angelite, Carnelian, Bixbyite, Anglesite, Opal, Smoky Quartz, Green Fluorite, Pearl, Blue Quartz, Milky Quartz, Rose Quartz, Spirit Cactus Quartz, Imperial Topaz, Jade and Larimar also align with Piscean energy.

CRYSTALS & THE PLANETS

All the Vedic texts agree in relating gems to planets. This verse from the *Jatax Parijat* links each gem to a planet:

'The ruby is the gem of the Lord of the Day (the Sun),
The shining pearl is the gem of the cold Moon,
Red coral is the gem of Mars,
The emerald is the gem of noble Mercury,
Yellow sapphire is the gem of Jupiter, instructor of gods,
Diamond is the gem of Venus, instructor of demons,
Blue sapphire is the gem of Saturn.'

Each planet influences its gem, and their curative power varies according to the position of its planet in the zodiac. Ayurvedic medicine has always paid attention to these details in their healing practices, often advising people to wear their corresponding zodiacal stone as a ring or a talisman.

CRYSTALS & THE ELEMENTS

Crystals are inextricably linked to the four elements, from their original creation to their potency and use in magical rituals and healing. Formed by the combination, in varying conditions, of different physical elements, such as metals, non-metals and gases, some stones require the enormous heat generated by volcanoes or deep thermal currents to bond their molecular makeup, while others may require pressure or water sources. The effects of the four elements of Fire, Earth, Air and Water is evident in these formation processes. The heat generated by Fire, pressure from the Earth, and the chemical reactions involved in absorbing elements from the Air and Water, all demonstrate the four elements in action to produce the correct conditions and ingredients necessary for the creation of crystals, lending them each their unique qualities.

CRYSTALS & THE WATER ELEMENT

The depositing or the evaporation of Water is a component in the formation of many crystals, including stalagmites and stalactites. Water also finds its balance by assuming its appropriate state as a gas, liquid or solid (ice). Therefore, Water-inspired gemstones help to balance your emotions and influence your dreams by shifting notions between the conscious and unconscious mind.

Some Watery crystals are ★ Pearl, Beryl, Moonstone, Aquamarine, Selenite, Tourmaline and

Amethyst.

THE CRYSTALLINE SYSTEM OF YOUR TRADITIONAL RULING PLANET JUPITER

Associated with your traditional ruling planet Jupiter, are Amethyst, Beryl, Emerald, Sapphire and Turquoise. This is the fifth crystalline system, known as the rhomboidric system, that is having a parallelepiped whose six sides are diamond-shaped and of equal size, ideally represented by the Rhodochrosite or magnesium carbonate. This, it has been suggested, has a curative action on such Jupiterian afflictions as liver complaints, ulcers, asthma and congestion.

JUPITER'S GEMSTONE ASSOCIATION

Amethyst ★ Connected with the Crown and Third Eye Chakras, this beautiful purple stone is used to aid and promote spiritual wisdom, intuition, protection, focus, inner peace, pleasant dreams, meditation, power, spiritual awareness, psychic abilities and healing. Calming, balancing and comforting, amethyst is a stone commonly used and worn by healers and spiritual workers, as it has the power to focus energies, brings forth 'unseen' realms, and heightens one's psychic perceptions. Purple has long been considered a royal colour, so it is not surprising that amethyst has been so revered and so much in demand throughout history. Amethysts are featured in the English Crown Jewels and were also a favourite of Ancient Egyptian royalty. Enchanted by the stone's energy, Leonardo da Vinci wrote that amethyst could dissipate evil thoughts and quicken the intelligence. It encompasses power, spirit, beauty and magic.

PISCES'S FEATURE CRYSTAL ★ AMETHYST

The Spiritual and Psychic Stone

An extremely well-known, common, easy-to-source and popular stone, this is the stone of spiritual power and psychic energy. It has a high ethereal vibration and is an extremely powerful and protective stone, particularly for those born in February and under the signs of Aquarius and Pisces. Amethyst is the birthstone for the month of February, and its name is derived from the Greek word *amethystos*, literally meaning "not intoxicated." This charming stone awakens and activates our higher awareness and psychic abilities. Amethyst has strong cleansing and healing powers, and its serenity assists with enhancing meditation and the reaching of higher states of consciousness. Connected with the Crown and Third Eye chakras, amethyst offers protection, wisdom, focus, power, access to Divine understanding, ethereal awareness, and increases psychic abilities, healing and inner peace. It's best known use is for heightening and enhancing one's spiritual connections and insights; it can even open doors to other dimensions, planes and realities.

The radiation of violet light issuing from amethyst has been placed on record as providing a calming influence upon the nerves, making it balancing and comforting to the wearer, and is said to be instrumental in slowing rapid and agitated bodily movements, and helpful in easing neuralgia, headaches, gout and stress-related insomnia.

Amethyst can be worn on parts of the upper body to encourage conversations with your higher self, and is especially beneficial when worn over the throat or heart. Encouraging selflessness, intuition, spiritual wisdom and Divine visualisation, amethyst can transmute Earthly energies to the higher vibrations of etheric realms. As a stone of tranquillity and contentment, it can also dispel anger, irritability, mood swings, fear and negativity. Amethyst can act as a compassionate anchor and ensures that you are emanating your energy from a place of peace and understanding. Wear or use some of this beautiful purple-hued stone to elevate you to higher places today! After all, your dreams are waiting for you to join them up there ... it's high time to heed their call.

PISCEAN POWER CRYSTALS

Around six thousand years ago, in ancient Mesopotamia, the Sumerians started studying precious stones and minerals, as well as the stars, with a view of improving their lives in many ways by probing the secrets and mysteries of the Universe. Their esoteric interests and knowledge were such that they began to grasp the general connections between the Earth and the heavens, or the Solar system as they knew it, and the functions of stones and minerals as a link between the two. Their method of making these connections was by colour (for example the Sun was allocated all yellow stones), as well as other spiritual links. The gemstones listed for the portion of your zodiac sign are given their status as your 'power crystals' due to the links that can be made between your primary planetary ruler/s and your mutable planetary ruler (listed last), and each stone's particular colour, chemical and mineral compositions, healing properties, and the number they are given (based on the Mohs scale of hardness: for example, diamond scores a perfect 10 out of 10), all of which combine to align with your planetary rulers. Working mindfully with your planet's special crystals is one way you can increase the flow of power and magic into your life.

POWER CRYSTALS FOR FIRST HALF
PISCES * ★ (19 February - 4 March)

Influenced by Neptune, Jupiter and the Moon
Diamond, Aquamarine, Smithsonite,
Satinspar, Opalised Fossil

DIAMOND ★ Those ruled by the sign of the Fish are in a special situation. Three Moons influence them: Triton (Moon of Neptune); Io (Moon of Jupiter); and the Moon of our Earth. All are strong characters and demand the services of not merely one crystal, but two. The green-blue diamond is a wonderful option for Neptune, which is wrapped around with a covering of water and gases, which, seen from a distance, transmit a mystical pale green-blue hue. Triton too, produces this appealing shade. Diamond is pure carbon and is known as the ruler of the mineral kingdom, due to its hardwearing qualities, hardness and sheer brilliance. Diamond is the purest substance in nature and one of the hardest (10 out of 10 on the Mohs scale). The word 'diamond' has its origin in the Greek word 'adamas', which means unconquerable. Mined for over 4,000 years, ancient civilisations discovered that this amazing gem could cut any other stone. The Ancient Greeks believed that diamonds were actually splinters of stars that had fallen to Earth, and it was thought by some they were the tears of the gods. Universally considered the greatest of stones, the diamond has been revered throughout the ages for its beauty and strength. The diamond, known as the 'king of the crystals', is a crystalline form of carbon and is known universally as a token of love; quite simply, it is the ultimate symbol of purity. The carbon atoms in this precious gemstone are very firmly and closely bonded, giving it a tightly knit and extremely hard structure. In simple terms, diamond is the hardest natural substance on Earth and is from 10 to 150 times harder than the world's second hardest mineral, corundum. Diamonds are found in many colours - white, pink, blue, green, yellow, brown, black - and even blood red. This luminously brilliant gem, through its renowned purity and durability, offers incomparable proof of total perfection expressed in a single element. Its pure white light can help to bring your life into a cohesive whole, the first step in using your amazing power for optimum effect. It bonds relationships, is said to enhance the love of a husband to his wife, brings love and clarity into a partnership, and is seen as a sign of commitment and faithfulness. Psychologically, this precious gem imparts a sense of fearlessness, fortitude and invincibility, for diamonds are unbreakable in every sense of the word.

Diamond is also an amplifier of energy and is one of the few stones that never needs recharging or cleansing; in fact, it increases the energy of whatever it comes into contact with and is very effective when used with other crystals for healing as it enhances and draws out their power. However, as an amplifier of energy, it also increases negative energy as well as positive; the merciless light of diamond will highlight anything that is negative and requires transformation. Diamonds have long been valued for their magical properties, and indeed they are linked with such dazzling key words and concepts such as intensity, radiance, sovereignty, linking with the heart of the Divine, and awakening oneself to and attuning to the Music of the Spheres. In fact, diamonds were long believed to offer access to Divine energies and this is one reason why they were traditionally set in crowns. Putting such a gemstone near the brain, particularly around the forehead area, can enhance inner visions and intuitive connection with the higher domains of spirit. Diamond can assist in activating the prefrontal lobes of the brain, the base of most paranormal abilities and other-realm consciousness.

Diamond has been a symbol for wealth for thousands of years and is one of the stones of manifestation, with the ability to attract abundance; the larger the diamond, the more abundance will be drawn to the person asking for it. Worn in everyday life, diamonds can intensify the ability to focus one's visions and manifest one's goals and dreams. Diamond helps to clear emotional and mental pain, alleviates fears and brings about new beginnings. It also provides a link between the intellect and the higher mind, aiding clarity and enlightenment of mind. On a spiritual level, it allows one's soul light to shine outward, cleansing the aura of anything shrouding the inner light, and reminds you of your soul's aspiration; it activates the Crown chakra, linking it to the 'Divine light'. Indeed, clear crystals such as diamond will interact with your energy field by raising your vibration through clearing away any cloudiness or blockages within your subtle bodies. This stone can enhance and magnify the energies of other high-vibration stones, and worn anywhere on the body will affect one's entire energy system and auric field. With it may be worn a bloodstone, another Piscean gemstone, through which the beneficent influence of the diamond will be greatly increased. A highly creative stone, stimulating imagination and inventiveness, and aiding spiritual evolution, it seems the ever-inspiring diamond was made for the dreamy Piscean nature.

AQUAMARINE ★ This hard gemstone, which forms in long hexagonal crystals, is a pale blue-green variety of a mineral type called beryl, a group which also includes emeralds. Its name suggests its link to the water kingdoms - *aqua* is Latin for water, and marine means 'of the sea'. True aquamarine has a translucent pale turquoise colour. Aquamarine has been believed to bring good luck to lovers since the time of the Ancient Greeks and Romans. It works on the Sacral and Throat chakras and helps open you up to love by removing blockages and balancing the sexual urges against other qualities that attract you to another, leaving you more receptive to love and its influence. Aquamarine tallies with all three Moons and with the planet Jupiter itself, thanks to its composition. Triton, with its Lunar-type crust and density, it's Earth-like atmosphere and its limpid Neptunian depths, especially calls for this stone. Aquamarine has a hardness of 7 on the scale (just over Neptune's own number) and often occurs in giant crystals appropriate to the size of its planetary rulers. The energy of our body's life force is sky-blue, which is the same colour the Earth is perceived as when seen from space, and it is also the same hue as the tint reflected in the blue of the aquamarine. Many crystal practitioners, knowing this gem's healing value, may work through an aquamarine to examine a person's surrounding life-force, which manifests itself to those sensitive enough to see them in billions of fine, hair-like blue arrows. If the practitioner assesses this radiating energy to be steady and of consistent strength throughout its flow, then all is well in the subject's energy field. If however, it is seen to be inconsistent or to thin out here or there, then physical strength may be on the wane - this condition may or may not be healable, but the significant factor here is that it is detectable. Aquamarine once bore the title 'All Life' and is a gem that must be listened to, not ordered about; its powers will depend upon its user's receptiveness and it will work on the level that he or she is able to achieve. An effective balm for swollen feet (Pisces's potential vulnerable area) and a soother of frayed emotions and nerves, aquamarine refines the faculties of the intuitive mind and removes discordant vibrations. It is also a vital tool in cleansing and clearing the 'water element' of our psyches, a symbol of our emotions and feelings. Our bodies being over 70 per cent in watery make-up, keeping this element balanced is crucial to our wellbeing. Ultimately, aquamarine helps to cleanse the water element deep within ourselves, clearing away emotional toxicity and bringing inner peace. Its energy indeed is that of water - flowing but strong, gentle and compassionate, moving around obstacles with ease. Aquamarine shields the aura and aligns the chakras, and is also an excellent crystal to boost, stimulate, activate and cleanse the Throat chakra, enhancing immunity and keeping the bridge clear between the Heart and the Throat chakras. It encourages creative verbal expression and harmonious communications, clears up confusion, sharpens intuition, opens clairvoyance, invokes spiritual consciousness, endows us with courage, and soothes powerful feelings such as grief, despair and loneliness. It will enable to find deeper satisfaction when you are feeling discouraged or empty, being reassuring, uplifting and pointing the way towards spiritual fulfilment. It also helps in situations where you need to be or feel in control, imparting feelings of inspiration, calmness, peace, love and 'flow'. It promotes the courage to express one's self truthfully and openly, and Pisceans should wear this gemstone to enhance communication and enable their highest truth to be expressed to the world. It is also useful in helping this sign release self-defeating patterns, destructive habits, self-pity or a victim mentality. First-half Pisceans in particular are indeed lucky to have such a beautiful gem as their power crystal.

SMITHSONITE ★ This stone is reminiscent of the soft tranquillity of the Moon, the mutable celestial body of first-half Pisceans. Smithsonite has an exquisite range of subtle tints, and is for those who prefer chic to overstatement. Pink-lavender is the colour found in some varieties of Smithsonite, and these varieties have an energy that is soft, comforting, gentle and soothing. The heavenly feel of Smithsonite can help heal the child within, by easing repressed feelings. This stone also works well on the brain's pain centres so it can help with addiction-related emotional disorders. It also assists in remembering and understanding dreams, promotes spiritual growth, brings tranquillity to stressful situations, and overall softens the emotions.

OPALISED FOSSIL ★ Opalised fossil is found in the hot desert areas of Australia, often coming from the tapering pointed bones of extinct cuttlefish or from sea snails and many other animals, metamorphose and live on in movement of colour within this beautiful 'stone'. Opalised fossils are the product of 110-million-year-old fossils, which date back to a period of time called the Early Crustaceous. These extraordinary relics are of global scientific interest, and Australia is the only place on Earth where these Opalised animal fossils are found. Fossil wood is another variation, a wondrous example of ingenuity, with soft tints of opal dancing along ridges left behind by the departed creature; and Opalised Fire Cones, another variation, are from America's Virgin Valley. Opal fossils were chosen for first-half Pisceans because they have a Double-Water influence: their ruling planet, Neptune, has the same density as water, while their mutable body, the Moon, controls the ebb and flow of oceanic water we call tides.

POWER CRYSTALS FOR SECOND HALF PISCES * ★ (5 March - 19 March)

Influenced by Neptune, Jupiter and Pluto
Kunzite, Hiddenite, Transparent Euclase,
Chrysoprase, Blue Lace Agate, Fluorite, Apophyllite

KUNZITE ★ Discovered in America around 1900 and named after its mineralogist discoverer, Dr G. F. Kunz, kunzite draws much admiration by its flawless transparency and high lustre. Uniquely phosphorescent and with a great sensitivity, its pink-lilac to dark lilac-rose tints add to its appeal. Further, it displays visible flares of a blue-tinged green when viewed from a side angle, resonating with its celestial ruler, Neptune. Wherever the stunning kunzite occurs, so does another Piscean precious crystal: hiddenite. In crystal healing, kunzite is used to protect the heart and enable it to release emotional blocks in a gentle way. Its soft pink-purple hue has a soothing presence, encouraging a sense of safety and peace. As a stone which has an affinity with the Heart chakra, it exudes love, compassion and peace, and connects us with the unconditional love of the Divine, as it also aligns the Heart with the Throat and Third Eye chakras. This gem comforts and heals the heart on both a physical and emotional level, and helps one's heart to awaken after long periods without a meaningful relationship, when trust and opening up have been challenges. In this way, kunzite is a wonderful crystal to have around in the early stages of a new romance, helping one to usher in this new experience with a sense of joy and openness. Worn over the heart, it can attract new love into your life, or indeed simply support you during the first stages of any new relationship. Kunzite is also a protective stone that provides a shield against negative, unwanted energies; soothing and calming, it is also beneficial to people with addictions. Possessing the power to raise our vibrations, it is a useful stone for meditation that enhances intuition and connects one with the infinite source, thus allowing one to reach a state of higher spiritual awareness. Ideal for babies and children, its loving and innocent nature helps them to feel safe and secure. It also has the ability to ease nervous stress, tension and anxiety, and dissolves resistance to new ideas and directions, enabling life to flow and develop in a positive way. A good balancer on all levels, kunzite promotes emotional equilibrium, enhances self-esteem, encourages tolerance and acceptance, and enables the deeper inner dimensions of the heart to be experienced.

EUCLASE ★ Transparent Euclase is another choice for second-half Pisceans, and is a rare greenish-blue or colourless crystal of fragile appearance. It is brightly lustred and shares its bewitching charm with that of aquamarine. It is scored as 7 on the hardness scale, and has a body weight of just over 3, in correspondence with its planetary monarchs, but is not frequently cut for jewellery owing to its unsuitable structure.

CHRYSOPRASE ★ This crystal's magnificent rich tints, in cheerful shades of apple to lime green, are the main reason for its beauty and popularity. The most sought-after, nickel-tinted variety of Chrysoprase occurs in the town of Marlborough Creek in Queensland, and comes in almost equally fine quality from other parts of the world: California, Brazil, Russia, Poland and Tanzania. It corresponds with Neptune and Jupiter by its light bodyweight and basic colouring. Physically, Chrysoprase has the potential to purge its wearer both physically and spiritually, from the lowest plane upwards. It has an outgoing influence, promoting inner clarity and discipline, and is adept in deflecting negative vibrations before they reach the higher senses. As jewellery or a touchstone, this mineral soothes nervous disorders, calms the brain before bursts of mental activity, steady's hysteria and convulsions, and eliminates anxiety. It also possesses a 'guard dog' character, protecting its wearer from overreactions and discordant factors until a balance has been reached. It supports and expands the Heart chakra, easing negative feelings and promoting joy. Its affinity with the Heart chakra gives it the ability to open, activate and energise the heart, and also to mend a broken one and to heal relationships. It is useful for overcoming compulsive thoughts and actions, stimulating acceptance of oneself and others, fluent speech, mental dexterity, alleviating mental and physical exhaustion, reducing claustrophobia and nightmares, and encouraging forgiveness and compassion. Resonating also with the Sacral chakra, it can also be used to treat the reproductive organs, as well as fertility problems. Chrysoprase, when placed over the Heart, Throat or Third Eye chakras, soothes and balances the system, and enhances the flow of positive feelings. Additionally, it attracts new love and abundance, and helps to prepare the system for new phases in life. Carry or wear this gem to attract new relationships into your life, or put a piece under your pillow to improve the quality of your sleep. Overall, it encourages restful slumber and aids general relaxation. Curiously, Chrysoprase seems to be loyal to only one owner. On changing hands, or if its owner passes on, it may show no response at all under its new 'influence'. Furthermore, carrying this stone for long periods of time can attune one to the devic ^ realm.

^ The term 'devic' relates to the kingdom of the devas, or nature spirits, believed to inhabit or reign over natural objects such as trees, mountains or bodies of water. People with clairvoyance are sometimes able to see or communicate with these spirits, by gaining intuitive access to the devic kingdom, the energetic level at which these entities exist.

BLUE LACE AGATE ★ Agates are a kind of chalcedony and come in a variety of colours, each with its own special qualities, but all agates are protective and nurture natural talents and relationships, acting as shields to protect you on your spiritual journey. Blue Lace Agate is a soft, sky-blue, opaque gemstone which displays its innocent purity and gentle character in translucent, white lacy patterns. It is an effective healing stone and its soft energy is cooling and quietening, bringing peace of mind and nurturing and supporting its carrier or wearer. It is an excellent calming stone to place in a meditation or healing space to enhance the atmosphere. It can also be used in meditative 'journeys' to expand the mind into new realms or to help dissolve worries and cares, and taken as a gem essence, can bring a sense of peace and calm to the whole system, especially in cases of emotional trauma or severe anxiety. It can alleviate suppressed or repressed memories, encouraging their expression and dissolving old patterns. For males, it is useful in helping them get more in touch with their sensitivity and feeling natures. Spiritually, blue lace agate can link thoughts to a more spiritual vibration, and clears the Throat chakra so that one's highest spiritual truths can be expressed. In fact, it is a powerful throat healer, both physically and spiritually, so is most effective if worn around this area. It also harmonises the Heart, Third Eye and Crown chakras. Agate helps to keep words and thoughts in good order by keeping you truthful and genuine. It is a wonderful stone to use during pregnancy because it soothes, balances, and calms both mother and baby throughout gestation and labour. Additionally, it can enhance sleep quality, soothes angry feelings, promotes communication, neutralises aggression and encourages clearer thinking. Overall, this soft-toned crystal encourages patience, kindness, peace, honesty and wisdom, and calms and strengthens one's spiritual centre.

FLUORITE ★ Fluorite, also known as fluorspar, usually has a basic white body, but can be angelically coloured in the softest shades of pink, magenta, black, green, white, purple, yellow and blue. It is often found in limestone caverns and as a natural cement in sandstone. Fluorite derives its name from the Latin word 'fluere' meaning 'to flow' and has a very unusual quality - it gives off light in darkness when exposed to a source of heat; under ultra-violet lighting, fluorite emits a beautiful glow - hence the term 'fluorescence'. Fluorite crystals usually grow in cubes. Green and purple fluorite is a popular choice, and these two complementary shades are linked to the Heart (green) and the Crown (purple) chakras. Green is the colour of expansion, growth and reaching towards the light, while purple is the shade associated with spiritual expansion and awareness of higher levels of consciousness, making this a wonderfully useful stone for Pisceans. The two colours combined enable the wisdom of spiritual awakenings to enter the physical body and reside in the heart. Meditating with this crystal can encourage a gentle flowing sense of peace through the whole system, an ideal state in which to experience spiritual expansion and one's unfolding into new levels of insight and awareness. Furthermore, it has a harmonising effect on the body on account of its ability to balance the nervous system, as well as encouraging harmony and stability in relationships. As a stone which endows the mind with discernment and clarity, fluorite increases our concentration and is a useful study aide, enabling us to absorb information rapidly. It can also be used on the Third Eye chakra to bring about greater clarity of vision and light the way to a clearer path ahead. Purple fluorite is a wonderful stone for meditation that not only helps the mind to focus, but opens up our intuitive faculties, reveals truths, allows us to see through any veils of illusion, and enhances psychic abilities; very helpful qualities that most Pisceans could benefit from. Overall, it cleanses, purifies, dispels and reorganises any aspects within the body or surroundings that are not in perfect order; it can overcome chaos and reorganise/restructure the physical, mental and emotional bodies, so allowing higher spiritual energy to be quickly integrated and absorbed. Fluorite eases physical and emotional stress, helps to balance the mind, body and spirit, and cleanses and replenishes the energy field surrounding the body. As it cleanses and stabilises the aura, it is extremely effective against computer and electromagnetic stress.

* All Piscean birthstones can be set with diamonds, which appear to proliferate on their ruling planet, Neptune.

YOUR LUCKY NUMBERS

Your lucky numbers are ★ 8 for Pisces ^, 7 for Neptune, and 3 for Jupiter (your traditional ruler) (also, see 'Lucky Magic Square of Jupiter')

LUCKY MAGIC SQUARE OF JUPITER

In Western occult tradition, each planet has traditionally been associated with a series of numbers and particular arrangements of those numbers. One such method of numerological organisation is the magic square. Magic squares date back to ancient times, appearing in China about 3,000 years ago. The first Chinese square is seen in the scroll of the river Lo - the Lo-Shu, a scroll believed to have been created by Fuh-Hi, the mythical founder of Chinese civilisation. Certain squares came to be linked with the planets; these associations came from the Babylonians. Each *kamea*, or magic square, is linked with a particular planet, and each of the squares has a *seal*, which is the geometric pattern created by following the numbers in order of their value. This pattern touches upon all the numbers of the square and the seal is used to represent the entire square. An intelligence and a spirit are also associated with each kamea, derived from the key numbers contained within it, using a Hebrew form of numerology. This intelligence is viewed as an inspiring, guiding and informing entity.

The 'Magic Square of Jupiter' is divided into 16 cells, or squares, four across and four down. The sum of the numbers in the vertical, horizontal and diagonal lines is a constant of 34. The total of these numbers is 136. Therefore, the numbers 4, 16, 34 and 136 are also assigned to Jupiter.

YOUR NUMEROLOGY NUMBER & LUCKY SUN SIGN NUMBERS

"Everything that exists has a vibration. The vibration of sound, music, colour, matter, even our words, thoughts, and names show form. All vibration is measurable. To measure we need numbers. Numbers are the basis of all. Numbers are the key to all mysteries."
Shirley Blackwell Lawrence, *Behind Numerology*

Numerology is essentially the metaphysical * 'science' of numbers. The use of numbers in magic is its cornerstone of power. The ancient Greek philosopher and mathematician Pythagoras, born around 590 BC, embarked on a thirty-year spiritual quest studying with important religious and esoteric teachers and healers to find the mystery of 'The Hidden Light', and came to see mankind as living in three worlds: the natural, the human and the Divine. He asserted that all things can be expressed in numerical terms, because they are ultimately reducible to numbers. Pythagoras stated that "Numbers are the first things of all of Nature" and followed the theory that "Nothing can exist without numbers."

Many believe that numbers have an arcane, mystical relationship with words, and with inanimate and animate objects; the interpretations that arose from these relationships date back to a time when the dawning intelligence of primitive man first visualised the meaning of numbers and associated it with spiritual significance. Numerology is the science of the exploration of this relationship in order to discover hidden meanings, forecast the future or interpret the character of a person. In its more modern applications, a series of figures which correspond to an individual's name and date of birth are calculated, and practitioners believe one's prospects, fortune and character can be deciphered from the results ^.

So what is numerology and how does one use it? Everything in the Universe has a vibrational frequency, an energy, a force, all vibrating at various rates, and we as humans are no exception, the difference between one person and another is their rate of vibration. This force or energy is constantly in motion and changing, and we can even 'tune into' and feel our vibrations if we are still for long enough.

Along with letters, sounds, colours, crystals, and many other things, it is believed that numbers also have vibrations, and when we are able to familiarise ourselves with our own numerical frequencies, we can use this familiarity to add power and magic to our lives. The numbers of our birth date, the letters of our names, and the numbers of our Sun sign and ruling planets, all have a unique vibrational frequency, and herein lies the key to understanding our self and our journey through life. Numerology refers to the knowledge contained within the numbers of our birth date and our name, and this is our own personal magic which can greatly assist us through life.

* Metaphysics is the study of those sciences that extend beyond the physical or tangible

HOW TO FIND YOUR NUMEROLOGY NUMBER

^ Your Sun sign's number was added up according to the principle of corresponding a number with a letter, for example 1=A, 2=B, 3=C and so on in sequence and up to 9=I, then beginning again at number 1 for the next letter J and following this same sequence. Following this system, the sum of the letters in Pisces vibrates to the number 8.

Your personal numerology number is determined by adding up all the numbers in your birth date until they reach a two-digit figure. The two resulting numbers are then added together again to form a single digit, which is your personal numerology number. For example, someone born on 3 February 1983, would add the digits 3 + 2 + 1 + 9 + 8 + 3 = 26 = (reduced to two digits) 8. So that person's personal numerology birth number is 8.

Each primary number or birth number from 1 to 9 has a specific meaning and is governed by a planetary force. The principle of numerology reduces all numbers down to the following: 1 to 9, and 10, 11, 13 and 22 *. The last four numbers only apply to people specially concerned with the occult and spiritualism - and can be studied at greater length through other sources if so desired - and can in any case be reduced further to a single digit if preferred. Your birth number contains a unique power, and therein lie your strengths, shortcomings and opportunities. It is beyond the scope of this book to outline your individual numerology number possibilities, so for the purposes of astrological applications, I have only included your Sun sign and ruling planet's special numbers.

* The numbers 10 and 13, and the master numbers 11 and 22, can be further reduced to one digit if so desired; however, they can be interpreted as they are without further reduction. The choice is personal.

BASIC MEANINGS & KEYWORDS

1 ★ Sun. Masculine influence, beginnings, independence, inventiveness, originality, leadership, exploration, innovation, ambition
2 ★ Moon. Feminine influence, cooperation, partnership, tact, diplomacy, harmony, unity, emotions, imagination, adaptability
3 ★ Jupiter. Communication, expression, youthfulness, self-confidence, creativity, inspiration, optimism, curiosity
4 ★ Uranus. Order, form, security, stability, patience, restriction, work, values, practicality
5 ★ Mercury. Freedom, inconsistency, change, variety, travel, activity, learned
6 ★ Venus. Love, home, family, sense of duty, responsibility, marriage, justice, nurturing, balance, gentleness, peace, friendship
7 ★ Neptune. Analysis, wisdom, mystical, spiritual, solitude, precision, research, integrity, mystery, psychic perceptions

8 ★ Saturn. Money, power, success, organisation, hard work, business, health, purpose, control, authority, mastery

9 ★ Mars. Completion, endings, Universal, service, humanity, philanthropy, loyalty

10 ★ Fortunate, creative, vibrant, stable, optimistic, original, successful, determined, individualistic

11 ★ Master number. Prophecies, inspiration, moral courage, missionary, long-suffering, foolhardiness, enlightenment, invention

13 ★ Misunderstood, fearful, changeable, interested in the occult, fatalistic, flexible, sacred, beguiling

22 ★ Master number. Powerful, successful, idealistic, attracted to the occult, creative, wise, successful, masterful, spiritually understanding

★ THE NUMBER 7 - FOR PISCES ★

Names ★ Septet, Septenary, Heptad

Arithmomantic connections with the letters of the alphabet ★ G, P and Y

Ruled by Neptune, 7 is a considered a very lucky number. A mystical number which is associated with philosophy, spiritual insights and inner contemplation, it is linked with the dreamy planet Neptune and its colours are sea greens and aquamarines. Seven is the number of mysticism and illusion. The Septenary or the Heptad as it is sometimes known, is the most interesting and mysterious of the primary numbers. To the Greeks and Romans, it was the symbol of good fortune, being connected with periodical changes of the Moon; and the seven notes in music gave rise to the philosophy of the 'harmony of the spheres' and the depiction of the Universe as one vast musical scale. Often linked to the world of dreams, 7 governs the imagination and the study of magic. Number 7 is a deep-thinking, spiritual vibration; symbolically it is the number for perfection. It signifies fine powers of sympathy, intuition and insight, and has long been regarded as symbolising spirituality, mystery, magic and the occult. Seven is the number of wisdom and relates to the completion of cycles. There are seven personal planets in astrology, seven days of the week, seven pillars of wisdom, seven chakras, seven wonders of the world, seven musical notes, seven Gothic gods, seven worlds believed in by the Chaldeans, seven degrees of initiation in various eastern orders, seven colours in a rainbow, seven crystalline systems, seven virtues, seven vices and seven deadly sins. There are seven components of the personality - instinct, emotion, intelligence, intuition, reason, will and awareness - and in Buddhism thought humans are made up of seven primordial principles. On the seventh day, according to the Bible, God rested.

Number 7 is thought to have occult significance, and people born under its influence often have a strongly spiritual or philosophical outlook - they are usually not so interested in material things. Carrying the Neptune vibe, it is the number for spiritual purpose, contemplation and evolution, therefore is the most appropriate for those wishing for peace, quiet and periods of solitude. It also attracts learning and education associated with personal development of some sort, and is very nurturing for those who enjoy or prefer their own company, are self-motivated and have their spiritual growth and way of life as a focus, but not so compatible with those who do not like to be or live alone. Number sevens may be highly intuitive, even psychic, and need to take time and space to consider the effects of love, life and the Universe as a whole. Liking to delve into all things mystical, they would make great occultists, witches, wizards, magicians, musicians and artists. Number 7 people often exert a mysterious influence over others, but may also have a tendency to become too introverted. Moodiness, depression, social awkwardness, aloofness, leaving too much to chance, cowardice and duality, may be negative associations. Number sevens are also unusual, psychic, wise, reserved, knowledgeable, serious, intelligent, analytical, contemplative, persevering, focused, studious, introspective, gracious, refined, and possess great inner wisdom. They are original thinkers and regularly experience the inherent luck associated with their number. However, they do need substantial amounts of understanding, because they often find it extremely difficult to understand themselves. Seven's planet is Neptune, which is associated with water, and number 7 people often have a restless love of travel and the ocean. Monday is its day.

Your Character ★ Wisdom and discernment characterise those born under the influence of the number 7. You are the world's great thinkers, philosophers and writers, of the type called 'ascetic', being rigorous in the practice of all forms of self-discipline. Frequently you have to fight to maintain your theories and principles, for you are mentally so far-sighted you are ahead of your time and are therefore regarded as cranks or reactionaries. You will show great fortitude in the bearing of pain, both physical and spiritual, and are rarely heard to grumble at misfortunes. Pedantry and pettiness are especially distasteful to you, and your love for knowledge lies in the deepest and greatest things in life. Ordinary pleasures and amusements, unless they demand mental exercise which leads into new fields of thought and contemplation, will mean little to you. An excessive love of solitude, which may cause morbidness, is your biggest danger. When you find yourself forced to mix with other people, you often become disgruntled and resentful because your desire for privacy has not been respected. As a result, you may become over-critical regarding the actions of others, always making comparisons with what you yourself consider to be the right path or course of action. Moreover, you will often refuse to make any practical use of the knowledge you possess, preferring to store it up and to devote your time instead to acquiring further knowledge. You should learn to appreciate the value of friendship, and to develop and make use of your brainpower as a means of bringing material success.

Alchemy ★ Seven signifies a full range of differences. It contains diversity within a recognisable order, like the spectrum of colours in the rainbow. The seven days of the week are a familiar version of this, each day with its own character and magical correspondences. Something that has seven components in it has an identity of its own, above and beyond the individual ingredients. For this reason, a group is said to function effectively only when it has seven members or more. The warring fours and harmonious threes, their sum equalling seven, find their first conjunction here.

LUCKY 'MAGIC HOURS' OR 'TIME UNITS'

One rule of magic, luck and power, as already outlined elsewhere in this book, can be found within the well-known phrase, "As above, so below." From the most ancient times, the planets were said to rule Earthly destinies and powers. Days of the week were named after the seven planets which were the only ones then known: Sun Day, Moon Day, Mars Day (French: Mardi), Mercury Day (French: Mercredi), Jove Day (French: Jeudi), Venus Day (French: Vendredi) and Saturn Day.

The planetary hours are based on an ancient astrological system, the Chaldean order of the planets. The Chaldean order indicates the relative orbital velocity of the planets, and from a heliocentric (helios = The Sun) perspective, this sequence also indicates the relative distance of the planets from the Sun (the Sun switching places with the Earth in this sequence), and the distance of the Moon from the Earth.

Before an action is taken in daily life, or a transaction undertaken, for instance, it is possible to choose the appropriate day and hour that will provide the greatest chances of success. By studying the planetary hours system, you will discover which actions are propitious to which of the seven planets or 'star-gods' and at what time it would be advisable to undertake them.

The planetary hours system uses this Chaldean order to divide time, and each planetary hour of the planetary day is ruled by a different planet. The order is repeated, starting with the slowest: Saturn - then, Jupiter, Mars, Sun, Venus, Mercury, Moon, then back to Saturn, Jupiter, Mars, etc, ad infinitum. The planet that rules the first hour of the day is also the ruler of that whole day and gives the day its name. So the first hour of Saturday is ruled by Saturn, the first hour of Sunday by the Sun, and so on. It is important, for the purposes of using specific planetary energies for our magic and wishes, to note that planetary hours are not considered the same length as our normal time-keeping slots of sixty minutes. Each day is split into time periods, day time and night time, beginning at around sunrise and sunset respectively. These two time periods are each divided into twelve equal-length hours, which are the planetary hours. So the planetary hours of the day and the planetary hours of the night will be of different lengths, except during the equinoxes when light and darkness are balanced.

In sequence, the Sun, Moon and the five visible planets each exerts its own special influence over a twenty-four-hour period. I like to call your planet's special day and hour the 'Magic Hour'.

Magic rituals to draw luck and love to you should be conducted at astrologically correct times and with the appropriate instruments, tools, cards, herbs, flowers, oils and plants which are linked with the ruling planet. For example, a love ritual, spell or potion demands a concoction of any or all of the above ruled by Venus. Do not underestimate rulerships, for they wield an unseen power that can help make our dreams, big and small, come true.

Further, as specific hours of each day are ruled by certain planets, if you are really serious about attracting some power, luck or magic into your life, it is imperative that you wish, pray or ask at the most opportune times for your Sun sign. There are two methods you can use for fine tuning your magical workings. The first method is to perform your spell, ritual or wishing on the day your Sun sign's ruling planet during the planetary hour that signifies the essence of what you are asking for (e.g. A Piscean who is looking for love might perform a love-seeking ritual on a Thursday, during a Venus-ruled planetary hour). Alternatively, if you wish to summon the power of your Sun sign's own ruling planet, then that same Piscean might perform their love-seeking ritual on a Friday (ruled by Venus) during Jupiter's planetary hour.

The nature of that which you are asking for, such as love, travel opportunities, money, career guidance, protection or friendship for example, should always be considered when choosing the day or hour during which your magic will be heightened.

The answer to the question why are there seven days in a week, is a very important one to know in unravelling the secret of your Magic Hours. Ancient people recognised the supreme importance of the seven heavenly spheres, which comprised those which could be seen by the naked eye: The Sun, Moon, Mercury, Venus, Mars, Jupiter and Saturn. They then named each of the seven days of the week after one of those spheres and assigned that planetary 'ruler' to one day of the week. As viewed from Earth, these seven spheres appear to move at varying speeds, and the ancients used this factor to arrange them in order of varying speed. If you intend to use your Magic Hours to attract wonderful things, you must memorise that sequence because it is what forms the basis of the whole system.

Whenever you intend to use your Magic Hours or, perhaps more accurately, Magic *Time Units*, it is important to find out the exact time of sunrise for the area in which you live, as sunrise marks the time when your planet's magic is at its most powerful on its specific day. So, at sunrise on Sunday, the Sun rules the hour following the sunrise, the Moon rules the first hour following sunrise on a Monday, and through the week the pattern is repeated, with each day's ruling planet beginning the cycle in that first hour after dawn. It is logical then, that the rest of the planets, in sequence, follow on with one planet per hour for that day thereafter for the rest of the 24-hour cycle, creating a Magic Hour or Time Unit for each planet throughout the day and night, depending on which planet rules that particular day and is therefore the first in line.

If you wish to explore the idea in more depth, it is worth noting first and foremost that each day contains twenty-four hours, but, depending on the season, day and night will be of varying lengths. In summer, daylight is longer than darkness, whereas the reverse applies in winter. During autumn and spring, day and night are usually about equal. Therefore, although a complete day always contains twenty-four hours, there are not always twelve hours between sunrise and sunset and another twelve hours between sundown and the following sunrise. So, depending on the season (and location), a time unit may be shorter than one hour, longer than one hour, or equal to one hour. So whenever you intend to use your Magic Time Units, it is important to find out the exact time of sunrise and sunset for the area in which you live. The next step is to divide the amount of day time (if day when you wish to work your 'magic', otherwise the same following theory applies to night time) into twelve equal sections by calculating the number of hours and minutes between sunrise and sunset and divide by twelve. An example is if the Sun rises at 6.27 a.m. and sets at 5.49 p.m., the amount of time contained in this day is eleven hours and twenty-two minutes. Convert this total into minutes (682) and then divide that figure by twelve (57). Therefore, each of the twelve daylight time units will be 57 minutes on that day.

Although this wonderful method of using astrology is very ancient, it may be completely new to you. You are in for a pleasant surprise though, because if you are willing to delve into a little research and put the system to the test, rich rewards are in store for you!

YOUR LUCKY DAY ★ THURSDAY

Basic Energy ★ Expansion
Basic Magic ★ Luck, Money, Increase
Element ★ Fire
Colours ★ Purple
Energy Keywords ★ Aspiration, Benevolence, Charity, Philanthropy, Generosity, Mercy, Dignity, Mind Travel, Expansion, Religion, Faith, Philosophy, Success, Understanding, Growth, Extravagance, Kindness, Humour, Optimism, Luck, Hope, Pomposity, Radiance, Reverence, Confidence, Indulgence, Opulence.

Thursday is the day of Jupiter, your traditional (or secondary) ruler. In commonly used calendars, Thursday is the fifth day of the week, though in others it is the fourth. The English name is derived from Middle English *Thuresday*, meaning 'Thor's Day'. In Latin the day was known as *Iovis Dies*, 'Jupiter's Day'. Thursday is known as this king of the gods' day. Thursday has its origins in the Saxon *Thor's Day*, and the Latin *Jove* (which links to the Jupiterian trait 'jovial'), from which the French *Jeudi*, Spanish *Jueves* and Italian *Giovedi* may derive from. In the folk rhyme 'Monday's Child', 'Thursday's child has far to go' - you can interpret this as you please, but I don't feel it fits with Jupiter's generally optimistic, expansive nature; however, it can be taken to mean that your horizons may well open up before you on your life's journey and you therefore have far horizons that await your exploration.

Jupiter rules over business and material growth, justice, the higher mind, legal matters, ethics, publishing, luck and general increase and expansion, so if you are taking action to expand anything in your world, or seeking judgement on or clarity about your affairs, Thursday would be a powerful day on which to ask. Thursday is a day of Luck, Abundance, Optimism, Expansion, Higher Learning, Hope, Positivity, Risk, Philosophy, Speculation, Adventure, Creativity and Faraway Journeys, and an opportune day for making wishes or working magic involving higher education or tertiary studies, growth, idealism, philosophical endeavours, influence, worldly power, accomplishment, wisdom, overall fulfilment, games of chance, abundance, optimism, and long-distance or foreign travel. Good luck, and always be careful what you wish for - because, as Ralph Waldo Emerson so eloquently noted, you will surely get it!

JUPITER'S MAGIC TIME UNITS (BASED ON THE PLANETARY HOURS) FOR EACH DAY OF THE WEEK

SATURDAY ★ Second and Ninth time units after sunrise
SUNDAY ★ Sixth time unit after sunrise
MONDAY ★ Third and Tenth time units after sunrise
TUESDAY ★ Seventh time unit after sunrise
WEDNESDAY ★ Fourth and Eleventh time units after sunrise
THURSDAY ★ First and Eighth time units after sunrise
FRIDAY ★ Fifth and Twelfth time units after sunrise **

Choose the Hour/s of Jupiter for any transaction, initiative or venture which is likely to involve an expansion, increase, good fortune, faith, celebration, spirituality, more comfort, greater possibilities in a situation, to arrive at a soiree or a party, or to choose or give a present or charitable gift.

** Please note that for the purposes of simplification, the information regarding 'Jupiter's Magic Time Units' is a very diluted and simplified version of using magical times to your advantage. These hours cover only daylight hours, or the first twelve hours after sunrise, and do not take into account magical times after sunset or throughout the night. 'Hours' is also a deceptive term, as most 'time periods' used in this system are less than an hour, but for the purposes of simplifying the technique, I refer to them as Magic Hours (to keep with the tradition of the term 'planetary hours') rather than magic 'time units', which is what they really are. Should you wish to do further research on your ruling planet's most powerful time units, or require further information about the planet/s from which you are seeking 'energy' from in order to assist your wish-making, other sources may provide you with more comprehensive and detailed information.

A LITTLE NEW MOON / MAGICAL TIME UNIT WISH RITUAL

Step 1 ~ Choose the Magical Hour and/or day that matches your intentions. The first dawn hour of Sunday, ruled by the Sun, is a great time for all-purpose magic, success, joy, abundance, prosperity, bliss, personal power & all-round expansion.

Step 2 ~ Write out a little wish list with the appropriate coloured pen on the colour paper which corresponds to your desire.

Step 3 ~ Choose a small stone of your choosing that is connected to your wish (or a number of stones that are perhaps linked with your planetary ruler's number, for example 7 for Neptune).

Step 4 ~ Find a nice patch of soil in your garden or any special place to you, dig into it, affirm your wish in your mind, place the crystal/s and piece of paper in the hole, then place a plant on top of the crystal/s and wish list.

Step 5 ~ Fill the soil back in over the roots of the plant and feed it with a little water out of a magical vessel (a small genie bottle would be ideal).

Step 6 ~ Thank the Earth, the Universe and the Sun (or whatever planet you are summoning the power from) for bringing forth your desires.

Step 7 ~ Repeat all day long: "Thank You, Thank You, Thank You!"

Step 8 ~ Watch your plant - and your wish - grow bigger and bigger as time goes on!

YOUR LUCKY CHARM/TALISMANS

The following are three 'materials' or talismanic symbols from which to make your lucky charms, and the planetary energy under which to do it, corresponding with your Sun sign:

PISCES ★ Bloodstone, Fish, Tin, Jupiter

"When any star ascends fortunately, take a stone and herb that are under that star, make a ring of the metal that is congruous therewith, and in that fix the stone with the herb under it."
Henry Cornelius Agrippa, *On Occult Philosophy*

Charms, talismans and amulets are among the oldest forms of magic. A charm or talisman is a symbol, often used to communicate a thought, prayer or wish to, or to make a connection with the Divine. It is usually in the form of an object, which has been imbued with mysterious and magical powers. A charm may be as simple as a stone, a flower or a feather, or it might be a parchment bearing writing; the meaning and significance that you attribute to the symbol is what is important. It can be created by yourself (to best effect) or by someone else, and works as a tool to activate our subconscious mind.

You can use general charms such as a cross, or a universally lucky symbol such as a horseshoe, but you will exude and therefore attract more potency and protection if you make and wear the appropriate charms with the matching gemstone, set in the right metal and created under the corresponding planetary influence. While most people wear silver or gold, cheaper tin or copper may be more appropriate and indeed beneficial for your Sun sign. An amulet (for protection) or a talisman or charm (for luck), must also be made, ordered, designed or purchased on the appropriate day of the week for its power to be most effective. Your day, as previously described, is Thursday.

You can even go further and create or buy your amulet or charm at one of the hours and/or days when your planet is exerting its most powerful influence. It may sound complicated and requiring of forethought and effort, but if you are going to summon magic and are superstitious enough to truly *believe* that you can do this (and remember pure belief in something is the starting point of all manifestation), you should be scrupulous enough to do it properly. For your planet's day and time, please consult the information under the previous headings 'Your Lucky Day' and 'Jupiter's Magic Time Units'.

GODS, GODDESSES, ANIMAL TOTEMS & OTHER 'GUIDES'

Gods, goddesses and guides can be summoned to help you live your life to its optimal best. Some are connected with your Sun sign, while others may be of your own personal choosing, ones you may feel particularly drawn towards. Those which align with your ruling planet and your Sun sign, give a good indication of those who will shine a guiding light along your desired path, but you can choose your own too, based upon exploration, observations, research, meditation or simple intuition - I believe choosing your own, based on your inner *knowing* or guidance system, is a very powerful magical tool. However, to get you started, following are some animal spirit guide ideas for your contemplation. Good luck!

YOUR LUCKY ANIMALS & BIRDS

Sheep, Ox, Seahorse, Horse, Fish, Swan, Cougar, Stork, Eagle, Dolphin and All Sea Mammals, Wolf

"Somewhere beyond the walls of our awareness … the wilderness side, the hunter side, the seeking side of ourselves is waiting to return."
Laurens van der Post, *The Heart of the Hunter*

"(People) everywhere are being made acutely aware of the fact that something essentially to life and wellbeing is flickering very low in the human species and threatening to go out entirely. This 'something' has to do with such values as love, unselfishness, sincerity, loyalty to one's best friend, honesty, enthusiasm, humility, goodness, happiness … fun. Practically every animal has these assets in abundance and is eager to share them, given the opportunity and the encouragement."
Jay Allen Boone, *Kinship with All Life*

Some astrological systems, such as Shamanistic * or Native American Astrology, tell us that the Sun sign we were born under has a corresponding animal totem, which informs us about our characteristics and act as a kind of spiritual guide or mentor throughout our life's journey. These totems are described as Solar totems, because many of them share similarities with the Solar system and the sign the Sun was passing through at the time of our birth, and therefore relate to animals and animal behaviours which also correspond to environmental conditions and seasonal changes. These animals encompass many aspects of the Solar system, from seasonal relationships, to creature instincts, to reciprocal links with the planetary vibrations, and 'clans' within nature that you are inherently closely connected with through your date of birth.

Carl Jung, a master of dream analysis and interpretation, proposed that animals symbolise our natural instincts, operating through our dreams. He theorised that certain dream symbols, among them animals, represent core emotions and concepts, archetypes that will hold true for all of us the world over, regardless of so-called 'divisions' such as sex, customs, age or culture. In *Man and His Symbols*, Jung states that primitive societies believed that each person had a bush soul and a human soul. The bush soul incarnates as a tree or animal - a totem - and when the bush soul is harmed or injured, the human soul is considered injured as well.

Some of the most important and powerful spirit guides are those belonging to the animal kingdom. Both in ancient times and in some traditional modern tribal systems, people consult with animals for their wisdom and personal power. Even though most societies today have drifted away from this connection, it has never really left us, and different creatures continue to communicate with us on both the physical and spiritual planes in an attempt to speak to our souls and spirits.

As part of the teaching world, animals can bring us wisdom and survival skills, while others show us how to adapt, transcend or morph. Others still can remind us the importance of play and humour, and guide us around how to overcome life's challenges. Many are known for their loyalty and ability to love unconditionally and without judgement, while some have a grounded and healthy detachment, remaining true to themselves rather than pleasing others, an important lesson in itself. Whatever the qualities of the unique animal guides for your Sun sign, all have some enlightening soul-awakening traits that can teach us much about our own true inner selves. Ultimately, your animal spirit guides, and in particular your Solar totem animal, endow you with qualities that will enhance your life and help to activate your creativity, wisdom and intuition, helping to heal the broken or return the lost pieces of your soul and reconnect you to the natural world.

Your Solar totem animal (listed last on your lucky birds and animals list) is not the same as an animal spirit guide, which is based on metaphysical principles and is also based on your soul's mission in this embodiment - however, you can definitely make your birth Solar totem animal your spiritual guide if you wish, as you may find that its qualities, traits, symbolism and messages strongly reflect and define your own nature - or what you aspire to become, manifest or draw towards you. Your birth totem power animal comes from a place of trust and innocence, and represents the essence of your creative inner child. If you spend some time meditating on your Solar totem animal, asking what lessons it can teach, and reflect deeply on its character, life and habits, you may find it connects with you on a deep spiritual level and you can make the necessary changes to your life to draw in more magic and power.

Overall, if your life is stagnant or in need of healing or an energy boost, you can request your animal spirit or spirits to come and help you change your vibration, awaken your truth and arouse your inner forces. If you are aware of your animal spirit's presence in your life every day, you can use its particular energies to support, guide and teach you. And above all, pay attention to any signs and expressions of its lessons, and remember to thank your chosen animal guide for helping you.

* Shamanism is a traditional spiritual practice of the Native American culture. A shaman, one who practices this age-old art, is an intermediary between the human world and the world of the spirits. He inherits his magical powers at birth, but spends many years as an apprentice, so that he is usually much older in age before he is able to practice and call upon his skills. People ask for a shaman's help when there is a crisis on either a personal or wider spread scale, such as famine, drought, war or illness. The shaman makes contact with the spirits by going into a trance. First, he may perform a series of rituals, which usually include drumming, singing and chanting, and when these have brought on the right conditions, he leaves his body behind to travel to the other world. There he meets with the spirits of his ancestors, who inform him what must be done to relieve the suffering of his people. If the shaman is asked to cure someone of a dis-ease, then the spirits may accompany him to find the correct medicinal herbs or treatments for his patient.

YOUR FEATURE ANIMAL ★ WOLF

The Wolf's Message ★ The idea that freedom, compassion and passion can reside harmoniously together. Birth totem Wolf individuals arrive on this plane of existence to learn the gifts of the seer. Your life path is one of love and the application of spiritual knowledge.

Brings the totem gift of ★ Compassion, benevolence, generosity, sensitivity, identity, and the 'way of the seer'

Shares the power energies of ★ Liberation, intuition, trust, deep emotions and unwavering loyalty

Brings forth and teaches the magic of ★ Illumination, psychic ability, mysticism, creativity and freedom, cooperation, leadership

Certain animals have attained an historic symbolism that far transcends their biological reality; they are animals of myth, legend and stature. They become metaphors for qualities we despise or desire, and our perception of these animals can extend and expand well beyond the realm of the physical. We tend to imbue certain animals with often fantastical notions, depending upon our experience, and cultural and personal perceptions of them. As symbols, there are many examples of animals who represent both good and evil, for example. Depending on the community, society, culture, or one's religious or political beliefs, a certain animal may be considered friend or foe. Such is the case with the Wolf. Capturing the imagination of humans since the beginning of recorded history, the Wolf has always been singled out as a symbol of enormous good or devastating evil. The Wolf tends to embody a mythic vision of duality, possessing both masculine and feminine aspects, since the Wolf is considered both a gifted parent (the feminine) and a fierce hunter (the masculine). Also, because wolves can see well in both day and night, they are considered an animal representing both light and dark. The Wolf is ultimately associated with the dual roles of destroyer and provider.

The Wolf instinctively understands that all we need is love, and is perfectly capable and willing to provide it. Deeply emotional and wholly compassionate, the Wolf is the lover of the animal totem zodiac, in both the physical and philosophical sense of the word. A need for freedom sensitively coupled with gentleness and understanding, there is an element of the 'lone wolf' in this symbol, though this aloneness can be misinterpreted. Although impractical, timid and sometimes vindictive, the Wolf is always passionate, generous and deeply affectionate. The Wolf is also a messenger and a guide to otherworldly realms, especially at the time of the Full Moon.

The symbol of the Wolf has encountered many stereotypes, misunderstandings and misconceptions. Far from representing terror or ferocity and invoking fear, the Wolf is a creature with a high sense of loyalty and strength. Another misconception is that of the 'lone wolf', because to the contrary, the Wolf is a social, gregarious, sharing and giving creature. Fiercely protective, a mother Wolf is said to be able to defeat even a bear in defence of her young. She is famed both in myth and in recorded cases in India for raising abandoned human infants.

As a Wolf, you possess a gift of specialised wisdom and the skill of prophecy. You tend to draw a clear line between those who belong to your 'pack' and outsiders. You are intensely loyal to your own, and it can take some time for you to accept others outside of your own circle. But once you do, your sense of loyalty to the whole community is legendary. Due to your unique inner knowing and perspective, you can offer incredible insights and contributions to others within your clan.

The Wolf stands for endurance and balance and teaches us to tread the fine line between independence and dependence, between the needs of others and our own personal development. If it is time for you to move on and to start or lead your own pack, the Wolf will support you and guide you.

Overall, the Wolf is cunning, loyal, communicative, intelligent, generous, friendly and compassionate, with a depth of passion, faith and profound understanding of life's undercurrents. It represents our connection to nature; it teaches us to listen to and act upon our intuition. Wolf energy calls us to acknowledge our primal urges and helps us to take risks in pursuit of our desires. Wolves are faithful animals offering companionship through the most difficult stages of our spiritual journey.

As the Solar totem and spirit animal guide for Pisces, the Wolf can remind Pisceans of the importance of leadership and providing your insightful wisdom to your 'pack', but also of *belonging* to it, so all can live in harmony. As Rudyard Kipling so eloquently put it: "The strength of the pack is the wolf, and the strength of the wolf is the pack." This strength is inherent within you.

"In many cultures, the wolf appears as a psychopomp, a figure that acts as a mediator between the ego and the unconscious, between death and transformation. Historically, we have over-identified with the dark side of the wolf. But the wolf is not just one or the other. It moves between and throughout both realms. It embodies the light and the shadow … No one seems eager to confront and make peace with the wild wolf lurking around inside each of us, (for) it is easier to despise our projection than to do the personal work necessary to integrate our own inner dark wolf. But unless we can face and claim the dark aspects of the wolf, we are not free to enjoy the light aspects: the courage, intelligence, and fierce joy of living that the wolf also embodies. This is the wolf's challenge to us: to embrace it all."

Dr. Elizabeth Kirkhart, Jungian psychologist

SPIRITUAL KEEPER ★ BUFFALO

Your spiritual keeper guides your spiritual growth and brings illumination. Your spiritual keeper is determined by the season in which you were born. Regarded as the 'keepers' or 'caretakers' of the Universe, the four Directions or alignments were also referred to by the Native Americans as the Four Winds because their presence was *felt* rather than seen. The Direction to which your birth time belongs influences the nature of your inner senses. The North

Direction's totem is the Buffalo. The Buffalo is a symbol of the mind and its sustenance - knowledge. The Buffalo (or Bison) is a revered symbol and a mighty albeit confronting animal, each beast weighing up to a tonne. It teaches us the gifts of provision, gratitude, abundance, prosperity, blessing, stability, consistency and strength. Its medicine includes manifestation, protection, Earth creativity, courage, knowledge, generosity, sharing, and giving for the greater good. The Buffalo brings you the endurance and power to walk the Great Road of pure intent that leads to happiness, health and fulfilment, bringing the sustenance that offers renewal and rebirth after a long, arduous winter. The power of the North's influence is primarily with the mind and wisdom, and the specific influence of this direction on Buffalo people is on intuitive sense, enabling you to Divine hidden truths, and endowing you with a deep sensitivity both to others' feelings and to mystical matters. Having this animal as your spiritual keeper bestows you with the gifts of a clear and keen mind, a quiet wisdom, and the power of renewing your energies from your own inner resources. The Buffalo is a reminder of the greater whole and its symbolism illustrates, in magical ways, the interconnectedness of everything in the world - and the wider Universe. Your animal keeper the Buffalo is, above all, a potent symbol of oneness and abundance.

CLAN ★ FROG

Your clan animal comes from a place of inner knowing and intuition, helping you to discover the essence and magic of your true self. The Frog, a Totem of the Water clan, represents the song that calls the rain to Earth, and cleansing, teaching us the opportune times to purify, refresh and replenish our reserves. A charm or amulet in the shape of a frog is said to attract true friends and to help you find long-lasting love. To the Ancient Egyptians, Romans and Greeks, frogs symbolised inspiration, fertility, good luck and speedy recovery from illness, beliefs that carry over into some cultures today. People of the Frog clan have deep, easily flowing feelings, which enable them to have empathy for others and to heal. They have natural gifts for healing, sensitivity, creativity, and a deep appreciation for rain and being around water. Frog clan people are blessed with an abundance of emotions, feelings, perception, insights, and the ability to pick up on the innermost feelings of others. They are also able to delve into the incredible depths of the Soul. As the Moon is so strongly associated with emotional and watery realms, Frog clan people can connect with this deep Lunar magic by studying the cycles, patterns and energies of the Moon, the ruling celestial sphere of their clan animal, the Frog.

THE CHAMELEON & PISCES

The chameleon is a small reptile from Africa and Asia, whose name means 'dwarf lion living at ground level'. It is well-known for its remarkable ability to adapt to its background, and its mythical, sacred and symbolic characteristics are strength, power, wisdom, patience, domination, perseverance and knowledge of the beginning and end of all things on Earth. You may have heard Pisceans being described as chameleon-like; this association has been made through the fact that the chameleon, a truly magical animal whose appearance on Earth dates back 170 million years, is a very placid creature with the unique ability to remain motionless for hours on end, until it blends in perfectly with its surroundings, traits it shares with the very adaptable Pisces. To do so, the chameleon's body seems able to inflate and deflate at will as well as change colour. Its protruding, constantly moving eyes, allow it to see almost simultaneously what is going on from all angles - in front of itself, behind itself, and also to the sides. Both perhaps best known for their adaptability to their environment and surroundings, and their calm placidity, the chameleon and the Piscean have much in common!

THE COUGAR & PISCES

The cougar, or mountain lion, like all big cats, has perfect balance and harmony. It shows us how to protect ourselves from physical injury, and how to conceal our fears when confronted with adversity, and when leadership and courage are needed.

THE SWAN & PISCES

Swans are a symbol of true love and fidelity. Working with the swan as your spirit guide will help you find your soul mate. Swans teach us to express our love creatively through poetry and music, calling on us to make deep and heartfelt connections with our loved ones.

YOUR CORRESPONDING CHINESE ASTROLOGY ANIMAL

The Chinese Zodiac, known as Sheng Xiao (literally meaning 'birth likeness'), is based on a twelve-year cycle, each year in that cycle related to a particular animal. These animals are: Rat, Ox, Tiger, Rabbit, Dragon, Snake, Horse, Sheep, Monkey, Rooster, Dog and Pig. The selection and order of the animals that so influence people's lives, particularly in East Asian cultures, originated in the Han Dynasty (202 BC - 220 AD) and was based upon each animal's traits, characteristics, tendencies and living habits. Further, ancient people observed that there were twelve Full Moons in a year, and that, among other similarly related celestial observations, suggests its origins are also based on astronomical concepts.

The legend of the Chinese zodiac's story usually begins with the Jade Emperor, or Buddha (depending on who is telling the tale), summoning all the animals of the Universe for a race or a banquet. The twelve animals of the zodiac all appeared at the palace, and the order in which they arrived determined the order of the Chinese zodiac.

Each oriental animal corresponds with a Western astrology sign. For Pisces, it is the Rabbit.

"I am in tune with the
Pulse of the Universe.

> In my quiet and solitude
> I hear the melodies of the soul.
> I float above commonplace
> Dissent and decay.
> I subdue my ability to conform.
> I colour my world
> In delicate pastel hues.
> I epitomise harmony and inner peace.
> *I am the Rabbit."*
> **Theodora Lau**

Chinese name for the Rabbit ★ TU
Ranking Order ★ Fourth
Hours ruled by the Rabbit ★ 5 a.m. to 7 a.m.
Direction ★ Directly East
Season and principle month ★ Spring - March
Corresponds to the Western sign ★ Pisces

★ RABBIT ★ *Fixed Element Wood*

★ Keywords ★

Pleasant, talented, articulate, discerning, psychic, refined, conservative, ambitious, sensitive, successful, & peaceful.

The Rabbit is the fourth animal of the Chinese horoscope. The Rabbit is one of the most fortunate of the twelve signs. The Rabbit, or Hare as he is referred to in Chinese mythology, is the emblem of longevity and is said to be endowed with his essence by the Moon. You possess an air of refinement, and you love peace, quiet and homely comforts. Traditionally a yin animal, the Rabbit is sometimes symbolised as a cat. Rabbits are mysterious, talented, sensitive and artistic. You may sometimes appear to be secretive or even unfriendly because you are shy of strangers. Once at your ease, you are friendly and helpful, willing to offer wise advice and capable assistance. The Rabbit is extremely lucky in business and monetary transactions and for all your quiet and docile nature, you possess a strong will and a formidable self-assurance. Arguably the luckiest of all the signs, you are also the most likely to live a long, prosperous life.

YOUR METALS

Piscean power metals are Tin, Antimony, Pewter, Platinum, Titanium and Neptunium

Although the magic power of crystals is widely recognised and applied, the influence radiating from metals is often overlooked. Metal, too, emits a powerful energy and in fact, in Chinese philosophy, metal is considered so essential and powerful that it is classified as one of the elements, alongside Air, Fire, Earth and Water.

As already mentioned earlier in the book, throughout the writings of early philosophers and theorists, there are countless references to the unmistakable mystic connection between the seven known planets of the time, and Earthly affairs, ailments and objects. Seven metals were connected with the seven planets, to which seven colours and the seven 'transformations' were added. So the ancient alchemist came to share the astrological doctrine that each planet ruled a mineral: the Sun ruled gold, the Moon silver, Mars iron, Venus copper, Saturn lead, Jupiter tin, and Mercury quicksilver. Consequently, in alchemical symbolism the same sign came to represent the nominated metal and its corresponding planet.

TIN

Tin is planet Earth's 49th most abundant element and has two possible oxidation states. Tin is allied with your traditional ruling planet Jupiter, because it is one of the so-called 'temperate metals', easy to forge and work with, which is a Jupiterian quality. Tin can be worn as a pendant, engraved with symbols, and is usually used for money attracting charms and for luck in general. A white-silvery, malleable, highly crystalline and ductile 'other metal' that is not easily oxidised in air, tin is a chemical element whose symbol is Sn. It is a main group metal in group 14 of the periodic table, sharing chemical similarity to both neighbouring group 14 elements (lead and germanium). The first alloy, used in large scale since 3000 BC, was bronze, an alloy of tin and copper. Pewter is another alloy, of 85 to 90 per cent tin with the remainder consisting of antimony, copper and lead. In modern times, tin is used in many alloys, one significant application being the corrosion-resistant tin-plating of steel. Due to its low toxicity, tin-plated metal is commonly used for food and beverage packaging as tin cans, which are made mostly from steel. Some alloys which contain tin to greater or lesser degrees, and which can be used as a substitute for pure tin to make Piscean talismans, are: Bronze, Pewter, and Brittanium.

PLATINUM

Platinum is associated with Neptune also. Its grey colouring reflects the cloudiness and dreamy qualities of your ruling planet, and when worn, this metal is thought to provide an antidote to Neptune's heavy, hallucinatory effects, thereby clearing the mind and lifting the spirits.

The word 'platinum' originates from the Spanish word *plata*, meaning 'silver', referring to the colour of the metal. Platinum was discovered in the early 1700s. It is so rare that two million pounds of ore may only contain about one pound of platinum metal. Its rarity makes it even more valuable than gold. Platinum nuggets are rarely larger than a pea - anything larger would qualify as a major find. The highest quality platinum comes from the Ural Mountains in Russia. It can be used for jewellery, but has less glamorous uses too: it is placed in anti-pollution devices in cars to trap dirt and toxic gases.

PLANTS, HERBS, SPICES, TREES, SHRUBS, FLOWERS, SCENTS & INCENSE

Plants have long been associated with magic, medicinal properties, superstition, nutrition and even astrology. In ancient times, some were endowed with magical properties based upon beliefs of the time, but also upon anecdotal evidence that some herbal concoctions, flowers or essences helped alleviate and even cure uncomfortable, painful or dis-eased physical or mental states. Whether these were based upon 'old wives' tales' or beliefs in supernatural forces matters little, for in modern times we can prove and indeed *have* proven through scientific research and controlled experiments, that plants have their place in our health and medicine cabinets. Some 'magical' plants have aphrodisiac or narcotic properties, while others have formidable toxic effects, but all are considered in some way to affect the human system on physical, spiritual and psychological levels. Plants such as cocoa, tobacco and coffee, which have accompanied humans over the course of millennia, are still, more than ever, an integral part of our daily lives. They still incite the same pleasures, the same fascinations, and the same dangers, and some still carry the same taboos. It is interesting to note that more than 80 per cent of chemical medicines in existence today, and found in pharmacists' dispensaries, are made from plants.

In modern astrology herbs are often associated with the zodiac signs and have evolved from an old system where a specific planet rules each herb. The planet that governs a herb is chosen according to its appearance, scent and where it grows; herbs are additionally categorised as hot or cold, and dry or moist. In this way you can see how the nature of the herb corresponds to the nature of the planet. If you are familiar with your ruling planets' basic associations, you will find it easy to match it to herbs. Although you can simply buy whatever herbs you wish to use for your magic, the optimum effect will be obtained if you can gather them at a favourable astrological time. Once you are armed with astrological knowledge, you can choose a time when the planet that rules your chosen herb is in a position of strength. Keep in mind that each planet rules a substantial amount of plants, so if one isn't easily obtained, it should be simply to find another one to use for the same purpose.

There sometimes seems to be a wide variance in the list of herbs associated with a specific astrological influence. This is because the different parts of the plant have different rulerships and uses. For example, whichever planet rules it, a plant that bears fruit is naturally related to Jupiter, its flowers relate to Venus, seed or bark to Mercury, leaves to the Moon, wood to Mars, and roots to Saturn. So, as well as the planet that traditionally rules the plant, it can be regarded as having a secondary ruler according to the part of the plant being used. Although you don't need to work with a highly complex system of deciding which herb will suit your purposes, you can make your magical workings more powerful by paying attention to some of these nuances.

Essentially, different scents, herbs, flowers and plants have their own specific vibrations. Their essences should be worn on your skin (you can make up your own combinations using essential oils or flower waters), burned in an oil burner, inhaled from a cloth, diffused in a bath or bowl of steam, or burned as incense sticks. Many plants, herbs and spices, however used, contain gentle yet effective energies which will affect not only your wishing ceremonies, but also your moods, associations and emotions, which can assist in carrying your wonderful self in the direction of your dreams. Lifted up on incense smoke, for example, your wish is carried out to the wider Universe. Try making your own, out of any or all of your power plants, woods, flowers, shrubs, trees or herbs!

Thirty-three magical, mythical plants are: Cocoa, rosemary, tobacco, thyme, wheat, coffee, sugar cane, cinnamon, hemp, tea, pumpkin, foxglove, incense, amanita (a mushroom), tarragon, pepper, rice, belladonna, reed, ginseng, clove, ginger, sage, maize, mistletoe, lily, mandrake, St John's Wort, poppy, peyote, cinchona, verbena and the vine *. How many of your Piscean 'lucky plants' (listed under the next sub-category, 'Your Lucky Plants, Herbs, Spices', etc.) can be found on this Magical 33 List?

YOUR LUCKY PLANTS, HERBS, SPICES, TREES, SHRUBS, FLOWERS, SCENTS, OILS & INCENSE

Lotus **, Cedar, Eyebright, Birch, Lichen, Cinnamon, Sage, Mullein, Dandelion, Lime Flowers, Myrrh, Ash,

Willow, Orchid, Mugwort, Kava Kava, Hazel, Yarrow, Chaparral, Saxifrage, Mulberry, Chestnut, Oak, Irish Moss (sea lettuce), Elm, Bog Bean, Fig, Purslane, Angelica, Sweet Cicely, Fumitory, Evening Primrose, Red Poppy, Coriander, Forget-Me-Not, Pussy Willow, Iris, Sun Dew, Violet, Heliotrope, Nutmeg, Purple Loosestrife, Carnation, Sweet William, Lime, Woundwort, Chicory, Golden Seal, Echinacea, Water Lily, Rosehips, Seaweed, Mosses, Fern.

For Jupiter ★ Mint, Borage, Nutmeg, Balm, Birch. The plants associated with Jupiter are large and often contain an aspect that resembles a religious cross. Clove, Fig, Myrrh & Sage are connected with Jupiter *

For Neptune ★ Because Neptune rules plants which are used as intoxicants, transcendence-aides, or to otherwise alter the human mind, body or spirit, these plants can also be associated with Pisces. An example of these herbs, plants and trees are cannabis sativa, coffee beans, peyote, coca leaves, tobacco, psilocybin mushrooms, devil's weed, and the opium poppy. Additionally, Neptune has co-rulership with the Moon over many plants which possess magical and occult properties. *

* Some plant products can be poisonous, toxic, hallucinogenic or even fatal if consumed. Always research first.

** A Note on the Lotus Flower ★ The lotus flower - which has its roots in the mud but arises out of it beautiful and clean - is a symbol of how we can all rise, glorious and triumphant, from the muddiest of conditions. Indeed, Hindus and Buddhists consider the lotus an emblem of purity, as its beautiful flower comes from a plant that grows in slime. The Ancient Egyptians believed the goddess Isis was born from a lotus flower, and so they associated the lotus with fertility and sexual potency. The Hindus believe the creator god Brahma was born from a golden lotus flower that was cited in the navel of the Universe. And one legend about Buddha tells that everywhere he walked, he left lotuses behind him instead of footprints. The lotus holds a spiritual significance and meaning for many traditions. Across all, the lotus is a symbol of creation: out of the mud, the world can be born. It is also a symbol of wisdom, expressing the truth about the possibilities for all living things. The Buddhist mantra "Om mani Padme hum" translates as "Om, jewel in the lotus, amen." Reciting this mantra is said to bring peace to the chanter and to those nearby. A thousand-petalled lotus symbolises spiritual enlightenment.

YOUR SPECIAL POWER FLOWERS

PISCES IN GENERAL ★ Water Lily ★ In Greek and Roman times, the lily was associated with Venus, and symbolised purity and chastity. The early Christians adopted this symbolism and linked the white petals and sweet fragrance of the lily with the Virgin Mary. There is another, different interpretation of the lily however, associating it with virility and sensuality, for in Ancient Egypt it was connected with the goddess of fertility and creation, Ashtar. Lilies are frequently seen at weddings *and* funerals; at weddings they represent innocence and purity, and at funerals they symbolise the soul, free from the body and from Earthly sins. In the East, the day lily is believed to dispel grief and sorrows.

OTHER BIRTH FLOWERS ★ Jonquil, Poppy, Heliotrope & Carnation

FEBRUARY BORN ★ Violet ★ As a birth flower, thanks to Christian symbolism, the violet symbolises the gentle qualities of modesty, humility and shyness (which is where the term *shrinking violet* comes from), together with strength of character in adversity. The Greeks associated the violet with Io, who was one of many human women loved by Zeus. Napoleon loved violets, and he used them to give hope to his followers. When he was exiled to Elba, he told his supporters that he would return, just as the violets return each spring, and as a result they used the violet as their symbol. Napoleon became affectionately known as "Caporal Violet" and gave a bunch to

Josephine on their wedding day. On their anniversary each year he gave her another bunch of them, and after she died he placed a violet from her grave into a locket, and wore it around his neck until his own death.

MARCH BORN ★ Daffodil ★ The spiritually uplifting daffodil bestows dignity and chivalry on those born in March, the earliest month of the northern Hemisphere's springtime during which it first blooms. The daffodil has always been considered a cheerful flower that raises the spirits.

YOUR FOODS

Because Pisceans tend towards sluggish digestion, poor assimilation, slow metabolism, bloating and over-eating, you should guard against foods which may create or exacerbate these conditions. Pisceans love being near the water, and love nothing better than to eat the produce of it, such as all types of seafood, seaweed, kelp, sushi, algae-based 'super foods' such as spirulina and nori, and other foods which come from watery environments. Pisceans have a natural affinity with water, and particularly the ocean, so any foods which align with this realm, such as those which have a watery or salty content, will appeal to and nourish the Fish's soul and spirit. If you're a truly typical Piscean, you'll adore cooking for others, as you have a strong caring and nurturing streak, but you don't like to be 'tied' to the kitchen for long periods of time, so easy-to-prepare food is a good idea for your culinary style; after all, the less time you spend in the kitchen, the more time you have out of it at the dining table, eating and sharing the spiritually uplifting experience of drinking and dining with those you love. You also enjoy being pampered by others, and will make a delightful guest at any dinner party, savouring the pleasures of the table - and lingering for after-meals conversations as well. Overall, sensual, fluid, watery, soft-textured or gooey (think soft cheeses), exquisite and ocean-based foods belong on any menu for the Fish.

PISCES POWER FOODS

"Let food be your medicine;
let medicine be your food."
Hippocrates

Figs, Purslane, Chutneys, Lettuce, Melons, Rosehips, Bilberries, Green Leafy Vegetables, Sweet Cicely, Lychees, Chicory, Cucumber, Onions, Soft Cheeses, Prunes, Grapes, Strawberries, Raisins, Figs, Dates, Nuts, Pumpkin, All Seafood, Shellfish and Freshwater Fish, and All Fruit and Vegetables with a high water content. Your power beverages are H2O (water), Spirits mixed with Soda or Mineral Water, and Wine and Champagne. *

* Caution: Always use essential oils, alcohol and/or herbs with caution and research each one prior to use, as not all are safe for use by certain people, or under certain conditions such as pregnancy, intoxication or illness. Some herbs and oils may be hallucinogenic, toxic in high doses, or produce other undesirable effects, and may be considered potentially harmful or hazardous if used or consumed before operating machinery, driving, or combined with alcohol or other drugs. Always consult a qualified practitioner or undertake thorough research from reliable sources before use or consumption of any of the listed essential oils, herbs or foods.

YOUR LUCKY WOOD ★ OAK
(Great to make a magic wand out of!)

Native Americans referred to trees as 'Standing People' because they stand firm, obtaining strength from their connection with the Earth. They therefore teach us the importance of being grounded, while at the same time listening to, and reaching towards, our higher aspirations. In Norse mythology, Yggdrasil, the tree of life, is a cosmic map that represents all life. The tree has its roots in the Underworld, is linked to the Earth through its trunk and its branches reach into the air of the Otherworld of spirit. The dryad, or tree's spirit, needs to be respected and asked when 'taking' from a tree for the purposes of magic. The essence of tree magic lies in understanding the qualities of each type. These can be drawn on for such things as healing and spell-casting. For example, the rowan tree grows high up the sides of mountains, often in hard-to-reach places, so if you need to develop tenacity or access to difficult spiritual spaces, you can call on this tree; the oak tree is durable and strong, so if you are needing fortification or firmness, you can gain power from this tree. When respected as living, breathing beings, trees can provide insights into the workings of Nature, cycles, and our own inner essence. Each birth time is associated with a particular kind of tree, the basic qualities of which complement the nature of those born during that time. Appreciate the beauty of your affinity tree and study its nature carefully, for it has a connection with your own nature and lessons to impart.

★ **OAK** ★ Oak wood corresponds to the element of Water and the planets Jupiter and Mars, and is a symbol of strength, sovereignty, courage, wisdom, wealth, honesty, toughness, endurance, rulership, nobility, generosity, justice, protection, bravery and power. With its towering height and wide girth, it also symbolises and bestows luck, vigour, love, potency, health and prosperity. The mighty oak tree has a wide trunk, very deep roots and deeply lobed leaves. The older a tree, the larger it will be and mature trees can be well over 1,000 years old (their life span is up to 2,000 years). Held sacred in ancient times, its noble attributes have long been harnessed for use in magic, and today the oak is still valued for its great strength and durability.

Oak is known as the 'King of Trees' and has a strong association with English woodlands, which has its origins in Britain's Pagan past. It is connected with the Summer Solstice; its wood being used to fuel the sacred Midsummer fires. It also has links with royalty and kingship: King Arthur's round table was fabled to have been created from a single cross section of a large oak. In the 'old days', front doors were usually made from oak; this was because, although the thickness of the wood helped to keep the warmth in and unsavoury guests out, its magical properties also provided strength, fertility and protection to the house or building. The word 'druid' originates from the Celtic word 'duir', meaning 'oak' or 'door'. It was believed that the oak was a portal to the spirit world and nature gods were worshipped in oak tree groves.

Acorn nuts, the divine fruit of the mighty oak, are said to increase fertility, sexual potency, longevity, 'immortality' and youthfulness, fostering virility partly through the sensuality of their creamy texture and smoky flavour, as well as the protein richness they offer. Both nut and cone have been used magically in fertility charms. Acorns are also omens of wealth, happiness and extremely good fortune. The acorn and the tree from which it comes, is a portent which signifies successful outcomes to any venture you want to undertake, and prosperity and growth in the future.

Furthermore, the oak tree's essence helps boost energy levels and to achieve our goals and manifest our desires. Oak is a grounding wood, offering the gifts of stability and strength; imbued with the tree's powerful properties, it can be used to make magical tools or charms. The power and durability of the oak tree are demonstrated by the fact its root system extends as far beneath the Earth as its branches stretch above it. Its strength is further symbolised by enduring what others around it cannot; it remains strong through challenges, and is regarded as being almost immortal, as is often attested by its long life and ability to survive fire, lightning strikes and other similar devastations. Oak is one of the most sacred trees, traditionally prized by the Celts and Druids, the tree's commanding presence signifying true alignment of purpose, balance and fortitude, and Witches often danced beneath the oak tree during ritual. Carrying any part of the oak tree draws good luck to you, but remember first to ask for permission and above all, to show recognition and gratitude for this wood's amazing gifts.

YOUR SACRED CELTIC CALENDAR TREES
★ ASH OR ALDER

ASH ★ (18 February - 17 March)
ALDER ★ (18 March - 14 April)

The Celts and other ancient peoples had many beliefs and traditions based around the magical lore of trees. The system of Celtic tree astrology was developed out of a natural connection with the Druids' knowledge of Earth cycles and their reverence for the sacred knowledge they believed was held by trees. The Druids had a profound connection with trees and regarded them as vessels of infinite wisdom. Their calendar, being based on a Lunar year of thirteen months, contains a tree for each of these Lunar months, corresponding with (but not exactly) each of the twelve western astrology zodiac signs, which are based on the Solar calendar. Because there are some crossovers, I have included two possible trees for your zodiacal birth period.

★ **ASH** ★ The ash tree is the immortal 'Tree of Life' and its winged seeds, called keys, represent the keys to Universal understanding and knowledge. One of the most significant trees in Celtic and Nordic traditions, ash is associated with the ever living Yggdrasil Tree. Ash offers protection from outside influences, healing and powers of divination. Providing the ash tree finds itself rooted in ideal soil conditions, it can grow to a height (up to 25 metres) that rivals even the might oak (up to 30 metres). The think trunk and pale colour of ash can make it appear fragile, grey and withered, but the wood is extremely strong and flexible, making it ideal for sports equipment such as hockey sticks or rowing oars. A traditional wood of boat-builders, it is a tenacious tree which symbolises the meeting of Fire and Water, lightning and rain, and represents the awesome force and turbulence that results when two opposing elements join up (the ash rules the third month in the Celtic calendar, a wild seasonal time of rains, floods and storms). It is also associated with royalty, as its wood was often used in the making of thrones.

★ **ALDER** ★ Often referred to as the 'King of the Waters', alder is one of the thirteen sacred trees of Celtic and European witchcraft. Associated with the period of the year surrounding the Spring Equinox, it brings a sense of healing, balance, harmony and calm. Rebirth, fertility and equilibrium are other key features.

In Welsh mythology, the alder fought in the front line of the 'Battle of the Trees', against the Underworld. When cut, its wood turns from white to red as though it is bleeding, and this red colouring can be used as a dye for sacred cloths, bags and ribbons. Growing near water, the tree has feminine associations, yet its links to war also indicate masculine powers. Therefore, the alder symbolises the balancing of the masculine and feminine.

The survival strategies of the alder tree make it an excellent pioneer species, being an initiator and motivator. It spawns a vast quantity of seeds and grows rapidly. Alder thrives around water, from marshlands to rivers, and the otter often makes its home in the waterside roots of the alder tree. As a hard, oily, and water-resistant wood, alder was often used to build early bridges, as well as to construct buildings, churches and cities. It is also used to make woodwind instruments, pipes and whistles.

Alder types are trailblazers. A natural born pathfinder, you're a mover and shaker with a fiery passion, charm and the ability to mix well with a broad range of characters. Dynamic and self-assured, you can see through superficialities and will not tolerate fluff or deception. Motivated by action and results, you place a high value on your time and dislike wasting it.

ESPECIALLY FOR AUSTRALIANS
(OF ALL ZODIAC SIGNS)

If you live in Australia, here are two Australian-based magical woods, for those who prefer to source their woods closer to home and nature. Australia has a less documented history than many European civilisations, but still has no less mythology and legends swirling in its mists of time.

EUCALYPTUS ★ Eucalyptus is very plentiful and has a wonderfully intoxicating, distinctive, clean aroma which is reminiscent of the continent's vast areas of bushland, and has played an important ceremonial and medicinal role in the culture of Australian Aborigines, who have inhabited the nation for 40,000 to 50,000 years. Eucalyptus is a wood of feminine energy whose elemental association is Earth and main origin is Australia. One of the strongest healing woods known, eucalyptus wood has been used for centuries for medicinal as well as ritualistic purposes. Heady and Earthy, the energy of this wood is clean and pure. Eucalyptus is recommended for the promotion of good, robust health, and is also related to luck, especially if regarding knowledge. An excellent tool in divination, particularly when worn as a charm to invoke luck, it brings the wearer or user good fortune when used in rituals seeking positive results.

LEOPARDWOOD (or LACEWOOD) ★

Leopardwood or the Leopard Tree, so named because of its spotted wood, carries the energies of both the masculine and the feminine, Mars (Aries, Scorpio) and Venus (Taurus, Libra), and its main affinity is with the Water element (Cancer, Scorpio, Pisces). Leopardwood is a very useful tool for divination and is associated with positive luck, earning it the label 'gambler's wood'. Overall, its energy is very positive, making it an ideal wood for use in almost any ritual or spell, especially those concerning luck, magic and divination.

THE POWER OF LOVE

Each Sun sign exudes their own love and romance style. This style is an energy unique to that sign, and has the power to magnetise to that person their true, soulful match. Unhappy or unsuccessful relationships are often the result of incompatible Sun signs, personal values, goals, hopes, viewpoints or expectations. I believe everyone has a perfect soul partner (or three!) who is especially for them, and just knowing that special person or persons are out there, awaiting too a moment of serendipity to bring you together, can illuminate your life's romantic path. In this lifetime, we may not find that person or persons, but can still experience the joys and wonders of many other significant relationships which enrich and add tremendous meaning to our lives. Some partnerships are only fleeting, but the feelings they give us can last a lifetime, while others are more enduring, and the rewards they give us and lessons they teach us can last a lifetime too. Small gestures of love on a frequent basis, consistent nurturing and communication, and making the effort to accept and understand each other, are just four ways to keep the fires of passion and romance burning long after the initially roaring fire has diminished into glowing embers.

Your whole natal chart would need to be examined to form an overall picture of your romantic nature, and although the Sun is a fantastic starting point, it is not the sole consideration. Regarding these other planets, in Carl Jung's studies on psychological astrology, and in traditional synastry (the comparing of two people's natal charts to determine overall compatibility), the harmonious link between the Sun in one person's chart and the Moon in the other's (usually the man's Sun and the woman's Moon) is considered the best indication for a happy and enduring relationship. More specifically, the sextile aspect, an angle of 60 degrees, appeared most frequently between the Sun of one and the Moon of the other in fulfilling relationships. Other positive planetary contacts, such as one person's Moon to another's Venus, or the Mars to the Moon (again, traditional indications of attraction and harmony) also occurred frequently.

The feminine personal planets in a male's chart (Moon and Venus), and the masculine personal planets in a female's chart (Sun and Mars) tell a lot about the inner self and how this is projected onto relationships. However helpful chart analysis is in telling a story about your relationship style and approach, it all depends not on your chart, but on what you do with the resources at your disposal, which your chart can indeed tell you a lot about. Relationships and marriages involving harmonious planetary and zodiacal energies between the two people tend to last longer because they are simply more 'flowing' and easier.

The signs in which the four personal and 'relationship' planets - the Sun, the Moon, Venus and Mars - are placed, coupled with the aspects they make with the other planets in the chart, give important clues into understanding the often unconscious drives within you that shape your relating style, tastes, mannerisms and patterns.

Expanding upon the other planetary considerations is beyond the scope of this book, but it is useful to know, particularly if you are interested in examining the dynamics of a current relationship a bit deeper, or are wishing to attract a new one into your life. But for now, your Sun sign is a wonderful place to start! Your Solar sign is regarded as being at the core of the complex - and very fun - study of relationships! So for now, we will begin this study of love with your essence, your core self, the brightest light shining from within - your Sun sign!

SOME LUCKY-IN-LOVE TIPS
GENERAL HINTS

★ To attract and retain love, the Heart chakra (an energy centre within the body) needs to be balanced and clear from blockages. The Heart chakra is located in the region of the physical heart. Its Sanskrit name is *anahata*, and its symbol is a twelve-petal green lotus flower whose centre contains a green circle and two intersecting triangles making up a six-pointed star representing balance (and also could be said to symbolise six as the number of Venus). Its element is Air and its colour is green. Balance in this chakra is expressed as unconditional love for ourselves and others. Crystals that can be used to cleanse and balance this chakra are mostly green and pink stones.

★ Pink candles (two, representing a couple, or six, representing Venus, is preferable) can be used in love spells.

★ Any 'love-attracting' wishing rituals should be done on a Friday (ruled by Venus) night around the time of the New Moon (signifying the principle of increase and growth).

★ Basil, otherwise known as witch's herb or St Joseph's wort, is said to be the most potent lover herb of all. Basil vibrates to the energy of Mars, which is all about lust and sexual energy, and it is used prolifically in all sorts of love potions and rituals throughout the world.

★ Ginger has a reputation as a potent sexual tonic and aphrodisiac *. Arousing and warm, it can increase sensual vitality, particularly in men. Being warming and spicy, its vibration aligns with Mars. Saffron is also regarded as a potent, albeit expensive, aphrodisiac!

★ Wear red and pink (associated with Mars and Venus respectively), as these colours in all their shades are said to incite passion, lust and romance. Green is also connected with the heart by virtue of its association with the Heart chakra and the planet Venus, and its links with fertility, nature, abundance of all kinds, and new growth.

★ Call upon some higher spiritual help. When working your 'love magic', some planetary influences, goddesses and gods that you can call upon are: Aphrodite, Venus and Eros/Cupid, and other lesser known deities such as Juno Lucina, Demeter, Freya, Ishtar, Circe and Hathor.

★ The planet Venus has developed a rich culture of gods and goddesses associated with her varying levels of love and passion. These include the virgin - Brighid; the fertile woman - Aphrodite, (the Greek goddess); and of course Venus (the Roman equivalent); the mother and provider - Demeter; and desirous or physical love - Eros/Cupid (Venus's son).

★ The pine tree is sacred to Adonis (Venus's lover) and is said to balance the male and female energies. Pine is cleansing and protective and, as an evergreen, symbolises life. Its cones represent fertility.

★ Cardamom is said to have aphrodisiac qualities

★ The three almost universally recognised symbols of love are the goddesses Venus and Aphrodite, and the Cupid. Venus is the patroness of flowers and vegetation, and represents the regenerative cycle of creation, as well as beauty, herbs and physical love. She can be called upon for general love wishes and rituals. The dove, roses, rings, copper, apples, rosemary and the ankh are some of her sacred symbols. Aphrodite is a Greek goddess who has the ability to bring lovers together. Her names mean 'of the sea' as she is believed to have been born of the foam of the ocean. She can be called upon in ceremonies and spells for affection, love, marriage and partnership. Some of her associated symbols are the Flower of Aphrodite, swans, dolphins, frankincense and myrrh. Cupid, the cherubic winged boy with a bow and arrow, is the Roman name, and Eros is the Greek name for the same deity. The son of Venus/Aphrodite, he is an aspect that represents lustful love and desire.

★ Heartsease, another name for the wild pansy, Latin viola tricolour, was one of the most popular additives to the love potions of the ancient Romans and Greeks.

★ In centuries past, when people were more in tune with nature and its cycles, ceremonies, rituals and festivals were held on certain dates or times of year. The following are some examples, and you can reawaken their powers through craft and ceremony: February 2 is Bridhid's Day, or Bride's Day, and represents the white goddess; February 14 is Valentine's Day, traditionally the greatest and most well-known love 'celebration' of the year; March 1 is one of the festival days of Juno Lucina, the light bearer and goddess of women and marriage; the month of April is especially linked to the love goddess Aphrodite; the Summer solstice which falls on or around June 21 is an important time for reconnecting with the spirit of love, fertility and marriage; August 1 is the first of three harvest festivals in the Celtic calendar: The Harvest Festival honours Demeter, the goddess of love, as bountiful mother and faithful wife; the Festival of Lights, Diwali, in October, is sacred to Lakshmi, the Hindu goddess of happiness, love, and good fortune; the Winter solstice which falls on or around December 21, marks the turning point from long dark nights to lengthening days, and is the time of the wheel of love when virgin goddesses gave birth to their children - it is also fittingly symbolised by evergreens such as pine, ivy and holly; in Mexico, December 31, the last night of the year, is traditionally 'wishing night' and is an opportune time to make a wish for a lover in the coming year, using evergreen branches to enhance your request.

* The term 'aphrodisiac' is derived from Aphrodite, the Greek goddess of love, beauty, lust and sensuality

★ GEMSTONES ★

When it comes to calling love into your life using crystals, the general rule is that any of the pink or green stones are closely aligned with matters of the heart and can therefore help you to entice the affections you seek. Although your Sun sign has its very own special gemstones, outlined elsewhere in the book, the following stones can be used by all the signs (except for the first point, which are your own sign's feature stones), as their energies and qualities contain the power to attract and create love in all its forms, from self-love to deeper soulful connections with another, or to increase states of being which open the heart, thus enhancing your abilities to magnetise love.

★ Amethyst, Turquoise, Aquamarine and Bloodstone

★ Using your Piscean luckiest crystals is a fabulous start to working on heightening your romantic zest, and making your sensual energy more potent. Beryl,

Emerald and Sapphire are also useful in raising your attracting powers.

★ Rose Quartz is the ultimate love stone. It invites love into your life by helping to open your heart to receive love, and gently reminding you that you are worthy of love. Connected with the Heart chakra, it is the stone of unconditional love, enhancing all forms of it and opening up the heart. It is excellent for increasing self-worth and acceptance. The colour of rose quartz is pink, the colour of Venus, the amorous planet of desire and nurturance. Balancing and calming, it helps to heal emotional pain. Wear this stone, keep some beside your bed, or sleep with some under your pillow to remind you that love it coming your way - and that you whole*heart*edly deserve it!

★ Green Aventurine is considered the 'opportunity and luck stone'. Connected with the Heart chakra, it helps us to recognise opportunities and is said to place us exactly where we need to be for good things to transpire, as energetically it opens our mind and heart to increased perception to recognise lucky elements. It also promotes new growth, optimism, and is an overall attractor of good fortune, adventure and abundance.

★ Jade, on a spiritual level, has an affinity with the Heart chakra. It harmonises relationships, and encourages compassion and the establishment of strong bonds.

★ Emerald is reputedly a stone of constancy in love, and is said to have been brought to Earth from the planet Venus. Because it is green, it also holds deep associations with the Heart chakra.

★ Rhodochrosite can be used to attract one's soul mate. This stone, as with all the pink stones, can be used as an effective love magnet. It encourages you to appreciate yourself by teaching you that you are worthy of love, wholeness and happiness - and so opening you up to receive.

★ Malachite, Citrine, Rhodonite, Moonstone, Morganite, Beryl, Ruby, Mangano Calcite, Garnet, Red and Pink Tourmaline, Tugtupite, Rutilated Quartz, Lodestone, Peridot and Lapis Lazuli are also known for their love properties, and can be used or worn to invite romance into your life, or to bring and retain enduring love.

★ Clear Quartz can be used with any of these listed crystals to amplify their metaphysical properties.

★ Shells: Although shells are not technically a crystal, but rather a natural elemental material, they are associated with love and are sacred to Aphrodite, the Greek love goddess, and are often used in magic talismans to attract romance.

★ ESSENTIAL OILS ★

The following essential oils are known for their aphrodisiac or love-attracting properties also, and can be worn as perfumes on the skin, used in an oil burner or vaporiser, dispersed in a bath, used in spell-casting and wishing rituals, sprinkled on your pillow to imbue your dreams with inspired romantic notions, or in any other creative ways you can think of! **

★ Essential oils, flowers and herbs which contain natural pheromones or like substances, or increase pheromone levels in the body, are: Lavender, Frankincense, Jasmine, Nutmeg, Ylang Ylang, Sandalwood, Patchouli and Asian Agarwood (Oud).

★ The prime love oil, which holds Universal appeal, is rose. Reputedly excellent for both the mind and body, roses are the basis of more than 95 per cent of women's fragrances, and the petals have a long tradition of uplifting the spirits and soothing the soul. *Rosa damascena* is believed to be good for attracting love, while *R. centifolia*, the French rose oil base, is regarded as an aphrodisiac. Rose is traditionally accepted as the all-encompassing Universal fragrance of love, blessed with a reputation for opening up the hearts of all those who come under its spell.

★ Cedarwood oil has been used since ancient times in incense and perfumes. Its deep, woody scent helps to stimulate the Base chakra, increasing sexual passion and desire. Its sedative qualities aid relaxation and encourage openness. In herbal magic, it is also associated with spells for wealth and abundance.

★ Neroli, Geranium, Almond (as a base), Basil, Thyme, Vetiver, Gardenia, Vanilla, Rose Otto, Apple, Cardamom, Lotus, Orange, Ginger, Bergamot, Rosewood and Clary Sage are also exquisitely seductive and sensual, and can be used in any way you like to bring to you that which your heart desires. These oils, when mixed with your own pheromones and magical intentions, will naturally enhance your point of attraction!

** Always research first and use with caution.

PISCES ★ LOVE STYLE

"There is a quality in Pisces which is essentially untouched and unpossessable, no matter how formal the contract is, no matter how long you've known (her). Some part of Pisces will always belong to the cosmos, to (her) own inner self, but not to you."
***Star Signs for Lovers*, Liz Greene, Arrow Books, 1980**

People born under the sign of the Fish have mixed fortunes in relationships. You are difficult to understand, even harder to hold on to, and moreover, you have a tendency to choose difficult partners, sometimes hopeless people, whom you try to nurture back to 'normality' or rescue in some way. Either way, Pisceans are usually in love, whether it be with a person, an ideal, a deity or a daydream, for it is almost impossible for you to conceive of a life alone. But you are unlikely to only notice one person, because not only are you interested in everybody, you are also strangely attracted to everybody. You tend to lack common sense when feelings are involved or aroused. But if you can find the right partner, you grow in character and go a long way towards emotional fulfilment.

Although Pisceans can be relatively difficult to pin down, once a relationship is well established, feelings are likely to run deep and be lifelong. The Fish's love is so readily poured into a romance that it can be overwhelming (for all parties) at times, but if you are able to take charge of your emotions you can bring something very special, ethereal and magical to a partnership. You have a tendency to wear rose-coloured shades and to put your lovers on a pedestal, and are thus particularly vulnerable to deceit or being taken advantage of should you leave your hazy specs on for too long. Sexually, you are more likely to be tender, sensual and romantic rather than passionate, Earthy or spontaneous. Sensitive and temperamental, you need a partner who believes in the same magic as you do, who desires to share similar experiences, and is on the same fairy tale page as you are. Above all, you need a lover who is tolerant, calm and stable, to offset your whims, inconsistencies and dreamy nature. It also helps if your partner is creative and fanciful like you are, because someone with artistic leanings is likely to understand your shifting moods and changeable, chameleon-like temperament. Being born under a Pisces Sun, you are sensitive and impressionable to outside influences. Your actions and decisions are motivated primarily by feelings, impressions, emotions and intuition, a drawback being that you are made vulnerable to every influence in the environment; your whole being is receptive to changes of atmosphere and you are easily swept off your feet. Consequently, undesirable associations may have an adverse effect. Pisces, being the most flexible of all the signs, makes you very adaptable, and you can adjust to relationship changes, fluctuations and cycles better than most. You have loads of sympathy and compassion for your lovers, but you may flounder when it comes to taking positive action. Some of the weaknesses of Pisces are a timid, self-effacing attitude and a tendency to apologise or constantly make excuses. Indecision is also a Piscean fault, and by stalling or succumbing to confusion, you risk missing out on love opportunities. Being so sensitive, you are likely to find it difficult to cope with the harsher realities of this materialistic world, with its tensions, struggles and fierce competitiveness. As a result, you may retreat into your relationships, even if they are not ideal, or even into yourself, to the detriment of your relationship.

A born idealist, you possess a vivid imagination, so you often have your head in the clouds, but on the plus side, have the ability to 'dream' a lover right into your life. Being the recipient of a Piscean's feelings can be the most healing and regenerative relationship one can experience; the only condition is to never trample on her dreams, and she will give you her Universe. Pisceans also like to fantasise, and tend to idealise your partners, which can be both a good thing and a bad thing: good in that it makes the other person feel loved and needed, bad in that it can be difficult for your partner to live up to the high ideals you hold of them. Ultimately though, despite your overly trusting nature and unshakeable belief in love,

Pisces are great romantics at heart and make exquisite and caring partners, but you do need time out just for yourself from time to time - or at least to swim off in your own whimsical direction occasionally.

LUCKY IN LOVE? PISCES ★ COMPATIBILITY

* Please note the following is based on your Sun sign alone. For a whole and integrated approach to relationship compatibility, your whole natal chart would need to be taken into consideration. Synastry (*syn*: acting or considered together, united; *astry*: pertaining to the stars) is a branch of astrology which delves into more complex areas, and is based upon the natal charts of the two people concerned, to determine overall compatibility, potential conflicts and suitability based upon celestial influences. For the purposes of length, the below information is simplified and only refers to Sun sign connections.

Pisces ★ Aries ♓ ♈

Aries and Pisces seem to understand each other's vulnerabilities and can develop a deep rapport. However, the Ram may find the Fish's 'poor me' attitude and tendency to daydream without taking affirmative action rather hard to take. The interaction between your ruling planets, Mars and Neptune, and your elements, Fire and Water, ensures there will indeed be a tremendous strength of romance and passion between you two. Pisces may be a little dreamy and dilly-dallying for the more active, on-the-go Arien, and Aries's sharp, direct tongue may upset the sensitive Piscean soul once too often. Pisces' tendency towards indolence and co-dependence on their partner may not sit well with the free-spirited Arien nature, which strives for independence, freedom and adventure. Being youthful at heart, however, the Ram is likely to feel inspired by the Fish's creative, unique and idealistic nature, but may lose patience when the Fish fails to deliver the goods; Aries needs immediate, snappy results, and Pisces lacks any sense of immediacy. The hot-headed and passionate Aries may place demands upon the delicate Pisces, who may in turn swim off in the other direction; both love their freedom, but in entirely different ways. Aries likes to always be right in the centre of the Universe, and will find the Pisces readily and happily accommodates this need. If used constructively, the Water needn't put the Fire out; instead, it has the potential to produce much romantic steam. If the Ram can somehow fathom the nebulous, mysterious substance of which Pisces is made without becoming frustrated, this pairing has the potential to fulfil, uplift and inspire both signs.

Overall compatibility rating ★ 6 out of 10
Lucky Romance Tip ★ To attract an Aries, wear the colours red or orange, and use the crystal diamond

Pisces ★ Taurus ♓ ♉

Tender Pisces melts Taurus's heart and waters her seeds of desire. But if the earthbound Bull tries to crush Pisces's dreams, the slippery Fish will swim away. Although Pisces is extremely flexible and adaptable, and Taurus essentially inflexible and unchanging, you do share similar natures, being peaceful, placid, kind and gentle. This combination of Earth and Water is very compatible because your ruling planets, Neptune and Venus, also share similar qualities, Neptune being the higher octave of Venus, vibrating at a higher frequency but still exerting a complementary influence. While Taurus is possessive and Pisces is 'slippery', these two can make their relationship work if they capitalise on their romantic and affectionate natures. Challenges may arise if the Taurean tendency towards materialism is not controlled, as Pisces never seeks to own or possess, only to understand; one thing the Fish cannot understand, however, is the Bull's need for luxury, ownership and 'having' things. Both are sensual, easygoing, friendly, artistic, soft, romantic, have a love of beauty and appreciate life's pleasures. These two seem to have just as many differences as similarities, and as a result, have the potential to ultimately balance each other out. Taurus is down-to-Earth while Pisces floats up in the clouds; the realist complements the dreamer; Taurus deals with tangible and practical realities while Pisces is inherently impractical and other-worldly. If the Bull keeps her feet firmly planted in the ground and maintains patience with the wanderings of the oft elusive Fish, she will find that the Fish will always swim back when she's ready - or at least return to Earth to pick the Bull up on her magical carpet so that the Taurean spirit can soar amongst the clouds as well. If Pisces can understand and fulfil Taurus's need for exclusivity in a relationship, and withstand the Bull's tight grip, these two have much potential - if a little clouded over by emotion at times.

Overall compatibility rating ★ 6.5 out of 10

Lucky Romance Tip ★ To attract a Taurus, wear the colours pink or green, and use the crystal rose quartz

Pisces ★ Gemini ♓ ♊

Pisceans are deeply feeling and idealistic partners, and Gemini's light-hearted and uncomplicated approach to love may upset the Fish. Emotional storms could be triggered by Gemini's flirtatiousness. Pisces, however, will delight in the Twins' playful, romantic gestures. And you both share the changeable and whimsical qualities the Mutable mode endows you with. With Gemini's tendency to play the field and Pisces's vulnerability, it's a small miracle that you two even come together in the first place. This is a challenging duo and the Fish's sensitive nature and changing whims may prove too emotional for Gemini. But, both being so versatile, you do have the potential to adapt to each other. Gemini can usually accept Pisces's dreamy and elusive nature, but may find it difficult to swallow the Fish's emotions and deep sensitivities. Both will give each other the space they need in the relationship, but for different reasons; Gemini, because he above all seeks freedom of movement, and Pisces because she above all seeks to dream her way through life and live amongst the clouds undisturbed by Earthly concerns. Gemini is intrigued by Pisces's ethereal and spiritual nature, and Pisces in turn is inspired by Gemini's lively and impressive intellect. However, this is where the similarities and interests in one another may end; the marked contrast between Air and Water is clearly illustrated here. Gemini is logical, factual, mentally-orientated and lives in a thought-based world, whereas Pisces is imaginative, dreamy, feeling, and lives by emotions, impressions and intuition. As a result of these conflicting elemental qualities, Gemini will often be unable to see reason in the illogical ways of Pisces. Both signs are very adaptable and tolerant of other people's ideas, so although you will rarely understand the way the other's mind works, you have the potential of reaching a middle ground and settling in for the ride. Gemini is efficient, active, intellectual, flashy and handy, while Pisces is easily confused, indecisive and for the most part passive. The Fish may spend so long whiling away the hours sitting on the fence, that when she looks around, the Twins have found a new, novel adventure somewhere over the horizon and cannot be seen for the dust they leave behind.

Overall compatibility rating ★ 5.5 out of 10
Lucky Romance Tip ★ To attract a Gemini, wear the colours light blue or yellow, and use the crystal citrine

Pisces ★ Cancer ♓ ♋

This combination unites two Water signs, and since the Water element is related to feelings, emotions and intuition, these will always take priority over logic and reason in your relationship. As a result, some of the more practical considerations of life will often be neglected, muddled or confused. But if you can both reside in your Watery realms quite happily, this pairing should bring much romantic fulfilment, caring, understanding and sharing. You are both sentimental and feel things very deeply, and there is potential for great intimacy and a meeting of the hearts here. You are also very romantic, with a strong need to love and be loved. Difficulties may only arise when the Cancerian, being naturally possessive and clingy, feels abandoned by the Pisces's innate need for solitude, indulging in fanciful whims and solo astral travel from time to time. One thing is guaranteed however: no matter how often the Fish retreats into her own Watery depths, she will always eventually swim 'home' to find the loving her nurturing Crab waiting faithfully with a home-cooked meal and a warm embrace.

Overall compatibility rating ★ 9 out of 10
Lucky Romance Tip ★ To attract a Cancerian, wear the colours silver or white, and use the crystal moonstone

Pisces ★ Leo ♓ ♌

You two have the potential to make a charming and romantic pair, but this is either a creative combination or a quagmire! The mushy Piscean emotions can either bog the Lion down or inspire his best efforts. Your ruling planets, Neptune and the Sun, exercise two very different energies in the relationship; the Sun may indeed outshine the more retiring, timid Neptune. Further, your elements, Water and Fire, and your modes, Mutable and Fixed, don't blend easily. Pisces has deep, mysterious and elusive qualities, which are unfathomable to most people, including the big-hearted, open Leo. While Pisces admires the strength and purpose of Leo, you both live in different worlds and may fail to really 'see' each other - Pisces, due to having rose-coloured glasses on, and Leo, due to wanting to be centre stage and being blinded by the spotlight. The Fish will sometimes prove too emotional and 'out-there' for the 'here-and-now', frank Leonian extrovert. The Leo needs recognition, admiration and praise, which the Pisces is only too happy to give, but the Fish can be so often residing in the clouds, that Leo may have trouble bringing her back down to Earth for long enough to watch his performance. Both are romantic, emotionally expressive and a little dramatic, but express these in entirely different ways, although both being big-hearted, are equally as capable of bringing out the best in the other, and as such, this can be an exquisitely inspiring match. The Leo thrives on ego and pride, and may hurt the much gentler, quieter Fish's sensitive feelings by being too direct, bossy or dominating. The Fish will rarely have her spot in the Sun with the Lion around, and may swim off in the other direction if her needs aren't being fulfilled. Nonetheless, with a love of receiving flattery and just as big a love for giving it, Leo will court Pisces with all the grandeur and romance of a Knight in Shining Armour if he feels the catch is worth casting his line for - and Pisces will more than likely be reeled in and swept off her feet by her bold King.

Overall compatibility rating ★ 6.5 out of 10

Lucky Romance Tip ★ To attract a Leo, wear the colours gold or orange, and use the crystal ruby

Pisces ★ Virgo ♓ ♍

Virgo's natural opposite Pisces has many qualities which the Virgin secretly desires, such as the Fish's imagination, compassion and even emotionalism. Yet the Fish's eternal dreams, with no real sense of direction or purpose, can contradict the Virgin's own sense of purpose. Pisces's vagueness and indecisiveness may also irritate Virgo. While you are astrological opposites, you are not necessarily psychological opposites, as your elements, Water and Earth, blend well together. In fact, being cosmic opposites, you have much to teach each other, and each can learn invaluable relationship lessons from the other. Both being Mutable signs, you also share agile minds, and adaptable and flexible natures. These qualities can be used constructively to form a wonderful bond between you, but as with all 'opposites', there will inevitably be clashes and differences. Further, your ruling planets, Neptune and Mercury, operate on different levels and have differing functions. While there may be an Earth/Air affinity between these two very different signs, there won't be much of an emotional bond, and you will tend to 'help' each other more than deeply love each other. Virgo can help the Piscean be more practical, while the Piscean can help the Virgoan 'think' more from their heart rather than their head. Virgo's nit picking, pessimism and fussiness may inadvertently upset the sensitive and easily hurt Pisces, and Pisces's tendency towards laziness, indecisiveness and daydreaming, will unsettle and test the orderly, rational and sensible Virgo's patience. The Virgin's naturally cool and essentially unemotional expression, may not sit well with the deeply compassionate and feelings-based Fish, and Virgo's natural tendency to anxiety and worrying will only exacerbate Pisces's tendency towards the same. Although you can complement each other nicely, you both see things through different eyes and each will always be a mystery to the other. Overall, Virgo's need for logic and order are the furthest things from the scattered and dreamy Pisces's mind, and Virgo's natural, almost obsessive, tendencies towards cleanliness and tidiness are not concerns at all for Pisces, who is more concerned about the state of the cosmos than the state of her house. If you two can overcome your many differences, Virgo can bring method to the Pisces's madness, and Pisces will return the favour by adding a bit of ethereal wonder and magic to Virgo's life - keeping the Virgo enchanted by keeping it all just a little out of their reach.

Overall compatibility rating ★ 6 out of 10
Lucky Romance Tip ★ To attract a Virgo, wear the colours white or yellow, and use the crystal sapphire

Pisces ★ Libra ♓ ♎

While Pisces is driven by emotion, Libra is driven by logic. However, Libra's ruling planet Venus complements the Fish's Neptune and this should smooth any ripples. And while Water and Air don't tend to blend easily, this is the exception rather than rule in this coupling. Both are naturally romantic, tender, affectionate, and have a fond appreciation of art and beauty. The harmony between your two ruling planets, Neptune and Venus, helps to bridge the gap between your differing elements, so although you may have essentially different natures, there is potential for great affinity and rapport between you. You both enjoy and seek harmony, gentleness, love, togetherness and the magic of intimacy and sharing. You also both have a need and love of peace. Libra's innate sense of good judgement and balance will help to counteract Pisces's tendency towards confusion, escapism and impracticality. Conflicts may arise over your differing emotional qualities; Pisces feels deeply and sensitively, while Libra tends to 'feel' with the intellect, and rationalises love. To Pisces, love is intangible and ethereal, whereas Libra has no trouble articulating what he thinks of the subject. Further, the Fish's Watery depths may intrigue the Scales, but Libra will soon lose interest if the mental rapport slips beneath the surface. Libra needs to be in a relationship like he needs to breathe air, while the Fish doesn't actively seek out a soul mate and is quite content to swim solo, enjoying serendipitous moments and romantic encounters along the journey; both, however, will easily climb aboard the magical carpet of love if it presents itself, and enjoy an entrancing ride across the galaxy. If these two can overcome their different elementary emotional natures, they have the potential to be a beautiful and successful match.

Overall compatibility rating ★ 8 out of 10
Lucky Romance Tip ★ To attract a Libran, wear the colours pink and blue, and use the crystal opal

Pisces ★ Scorpio ♓ ♏

Scorpio feels safe and free to be herself around the Fish. You can create deep empathy and tender passion together, but the Scorpio needs to beware of using force or trying to exert control, for the Fish is a slippery character and will not hesitate to swim away. Water harmonises with Water, and you two have the potential to have an intense and passionate meeting of the hearts. Since your signs are naturally emotional and sensitive, you can usually share these qualities with each other, feeling understood without the need for words. There is a magnetic attraction between the Fish and the Scorpion, and in combination you will generate a deeply romantic and feeling bond. Scorpio has an innate desire to dominate and conquer people or situations, and so needs to have others who will succumb to her will, to which the Piscean will usually oblige. However, being a sign of illusion and deception, Pisces can give the impression of being submissive to disguise an inner truth: that she is actually deviously manoeuvring or manipulating the situation. Scorpio is a dab hand at power plays and complexities however, and will not find this daunting or even off-putting, even when she inevitably finds out (and Scorpio will *always* find out). The compassionate and sympathetic Fish is a great balm and soother for the Scorpion's inner tensions, compelling desires and consuming obsessions, and each will intuitively be able to sense the other's moods, fears, needs and shortcomings. If trouble arises in the relationship, emotions can cloud the issue, and Pisces may be easily hurt by the Scorpio's sharp tongue and even sharper sting. Scorpio will also need to curb the need to control Pisces, as the elusive Fish is easily frightened and apt to slip easily from too tight a grasp, swimming away if she feels restricted. The mysterious, charismatic and magnetic Scorpio will usually reel the slippery Fish back in, though. Both are enigmatic in their own ways and will captivate and enchant each other for the most part. While Pisces is gentle and easygoing, Scorpio is much more intense and complex, but if you two can overcome your differences in nature, you have the capacity to swim happily along with the current of life's stream. Your emotional rapport alone suggests deep potential here, and this can take your relationship to whimsically dizzying heights!

Overall compatibility rating ★ 9 out of 10
Lucky Romance Tip ★ To attract a Scorpio, wear the colours red or burgundy, and use the crystal malachite

Pisces ★ Sagittarius ♓ ♐

While Water and Fire generally don't share a strong affinity, you seem to share many similarities as well as a ruling planet, Jupiter (albeit a secondary ruler of Pisces, since the discovery of Neptune). Both ruled by the expansive and optimistic Jupiter, you dream big and love large. Sagittarius loves to listen to Pisces' whimsical fantasies, but her tales of woe and sensitivities may set the Archer firing - either arrows of desire or derision. You are both idealistic, giving, generous and helpful, and have a mutual appreciation of religion, Universality, philosophy, philanthropical interests, charitable causes, travel, and humanitarian and other lofty ideals. Jupiter, the god of thunder, combines well with Watery Neptune, but this combination of energies can just as easily create waves and turbulence. This pairing is full of complexities and although it presents a multitude of possibilities in some types of human relationships, such as marriage, friendship and family, it can also can present issues around confusion, uncertainty or wishful thinking. Both being idealistic, many ideas may never make it past the talking phase, which you two love to do - share thoughts and ideas. Pisces and Sagittarius are likely to have a wonderful chemistry between them and make a strong impact on each other, and when the need arises, they both give each other the freedom they so desire. But while the Archer is head-based, the Fish is heart-based, and the Archer may feel stifled by Pisces's oversensitive, dreamy, and deeply emotional nature. Further, direct and frank Sagittarius may feel impatient with the Piscean tendency to be indecisive, vague and weak-willed. Sagittarius is rarely sentimental, and although spirited, chivalrous and charming, it is all one big fun adventure and the Piscean can feel hurt by the Archer's bluntness, nonchalance and apparent indifferent attitude towards their relationship at times. The Fish will easily fall hook, line and sinker for the warm Sagittarius heart, but her vivid imagination will conjure up the worse possible scenario when Sagittarius feels the need to break free for a little while. Overall, if Sagittarius can tolerate Pisces's tendency to be disorganised and scatterbrained, and if Pisces can accept Sagittarius's ongoing need for independence and far-reaching horizons, these two can make it work - and may even explore those glistening greener pastures *together*.

Overall compatibility rating ★ 7.5 out of 10
Lucky Romance Tip ★ To attract a Sagittarius, wear the colour deep purple or royal blue, and use the crystal zircon

Pisces ⋆ Capricorn ♓ ♑

Pisces brings out the Goat's protective urge, making Capricorn feel lighter and somehow enriched. The Fish's patience, gentleness, acceptance, persuasive charm and soft manners are food for the Capricorn's soul. But she might try to swim away if Capricorn tries to control her. Earth has an affinity with Water and although there is a great difference between your two signs, you do complement each other in many ways. Pisces finds it easy to merge with and adapt to people and situations which are safe, strong and secure, and Capricorn is the epitome of safety, strength and security. However, while Pisces is elusive, indirect, sensitive, emotional, fluid, sentimental, unworldly and romantic, Capricorn does not wear her heart on her sleeve and is serious, practical, solid, competitive, worldly, sensible, practical, conventional, structured, organised and worldly. While sensual, Capricorn is not known for being overtly romantic or readily charming, which doesn't seem to bother Pisces too much, as long as the steady Goat can provide a shelter and protect the Fish from the harsh elements of life. Pisces may be a little over-sensitive to Capricorn's lack of outward emotional expression, and Capricorn may find Pisces's deeply feeling nature a little difficult to handle. In Capricorn's ordered and organised world, there seems no place for a slippery and timid Fish, and Piscean behaviour often undermines Capricorn's desire for stability and consistency. The traditional Goat, however rigid, is conservative, traditional and respectful, and will treat the mermaid or merman with an inner tenderness, devotion and kindness like no other sign. A mutually fulfilling relationship could very well develop if Capricorn can learn to live with Pisces's tendency to dilly-dally and waver, and if Pisces is not intimidated or hurt by Capricorn's biting, ambitious, striving, win-at-all-costs nature. While you both have different motivations and needs, you also share a need for peace, occasional solitude, profound connection with another, the deep sharing of thoughts, and gentle, sensuous affections.

Overall compatibility rating ★ 6.5 out of 10
Lucky Romance Tip ★ To attract a Capricorn, wear the colours brown or black, and use the crystal garnet

Pisces ★ Aquarius ♓ ♒

This is a surprisingly magical mix. Indeed, it would be hard to find a more unusual - and enlightening - combination than these two, for the simple reason that your ruling planets, Neptune and Uranus, are quite literally out of this world. Both signs have an elusive quality about them, and have a level of understanding that seems to contradict the usual Water/Air relating difficulties. You are both unique and different to most other people, and you sometimes feel like misfits, that is except around each other. Although the Piscean psyche is deep, emotional and complex, the Aquarian can still manage to sense the unfathomable depths of the Piscean soul. Feeling, sensitive and romantic, the Pisces seems to intuitively respect Aquarius's need for independence, freedom and friendships outside the relationship. You are both compassionate, caring, kind, humanitarian and believe in all things mystical, and although you express these in different ways, you can still find a way to live together in relative harmony with little effort. Perhaps this is because you are both lovers of solitude, for different reasons of course, but you understand each other's occasional need for retreat. If you can forget your elementary and modal (Mutable and Fixed) differences, you may just make a beautiful symphony together - indeed, you can swim along happily through life's meandering waters together, as long as Pisces doesn't try to escape or get lost along the way.

Overall compatibility rating ★ 8 out of 10

Lucky Romance Tip ★ To attract an Aquarian, wear the colours electric blue or turquoise, and use the crystal aquamarine

Pisces ★ Pisces ♓ ♓

On the surface, both of you, sharing the same Sun and the same ruling planet, appear to be the picture of Watery excitement, thrills and oddball adventures. However, too much Water may create two people who seem to roll along like, well, a tidal wave. Outsiders may not be able to fathom this complex Piscean wavelength because it takes one to know one, and only these two can truly know why the other thinks or behaves as they do. You are both imaginative, intuitive, emotional, feelings-based, dreamy, other-worldly and hypersensitive, and these qualities will always take precedence over logic, rationality and cold, hard facts. Both being Water signs, there is naturally a deep resonance and unspoken understanding at play between you both. Your ruling planet Neptune, may make your relationship feel lost and confused and disoriented at times, and you may even find yourselves swimming in completely different - or plain weird - directions! Neither can provide a solid base for the other, but you more than make up for this by daydreaming your way through life and creating a beautiful, if completely chaotic or disorganised, home together. You both share an appreciation for artistic pursuits and encourage each other in these fields, but you are also prone to being directionless, vague and led astray by others, and may all too often find yourself without even two coins to rub together. You each have your own private world of make-believe to fall back on however, and this shields you from the harsher realities of the world. You can also sense things about people, including each other, without a word being spoken. Ultimately, sharing the same Sun sign gives this relationship great potential - just don't spend too much time in your separate fantasy worlds, or indeed, climbing aboard different magical rugs.

Overall compatibility rating ★ 7.5 out of 10
Lucky Romance Tip ★ To attract a Pisces, wear the colours mauve or sea green, and use the crystal amethyst

* With all Fire and Water combinations (i.e. Pisces with Aries, Leo or Sagittarius), it is easy to see how and why fire and water are natural enemies. Water can quickly put a fire out, and fire can dry up water. Fire usually works quickly, and water gently. In alchemy and astrology, both are important, and both must be carefully manipulated and controlled to make full effective use of their powerful, albeit vastly differing, natures. Fire can be brought back to a steady heat, whereas the pressure and force of water can be increased vigorously or to circulate more actively. As warm and watery beings, the human body demonstrates the miracle of fire and water combined. Water connects, flows and lubricates, and brings healing, its passive, gentle nature soothing away the scorching harshness of fire. One ancient text offers a mystical view of how water and fire are intertwined in the body, and suggests that it is through consciously combining these two elements that we can transform our inner state. Fire can initiate and inspire this quest for self-transformation, but once the fire burns down, life can be restored anew by water. Natural enemies? Mostly. Astrological passion? Absolutely!

YOUR TAROT CARDS ★ FOR LUCK, MAGIC, ENERGY, ABUNDANCE, QUESTING & MEANING
THE MOON, THE HANGED MAN, WHEEL OF FORTUNE & THE HIGH PRIESTESS

Tarot and astrology are inextricably linked. All the cards of the Major Arcana, which comprises 22 of the Tarot's 78 cards, are 'ruled by' or connected with either one of the twelve zodiac signs, the planets and luminaries, or one of the four elements.

The 22 Major Arcana cards contain the richest symbolism of all the cards in the Tarot deck, each carrying a myriad of messages for the reader to decipher. The symbolism contained within these images represents the archetypal aspects of your character. It also describes the path your soul takes through each stage of life, revealing clues through which you can explore different parts of yourself. Each of the cards also represents an aspect of Universal human experience and has a name that either directly conveys the meaning of the card, such as Strength or Justice, or depicts individuals that represent these human archetypes, such as the Hermit or the Empress. The illustrations on each card contain one or more figures and tuning into a card's imagery enables you to grasp its meaning intuitively. Consider the demeanour of the characters, whether it is day or night, the background, any symbols, the buildings, the colours, the vegetation, the weather and the season. Every card has its own story to impart, and through entering that story you can gain deeper insights into the full picture of your journey so far, as well as illuminating your path ahead.

I have outlined four cards here for your sign: The Moon, The Hanged Man, Wheel of Fortune and The High Priestess, all of which have links to your zodiac sign itself Pisces, your ruling planet Neptune, your traditional ruling planet Jupiter, and your element of Water. All four cards will have special meaning for your sign, and can carry powerful messages and lessons for you to reflect upon.

★ THE MOON ★
Ruled by Pisces

Keywords ★ Hidden Depths, Illusions, Awakenings

★ KEY THEMES ★
Dreams ★ Illusions and Disillusions ★ Subconscious ★ Mind ★ Betrayal ★ Bad Influence of Friends or Family Circle ★ Private Life and Thoughts ★ Self-deception ★ Uncertainty and Confusion ★ Unforeseen perils ★ Intuition ★ Lack of Clarity ★ Psychic Awakenings
The Primitive Subconscious ★ Premonitions

Meditation ★ "I trust my intuition; it always knows what to do"

Number ★ 18
Astrological Signs ★ Cancer & Pisces

By the light of the Moon, things aren't always what they seem. The Moon reminds us that illusions and hidden forces can obscure what is really happening. But this card also represents our psychic, imaginative, or emotional sides, the Pisces or Cancer in us all.

THE MESSAGE ★ The Moon is the intuitive clairvoyant, who opens you up to your deeper self and uncovers your hidden depths. The kingdom of darkness represents all that is hidden, concealed, buried and deep inside each one of us. The darkness contained within the night symbolises the hidden side of our personality, the Divine part of our self. When the symbolic dark intervenes in our lives through hardships, setbacks, trials and obstacles to be overcome, it tests our strength and self-knowledge. Trials lead us to question ourselves and also to search for the light - which we would not do if life was smooth, serene and going well. Everyone experiences times in their lives when they are fearful or insecure. Sometimes these fears are based on the 'seen' and that which we can recognise, while other times they stem from the unknown, irrational, hidden or illusory forces. In both cases it is important to go within and be guided by your intuition. Ask your inner self about the true source of your fears, and trust its answer. The Moon card appears when we are experiencing times that open us up to our intuition and psychic abilities through increased self-awareness and the acknowledgement of past blocks that have held us back - or things which have been suppressed and need to rise to the surface. It is from our shadow selves that we must endeavour to draw regenerating energies so as not to become overcome by our emotions or ravaged by insurmountable circumstances. Its main message is to encourage us to face the unknown without being afraid, to acknowledge our anxieties, weaknesses and mistakes, and to conquer the inner darkness within us. You need to awaken to the truths about yourself that you have so far kept hidden, and reawaken to your brilliant light and power.

THE STORY ★ Under a waning Moon, upon a dark and eerie landscape, a lost soul stands with her faithful dog. She gazes up fearfully at the Moon, remembering terrifying stories of a Moon Witch who plays cruel tricks on those lost in the night. She raises her hands, as if in prayer, and hopes that she will be saved and guided through this haze. Across a moat of turgid water, inhabited by fearsome, unseen things, the turrets of her castle home can be seen. But the drawbridge is up, the gates are locked and no one can hear her wails. Has the Moon Witch's trickery and magic barred her way home? Just as the child is about to succumb to overwhelming feelings of despair, peril and sadness, the Moon beams out more strongly from behind the clouds and suddenly appears warm yet pensive. The Moon persuades the land to swell up higher than the moat and the gate surrounding the castle. The lost soul then clearly sees the way home, and gives thanks to the Moon as she proceeds towards it.

THE AWAKENING ★ This is the darkness before the dawn. You must separate illusion from reality. Even though the path may seem daunting and treacherous, you need not fear the mysterious unknown. Your natural intuition can guide you to hidden opportunities. Remember to save your energies for the challenges and obstacles ahead, and not squander them with needless worrying. The freedom allowed by the previous card the Star takes you deeper within yourself. You become more reflective, aware of the messages of your subconscious mind, intuition and dreams. This leads you to explore a deep sense of connection within yourself and to see the threads of your life woven as a rich tapestry - you need only to join them all up through the use of your imagination.

THE LESSON ★ The Moon's face on this card is beautiful but the light she sheds on the world is deceptive; under it we tend not to see things as they really are. The wolf-dogs baying at her do not trust her influence. But she is teaching us that we should allow ourselves greater freedom and avoid holding back or suppressing feelings, as the Crab emerging from the water in the picture is prone to doing. You may also be living under some sort of illusion by refusing to see things as they really are. In the long-term, this self-deception will harm you. The Moon also warns you to be wary of outer-deceptions as well - your friends or family could be much less trustworthy than you imagine. This card will show up when you are encountering difficulties, conflicts, disappointments or disillusionment in your life, which have originated from your errors and shortcomings. They manifest themselves to you as a test, so that you may become aware of them. Outside, under a waning Moon, visualise a circle of protective white light around yourself as you stand by a body of water. Concentrate and project a specific and deep-rooted personal fear into a special stone, then strongly hurl it out of your circle of light into the body of water as you chant: "With this stone, fear is banished, into the water it has vanished."

SYMBOLISM ✳✶ The Moon reflects the realm where the unconscious meets the conscious. In astronomy, the Moon reflects the light of the Sun. Its mysterious, veiled qualities reveal only portions of itself and this symbolises the need to use the power of our imagination to move into that mystery and attempt to decode it.

The crayfish or crab emerging from the water is a symbol of the deepest fears that haunt us yet never fully materialise. It represents the surfacing of our inner nature, which we often push back down into the depths again. Therefore, the Moon highlights the need to face our fears by bringing them to the surface rather than keeping them hidden and submerged.

The Moon is the card of hidden emotions. The Moon tells us that there is illusion all around us; the waters can mislead and confuse. The waters around you might look calm on the surface but a powerful current might be brewing just beneath. The water can tell us about looking past illusion, into the vision of what is really there. Its reflective surface challenges us to look at ourselves and the image we present to the world. It also tells us that only a person of truth will have the truth shone back at them.

This card signifies that the landscape beneath the Moon is full of threats. It is the card of hidden meanings, and represents frustrated and seemingly impossible desire. But the Moon's light can also reveal a great deal. Its link also with the star sign Cancer shows that a tough shell cannot conceal or stifle tender love, and that illusions can blind us to what lurks beneath.

This card's symbolism can suggest unforeseen perils and deception, but is also shows great possibilities can be accessed through intuition, latent psychic powers, and astral travel. Its other divinatory meanings are twilight, disillusionment, danger, obscurity, bad influence, ulterior motives, frustrations, false friends, selfishness, insight/intuition, craftiness, deceit, slander, disgrace, unknown enemies, libel and superficiality.

The Moon card depicts two animals, a dog and a wolf, baying at the Moon, and in the foreground a crab crawling out of a pool disturbs its waters, symbolising that the innermost fears are forcing their way to the surface of consciousness. The idea of dogs and wolves baying at the Full Moon is a powerful image suggesting madness or lunacy, and the two animals represent our 'animal self' roused by the Moon. A werewolf howling under a Full Moon is a vivid metaphor of the power of the unconscious to bring out the primitive, 'unknown' side of ourselves. The Moon rules the waxing and waning rhythms of life, of tides, and all natural cycles, particularly the feminine ones. It also symbolises feelings and emotions that are by their nature often volatile, nebulous and uncertain. But it also represents the power and mystery of women's fertility, and power does not have to be destructive, threatening or frightening.

Indeed, if respected, this Lunar psychic awakening enriches life. Ruling the realm of subconscious thoughts, fantasies and dreams, these aspects, when made conscious, can become wisdom. This card indicates that both our primitive animal instincts and our tamed mundane domesticity are a trap, in that the truth lies between them on the rocky narrow road that leads over the horizon under the watchful gaze of the silent and mysterious Moon. The idea of the crab in the foreground forcing its way onto the land from out of the depths of the water, is symbolic of our innermost fears emerging from the depths of our souls and rising to the surface. This crab might represent childhood fears reappearing in adult life, still managing to cause fear and anxiety even when these fears have lost their rationality or logic. As the crab crawls up into our consciousness, we often try to push it back down into the subconscious. However, when we do this, it continues to exist and persist there, still giving rise to vague fears and unacknowledged stress until such a time arrives during which we allow it to fully emerge and in turn, confront it.

When the Moon appears in a reading, it usually points to a period of fluctuation, change, uncertainty and illusions. It can also suggest that solutions to problems can be found through dreams and intuition rather than logic and reason. The path you are on is difficult and may cause fear, but continue along it even if you are doubtful, because all will eventually turn out well. If you are involved in a secretive love affair or harbour secret feelings for someone, this card is favourable.

It can take on the Piscean quality of sacrifice, by urging you to be more introspective, to turn away from outer concerns, to give up some specific activity or simply allow a period of withdrawal. The Moon reminds us that the Star and the Sun give off their own light, whereas the Moon herself reflects the hidden light from the Sun. In fact, the Tarot Sun comes after the Moon, suggesting that simplicity can only be appreciated after a journey through dark, strange Lunar landscapes. Ultimately however, the Moon can be our guide if we let it, and the road leading towards the horizon between the two mountains, need not always be perilous if we can join the unconscious and conscious forces of the mind together harmoniously to create a well-integrated personality.

All the irrational, supernatural associations of the Moon can make this seem an unfortunate card for the rational person, because it indicates a time when only intuition, the non-rational side, can overcome obstacles. Yet the non-rational must be used with care, for it can lead towards a dangerous fantasy world. On the other hand, it warns against fearing this non-rational side of ourselves, in case we settle for a life of sterility and stagnation.

It is time to ask yourself: What about me seems murky or polluted? What can be done to clear up the waters of my inner channels? Now is the time to take stock of the current you are standing in. Where does it pull you? How strong or gentle is its force? Sometimes it feels as if we are swimming with the current and towards our authentic self, but others it feels as though the waters around us will never be clear enough to peer into. In other words, it can seem like nothing is true and all around us is merely an illusion. Communion with water and The Moon can empower us to see past the façade and down into the bedrock of the ocean floor. What sits there, in its truest, clearest form? Trust your gut - for Water always knows where it's supposed to go.

Pisceans are recommended to carry one of these cards with them to illumine their paths, and to magnetise that for which they are asking. Go forth and claim the magic which is yours!

★ THE HANGED MAN ★
Ruled by Neptune & the Element of Water

Keywords ★ Suspension, Sacrifice, New Perspectives

★ KEY THEMES ★
Sacrifice ★ Period of Inactivity, Respite or Transition ★ Forfeiting one thing to gain something more valuable or desired ★ Trust ★ Faith ★ Letting Go ★ Surrender Introspection ★ Suspension ★ Stepping Back ★ Inner Journeying ★ Opportunities for Transformation Progression ★ Renewal ★ Rebirth ★ Epiphanies ★ Unexpected Life Changes ★ Unusual Solutions ★ The Need for Patience ★ New Perspectives

Meditation ★ "I am willing to sacrifice one thing to make way for another, improved thing"

Number ★ 12

Astrological Sign ★ Pisces

THE FOOL'S JOURNEY ★ Hanging by a thread, the Hanged Man is learning the lessons of letting go and of not being ruled by the material or the mundane. This is the Fool searching for spiritual enlightenment and psychic revelation.

THE MESSAGE ★ The Hanged Man represents change, but it is usually an alternation in mental attitudes rather than physical circumstances. Look at things from a different perspective. The Hanged Man indicates a temporary standstill. It seems that time is frozen, that the unfolding of events and circumstances has stopped or, more precisely that you find yourself at a time in your life when you are unable to take action but have to undergo the consequences of your actions, good or bad, and draw lessons from them. When the Hanged Man shows up, it means that you are temporarily out of the game of life, either because you have chosen to do so, or you have been forced to take some time in suspension.

THE STORY ★ Under a calm, blue sky and above a radiant, flourishing Earth, a man hangs upside down, suspended by one foot from the tail of a dragonfly (in at least one version of the card). The dragonfly emphasises that this scene is not one of torture or punishment, but part of a natural and even necessary, process. The young man's life appears to be in limbo, but his expression shows only acceptance and absolute faith at this moment of total surrender to a higher force. He may be listening to an inner voice, speaking to him the truths that are completely the opposite to all that he has previously believed. He may also have deliberately sacrificed himself to attain some desired goal. He seems to be in a trance and a state of illumination as a result of the increase of blood flowing to his head, both metaphorically and physically speaking, blood containing abundant life force. It does appear, however, that the pattern of his everyday life has been reversed to provide a new outlook. The water flowing beneath him symbolises that the young man has risen above emotional turmoil and upheavals to accept the suspension of his usual, or old, way of life. The enforced period of waiting may be viewed as a way of gaining new eyes and a fresh perspective.

THE AWAKENING ★ New perspectives are required in your life. You are reluctantly forced to accept that it is necessary to adopt an attitude of surrender while you wait for the tide to turn. The Hanged Man signifies the ability to accept delays, and to recognise that correct timing is essential. This period may seem restrictive, but you are being forced to step back from the situation and become introspective in order to listen to your higher, stiller mind. Waiting has its place in any plan. Try not to become a martyr but do not be afraid to make sacrifices or be unwilling to adapt to changing circumstances. If you feel powerless, stuck in a rut or blocked in some way, you must lift yourself up by your own boots and suspend yourself.

THE LESSON ★ Do not be disconcerted by the appearance of the Hanged Man. He is not in distress; he is simply, literally 'in suspension', in limbo, waiting for something to happen. He signifies that you are between two phases in your life, perhaps waiting for news before you can move forward. But the Hanged Man encourages you not to take premature action. Waiting, not knowing what to do next, is trying, but you must control restlessness and be patient and philosophical in outlook. As you 'wait', be forgiving of those who have harmed you and aim to balance materialistic progress with spiritual development. The word 'yoga', a Hindu spiritual and ascetic discipline, means 'to unite'. To create a unified, integrated psyche, try the yoga posture called The Bow. The flow of energy it helps circulate through your body will direct and focus your mind on the lessons you need to be learning.

SYMBOLISM *★ The Hanged Man symbolises the patience involved in waiting to see what unfolds naturally, and gives you acceptance that everything happens in its own good time. He symbolises a state of inner peace and a spiritual surrender to the natural order. The upside down man's pensive and resigned facial expression symbolises the need to go inward to find a new perspective on the situation. The plank of woods from which he is suspended has been cut to fit between the two trees, indicating that this state of suspension in life is deliberately engineered. In some decks, a halo of light surrounds the man's head, symbolising that he is attuned to - or becoming attuned to - his spiritual nature.

This card depicts a young man hanging from a tree or suspended from the gallows by the ankle. His other leg is folded behind him, forming the shape of the number 4 or an inverted triangle, symbolising the descent from higher to lower, or conscious into unconscious. This suggests a sacrifice, giving up one thing for something more desired. His arms are folded behind his back. The man's face does not look tortured or fearful, but rather it is serene and calm. He wears a green shirt, and one of his stockings is red and the other one white. A pool lies beneath him, and despite his perilous position, a halo glows around his head and his expression is not unhappy. The twelve branch stumps on the two wooden pillars supporting the scaffold from which he hangs, represent the twelve signs of the zodiac, suggesting that the Sun has run its course through the signs and seasons of the year and is ready to enter the final phase. Pisces represents a death or a letting go, once a person has thoroughly experienced an entire cycle of life, and symbolises the subsequent turning toward the soul or higher self.

The man hangs from his foot, the part of the body attributed to Pisces, and the sign of purification and sacrifice. The card's ruler, Neptune, is a planet associated with self-sacrifice, dreams, mysticism and inspiration. Its watery nature suggests that time is fluid and dissolves all undesirable circumstances eventually. Its divinatory meanings are transition, change, reversal of the mind in one's way of life, renunciation, abandonment, the changing of life's forces, the approach of new life forces, a period of respite between significant events, sacrifice, repentance, regeneration, readjustment, and that life is in suspension.

The Hanged Man card represents a sacrifice of some kind which results in transformation, and is identified with the Norse God Odin, who hanged himself voluntarily from the World Tree for nine days and nights in order to gain spiritual insight and wisdom, and was reborn anew. Like Odin, none of us can know the full meaning of being alive until we having ourselves on the World Tree and allow its roots to extend far beyond our deep wells of worldly experience, and its branches pointing upwards towards the endless stars. Another interpretation is that the traditional values of society are turned upside down and that things can then be looked at from a different angle.

This card bears the message of independence and feeling life through an inner awareness rather than doing what others expect or demand from us. Interestingly, reversed, The Hanged Man symbolises fighting your inner self in some way, denying your inner voice a hearing, and battling uphill against life. The essential meaning of this card is sacrifice: the voluntary surrendering or shedding of something in order to gain something of far greater value. It can signify that one's life is at a standstill, however, although circumstances may not be to one's liking, it is not as bad as one thinks it is. It tells us to take life patiently until we see that the time is right to make the necessary improvements to the situation. It represents the turning point in psychological development, the point at which we must come to grips with the unconscious forces within and surrendering the conscious ego in order to delve into the oft unknown territory of our inner world. The conscious mind is volunteering to 'die' in order to bear a new and fruitful life in the unconscious, despite the inevitable fears we hold. This involves faith, hope and trust.

The Hanged Man indicates a time of greater self-understanding, and perhaps a decision to abandon worldly values. Here, the Fool must take a risk and dare to take that inner journey, to plunge into the depths of the self, to seek the inner reality needed to become whole. And from that sacrifice come things of infinitely greater value: enlightenment and renewal. Overall, this means it is time to review your plans, and look at things from a new perspective.

The Hanged Man encourages you not to take premature or hasty action, but rather you should wait, for even though waiting is trying, you need to control your restlessness and be philosophical in outlook. Accept the fact that you have already achieved a great deal, and trust that your experience will stand you in good stead for what is to come. Be forgiving of those who have harmed you, and aim to balance materialistic progress with spiritual development. The task it sets is to explore the mysterious gift of life and ultimately, experience rebirth.

When this card appears in a reading or your life, it does not mean you are going to die, but that you are going to lose yourself; this does not imply crucifixion or pain, but rather a sense of ecstasy and surrender to love. You may want to do something to literally turn yourself upside down temporarily, to change your perspective; in doing so, try to channel your pure inner child, and envision how they would laugh and squeal with delight if turned upside down by an adult.

The Hanged Man card prompts you to ask questions of yourself such as: What is the best way to spend my time during this period of waiting? Is it possible that a different approach would work better? What preparations can I make for the future, considering the options that are open to me? Am I avoiding reality or making a decision? Am I only deceiving myself about my concern for the future when my inaction is really caused by cowardliness or laziness? The Hanged Man signifies a temporary pause in life, and tells us to cultivate patience, go with the flow and accept the changes that are occurring. Ultimately, the symbolic descent from the conscious mind into the unconscious enables you to discover what is truly important to you. You may even need to step outside of the norm and the mainstream right now and embrace your unique and eclectic beliefs or attitudes. It's also a good moment to be generous with your time, attention and 'gifts' - this tithing will be returned to you manyfold by the Universe.

Pisceans are recommended to carry one of these cards with them to illumine their paths, and to magnetise that for which they are asking. Go forth and claim the renewal and transformation that can be achieved through sacrifice and inner journeying, by using the symbolism of the Hanged Man as your guide.

★ WHEEL OF FORTUNE ★
Ruled by Jupiter

Keywords ★ Change, Acceptance, Fate

★ KEY THEMES ★
A Miracle ★ Adjustment in Circumstances ★ A New Chapter ★ Changes in Fortune ★ Unexpected Turn of Events ★ Fate and Free Will ★ A Twist of Fate ★ Continual Movement ★ Responsibility for One's Own Destiny ★ Good luck ★ A Happy Accident ★ Balanced Karma ★ Destiny ★ Acceptance ★ Progress Possibility to Intervene or Act ★

Fortuna, the Goddess of good luck's energy is inherent in the Wheel of Fortune card, and when this card appears in a reading, it means that:

"Fortune is indeed smiling on you and you may as well surrender to the flow, because something remarkable - a big event - is taking place. ... Although fate does not in any sense control our lives, when something has been wished for and worked towards, it is the Goddess Fortuna who decides on the timing of the event. The Wheel of Fortune signifies a high point, a wish coming true, the manifestation of something anticipated."
***Mother peace: A Way to the Goddess Through Myth, Art and Tarot*, Vicky Noble, 1983**

Meditation ★ "I must take responsibility for my life to move forward in a positive direction"

Number ★ 10

Astrological Signs ★ Pisces, Sagittarius, & the Fixed Signs: Aquarius, Taurus, Leo and Scorpio

THE FOOL'S JOURNEY ★ Having completed the personal aspects of his journey, the Fool now encounters the outside forces associated with it. The Wheel of Fortune is all about destiny, the things of life that are beyond his control. This is exemplified by the Serenity Prayer, "God grant me the courage to change the things I can, the serenity to accept the things I can't, and the wisdom to know the difference."

THE MESSAGE ★ A time of positive change. A situation suddenly moves forward. Fortune is on your side! This card also offers a chance to step back from circumstances in order to notice life's seasons, or the natural 'turning of the wheel'. In doing this, you will know when to plant seeds and when to harvest.

THE STORY ★ Tarot historians believe the word Tarot itself derives from the Latin word *rota*, as in 'rotation', and reflects the ancient sense of life as a moving wheel. The 'wheels within wheels' that make up the Wheel of Fortune, rotate and turn like the ever spinning rhythms and cycles of life. A spin of the wheel may bring unexpected luck, opportunity and good fortune, or it may cause the reverse, and present obstacles to our desires. A confrontation with some 'demon' from the past may occur with a turn of the wheel. These could be fate, part of a Divine plan, or karma, but what seem to be beginnings and endings are in fact just part of the never-ending circle of life. Rising up from the horizon are two puffs of smoke that symbolise the form of spirit. In spite of all the changes, nothing remains but the elusive essence. Animals of varying characters and powers are depicted around the circle, and ultimately atop the wheel reigns a Sphinx, with flowing eyes that see all the cycles, evolutions, revolutions and recurring patterns. The Sphinx, in her quiet wisdom, knows that no one stays on top forever.

THE AWAKENING ★ It is not the Wheel of Fate but the Wheel of Fortune; this nuance is important. Indeed, the very fact that the wheel is activated by a handle, suggests the notion of free will at play. In other words, you have the choice to act or not to act, to use or not to use the handle in order to activate the wheel of your destiny. In any case, this card must prompt you to become aware of your share of active, conscious or unconscious responsibilities in the situations, circumstances or events we have to confront. Sometimes it indicates that we have to remain committed in order to progress; other times it means that for the moment, we can do nothing else but allow events to take their natural course. The turning of the Wheel of Fortune carries the message that what goes around, comes around, or what goes up, must come down. You will reap what you have sown, therefore you must think ahead and consider your actions today, wherever you find yourself on the wheel. To avoid being ruled by fate, take responsibility for your life and what happens in it. Be open to new and unexpected opportunities, allow for receiving, and above all, take risks. It is vitally important to always expect the unexpected. You must not worry about or fear the unexpected because it opens new perspectives for you.

THE LESSON ★ Ask your own spiritual guides or gods or goddesses to deliver to you your desires and just fortunes. Meditate on the Wheel of Fortune as you ask, and finally, take the chance and turn the wheel, for you never know where it may come to rest. The Wheel of Fortune represents the ability to understand and accept things, encouraging you to embrace changes in life wholeheartedly. There will always be highs and lows. Good or bad, trust that all is happening for your higher good. Accepting this brings a calmer, more holistic perspective.

SYMBOLISM *★ In Buddhist thought, the Wheel of Life is *Samsara*, the never-ending, going-nowhere spinning circle of illusion that represents the physical and emotional world of the senses. Buddhists believe the solution is to get off the Wheel by transcending these physical and emotional worlds. Some other religions and thoughts, suggest a coming to terms with the Wheel by understanding the laws of cause and effect, and by directing one's life accordingly.

The Wheel of Fortune symbolises the constant cycles that run through life. We may experience high and low points, yet the Wheel continues to turn. Therefore, the fundamental message of the Wheel is that you need to be attuned to the still centre within yourself, whatever the outer circumstances may be.

The Wheel of Fortune is turned by a blindfolded figure, looking in the opposite direction, symbolising that the ways of fate are a mystery and that you can only accept change, and work with it. The other figures, sitting on the Wheel and falling off as it turns, represent the varying experiences of life, and emphasise that resistance to change is completely futile.

Some Tarot decks depict the Wheel of Fortune as the Zodiac Wheel. This symbolism is quite apt, for just as we can do nothing about the turning of the stars in the sky, so we cannot avoid the turning of fate. This symbolism also suggests that we don't always have Earthly control over our fate and destiny. It further shows that there are higher laws set by a cosmic order.

Throughout history, the Wheel has been a potent image. In medieval times, when the Tarot first appeared, the Wheel represented not only the zodiac but also the cycle of birth and death, and the spinning wheel of the Fates. In this sense, the Wheel of Fortune denotes the uncertain nature of existence, as well as movement and change. Tarot historians believe the word Tarot itself derives from the Latin word *rota*, as in 'rotation', and reflects the ancient sense of life as a moving wheel.

This card signifies that a new chapter is beginning, a decision of importance is to be made, or that a new run of luck is commencing. The depiction of the turning Wheel of Fortune dates back to medieval times and, as a familiar Tarot image, it reveals four men who are attached to the wheel's rim. The goddess turning the wheel is blind, symbolising the element of chance that exists as fortunes of men rise and fall. The man at the top rules, the man descending has ruled, the man at the base of the wheel is without rule, while the man ascending will rule one day. Traditionally the card is said to be concerned with the beasts it portrays in some decks, and with the wheel itself; the Sphinx or Angel at the top says, "I rule," the serpent, "I have ruled," and the dog, "I will rule." (Other cards may have other animals aside from these, such as a monkey-like creature or jackal-headed man, and a hare. Some older decks still show two people celebrating together at the top of the wheel while a third man is hurled off the edge of a precipice. At the corners of some cards are figures: a bird, a lion, a bull and a human). These various depictions and meanings clearly reflect the ongoing peaks and troughs of life, and suggests that no one is exempt from a sudden change of fortune, be it for better or worse.

The Wheel of Fortune signifies that a new chapter is about to commence or an important decision must be made. The angels sent you this card because of positive changes occurring in your life, so expect and enjoy new beneficial opportunities as they present themselves. It is equally important that you always expect the unexpected. You must not worry or be afraid of the unexpected, because it opens up new perspectives for you.

The Wheel of Fortune's association with the planet Jupiter links it with the transcendence of time, ruling the higher mind of Sagittarius and the devotion to intangibles of Pisces. Its divinatory meanings are destiny, fortune, fate, outcome, culmination, approaching the end of a problem, good or bad luck, inevitability, a turn for the better, the end result of past actions and the workings of destiny, which no one can ever completely understand.

This is an optimal time to make big *and* small changes, major *and* minor adjustments. Take the next leap with the knowledge and faith that everything will work out well for you. Old blocks are lifting, and everything now moves forward swiftly. If recent events have shaken your faith, you will soon see how they were actually positive for you. In essence rapid and necessary advancement is possible and highly likely now.

This card suggests the course of events from beginning to end, advancement for better or worse. It also signifies the end to current problems and some marked strokes of luck. But the Wheel of Fortune is a curious mix of fate and free will, as suggested by the wheel itself. The Wheel in some cards is kept in balance by a figure who sits at its top and aims to keep the equilibrium; she may or may not be successful. Two creatures are pictured trying to unbalance the wheel. They represent both positive progress and possible difficulties, denoting uncertainty - the Wheel could turn in either direction.

This card is the symbol of the paradox of stability and change. The true self of man, which is hidden from his conscious mind, very often remains at the still hub of the wheel, like the blindfolded goddess pictured in the centre of the wheel. The hub remains stable and represents the true self, although the external or conscious situations around it change, as reflected by the moving outer rim. Fate is the circumference of the wheel, and this true self is at the centre. The hub enables the rim to turn and therefore controls all that comes its way. It indicates that each man turns his own wheel to whichever point his true self dictates.

Overall, this card alludes to the mystic idea of karma, individual inner growth towards wholeness and harmony, symbolised by the circular mandala, and is a fortunate card, implying that your rightful destiny will unfold positively. Fortune is indeed smiling on you, and you may as well surrender to the flow, because something remarkable - a big event - is taking place. The Wheel of Fortune signifies a high point, a wish coming true, the manifestation of something anticipated. Ultimately, this card carries the message that the more aware you are of your own power over your destiny, the clearer things will appear - and also, perhaps the most poignant message of this card that the wheel will turn in your favour eventually.

★ THE HIGH PRIESTESS ★
Ruled by the Moon & the Element of Water

Keywords ★ Intuition, Wisdom, Knowledge

★ KEY THEMES ★
Desire for Esoteric Understanding ★ Seeking to Uncover Mysteries and Secrets ★ Mystical Powers ★ Dreams ★ Psychic Abilities ★ Unconscious Mind ★ Reliance on Instincts ★ Patience ★ Guided by Intuition ★ Careful consideration before action ★ Inner Calm ★ Knowledge that is both inborn and acquired Experience ★

Forethought ★ Wisdom ★ Purity of Intent ★ Thoughtful Reflection ★ Secret Knowledge

Number ★ 2

Astrological Signs ★ Cancer, Scorpio, Pisces & Virgo

THE FOOL'S JOURNEY ★ Although the Magician can control the material world, another world is out there - the hidden, intuitive side of everything. The High Priestess sits between logic and spirit and is associated with the Jungian archetype of the Wise Woman, such as Grandmother Spider in Navajo myth.

THE MESSAGE ★ The High Priestess is the Seer who tunes into everything happening anywhere, anytime. She represents dreaming consciousness, latent psychic abilities, and the modes of perception many modern cultures have scorned, to their detriment and suffering. She embodies the highest spiritual values, representing an open door to the sacred realms of mysticism and magic. The High Priestess is telling you to learn from emotional situations. The answers you seek lie in your emotions and feelings, so trust your intuition and the power of your natural psychic abilities. Also, by paying special attention to your dreams and any intuitive messages you receive, you will be accurately guided by them. When she appears in a reading it means your intuition is functioning more strongly than your intellect. A wisdom is activated in you that is older and deeper than your ordinary mode of thinking. She signifies decision-making with an awareness of the hidden and the visible aspects of the situation. Stay open to your emotions and your feelings in order to come into contact with what you already know. Study spiritual topics, and remember that silence is golden.

THE STORY ★ The High Priestess is a private, all-seeing and spiritual woman with hidden depths and a deep compassion for others. Passive and quiet, she represents a vessel of memory and holy female wisdom. Her powers are so great that they are almost beyond actions, her timeless secrets communicated through an inner voice, and only those wise enough to retreat into silence and undertake thoughtful study will know them. The crown the High Priestess wears as headdress, is reminiscent of the waxing and waning Moon and the natural rhythms of the feminine cycle. These crescent horns of fertility connect her to the Lunar cycle - the waxing Moon forms one horn, the waning its opposite. It doesn't seem to be mere coincidence that the Greek word *delphi* is linked to the word 'uterus' and connects the High Priestess (and women) with prophecy, insights, divination and oracles. She effortlessly directs her psychic abilities in harmony with the desires of the Universe that is her child.

THE AWAKENING ★ Selective in your desire for knowledge, you aspire to know and hold the key to life's mysteries, the essential, primordial principles and secrets that are the unique and sacred nature of life on Earth. Silent, secretive, clairvoyant and enlightened, the High Priestess can guide us through the dark wood of ignorance, indicating that reason alone cannot guide us. Her task is to show us the way to the inner world of the collective unconscious. She has a book of wisdom on her lap, with its most esoteric secrets hidden under the edge of her cloak; behind her is the veil between the inner and outer worlds, or the spiritual and the material planes. And although we, as travellers on the Tarot journey, may not yet be ready to part this veil, we are being shown it exists. Her overall appearance is a message to go quietly within yourself to become aware of your eternal connection to All That Is, and the strength you gain from this knowledge will bring insight.

THE LESSON ★ The High Priestess imparts a simple yet meaningful message: Look for the answers to questions within your heart. Trust your insights, intuition and gut feelings, and act on your hunches. As she also represents learning, she indicates you should undertake a period of study - either formal, or that which comes about through your experience of life. It can suggest the start of training in the Tarot, clairvoyance, astrology, and other mystical studies which rely on intuitive application or psychic insight. She may also represent unnoticed 'power behind the throne', which indicates hidden influences at work and secrets to be revealed later. Something may not be currently known to you and you are not in possession of all the facts, so she advises that you wait until these are more fully uncovered to you before making any further moves. She could also indicate a female teacher or mentor will enter your life soon, or that you yourself will have some knowledge and wisdom to share with and teach to others. If you are in the process of trying to answer an important question about your life, the High Priestess invites you to relax and listen to your inner voice. Take a deep breath, and imagine an open, illuminated space in the centre of your chest where all wisdom resides, and let the answer come to you.

SYMBOLISM * ★ The High Priestess sits between two pillars representing severity and mercy. Her robes are patterned with pomegranates, suggesting the mystery and richness of life and death. Her robe, her posture, the scroll she holds in her hand, and her crown, symbolise intuition and the ability to listen to, and act upon, inner authority and guidance. Symbolising all that is subtle and 'hidden', she holds the keys to the mysteries of life. She carries the knowledge of occult wisdom, which is accessed through her connection with the deep emotional self, and whereas the Magician in the preceding card manifests his power in more tangible ways and using physical tools, the High Priestess contains the power within *herself*, using her abilities for spiritual growth rather than outward expressions of her forces, and uses only her mind and feelings to achieve this.

The staff she grasps appears to connect both the heavens and the Earth, and symbolises that the High Priestess is the gateway to the conscious mind through the subconscious. She is able to access both spiritual and Earthly mysteries.

The peacock pictured in some cards symbolises the High Priestess's ability to choose to display her beauty, or to keep it hidden from view.

The High Priestess is depicted as a regal-looking young lady sitting between two pillars, which represent opposing forces such as life and death; she acts between them. She has always had a spiritual meaning, and in older decks was known as the Female Pope or The Papess. She rules the shadowy world of the unconscious mind and imagination, and symbolises the creative process of gestation; indeed, the foetus must remain in the womb until it is ripe to birth itself, and nothing should be done to precipitate this moment. The lady shown on the card often wears virginal white, signifying unfulfilled potential. In some decks she appears holding a pomegranate, the many-seeded fruit of fertility, suggesting promise for the future. The High Priestess is connected with the Crescent Moon, which symbolises a new cycle of creativity, and she has links with Persephone, goddess of the underworld, and the Egyptian Lunar goddess Isis (in some cards the High Priestess is depicted wearing the horned crown of Isis).

This card can be a challenging card to interpret because of its hidden, elusive and shadowy quality. Her links with the underworld and the unconscious can suggest that she doesn't reveal her secrets easily. Despite its lack of apparent clarity, its divinatory meanings can be perceived as wisdom, sound judgement, serenity, common sense, penetration, foresight, objectivity, perception, intuition, self-reliance, emotionlessness, and platonic relationships.

When this card appears in a reading, it is necessary to seek understanding and solutions on an intuitive level rather than applying the rational mind. The mysterious world of the High Priestess is one of dreams and intuition, which are mediums through which she can best be approached in the search for meaningful answers. These answers may also come in the form of a secret which will be revealed to you. But some secrets need to be decoded first, in order to be deciphered. In this way, the High Priestess has a lock, but she also provides the key to those who seek it.

She also symbolises a budding potential, indicating that perhaps something is yet to come to fruition and it will only be realised and fulfilled at the right time and place. Her connection with gestation reinforces this, giving the strong message that tells you to make sure the time is ripe before you take action. There is no need to race into action. Take time to gain more insight, as things may not be as they appear on the surface.

If you are a female, the High Priestess is telling you to be confident in your approach to life, its problems and what it has to offer. You are far stronger than you may realise, but must avoid overbearing behaviour. You can maximise your potential by thinking before you speak, and making sure of your grounding before you commit yourself to anything. You may also benefit from higher study and knowledge.

If you are a male, the High Priestess is telling you that you need to become more aware of your feminine side, and allow yourself a freer flow of emotions. You should also listen to your intuition and heed its guidance; it could be a greater help than you realise. Often this card describes a strong feminine influence, and in a man's reading it can represent the most important woman in his life.

Regardless of gender, when this card shows up, it is compelling you to withdraw from the chaos and noise of daily life and seek counsel from your guides and angels. Meanwhile, know that everything you need to know will be revealed in time; you just need to foster patience and be led by your inner wisdom.

Know that the High Priestess only exists to help you and respond to your every question. While galaxies swirl above you, pose your query without any attachment to the answer you will receive. In time she will take her hands from behind her back, and in them will be the symbol of your answer.

* Please note that the images described are not found in all Tarot decks. The images in different decks can differ considerably.

THE TAROT'S SUIT OF CUPS ★ REPRESENTING THE WATER ELEMENT

The Cups correspond with the Water element and are an especially interesting and meaningful metaphor. Water is life-enhancing and sustaining when it flows freely; but if trapped or contained for too long, it becomes stagnant, blocked and unhealthy. And, like our emotions and feelings, water can change shape to fit any channel or container, as well as being able to transform into other forms, such as ice or steam. The Tarot Cups reveal the flow of our emotions, how turbulent or calm our inner seas are, how we express ourselves, and how this all influences the relationships we have with others. Their narrative tells the tale of our inner life and reveals hidden feelings. The symbol of the Cup resembles a chalice or sacred drinking vessel and brings to mind the Holy Grail or the cup of life. Consequently, the issues the Cups raise have a spiritual quality. The Cups are connected with the unconscious, artistic abilities, fantasy, feelings, attachments, intuition, love, pleasure, emotions, harmony, sensitivity, fertility, happiness and unity. The decorative imagery and themes that run through the suit of Cups are fish, mermaids and of course water. The fish is a symbol of creative imagination, and the element of Water represents the feelings and the depths of the unconscious mind. The Cups deal with the emotional level of consciousness and are associated with connections, expressions and relationships.

The Cups suit can indicate that we are being ruled by our hearts rather than our heads, our emotions rather than our intellects, and therefore they may reflect instinctive responses and habitual reactions to situations. The Cups are also linked to romanticism, fantasy, imagination and creativity. The Suit of Cups connects us to the wellspring of the spiritual source, helping us to develop our emotions and intuitive faculties, and to understand how we attract particular energies, relationships, experiences and events into our lives. The negative aspect of this suit include being overly emotional, relying too much on one's feelings, becoming disengaged or dispassionate, fantasising, idealising, and holding unrealistic expectations of ourselves or of others. All of these may manifest as repressed emotions, an inability to properly express our self, or a lack of creativity, self-confidence, faith or self-belief. In a deck of playing cards, the Cups correspond to the suit of Hearts.

THE LUCKY 13 ★ PISCEAN TIPS FOR INCREASED MAGIC, LUCK & MAGNETISM

1 ★ Incorporate Piscean symbols into your daily life to remind yourself of your soul's mission.

2 ★ Use the crystal Amethyst in any form in your daily life - wear it, meditate with it, hold it and carry it with you everywhere! Amethyst is the stone of the Third Eye, spirituality and psychic awareness, and so aligns with the Twelfth House, which is the astrological house ruled by Pisces. It also brings calm, peace, inspiration and balance, all of which are emotions or states of being that assist in attracting wonderful things to you.

3 ★ Wear or surround yourself with the colours sea green, purple and violet.

4 ★ Learn the way of the Virgin by learning practical application, focus, self-improvement, purity and perfection. Virgo has much to teach the Piscean soul. Come gently down to Earth … Put your hands in the soil and sow some seeds … Wear a daisy chain in your hair … Work harder … Discriminate with wisdom … Develop discernment … Feel the wonders of the Earth under your feet … Enjoy the sensual feasts and fruits of your journey … Celebrate your achievements … Sit in the field and feel the wonder of its vastness … it's all within you!

5 ★ Use your lucky numbers 3, 7 and 8, whenever you are needing an extra stroke of luck.

6 ★ Magnify and celebrate your selflessness, your giving nature, your compassion, your inherent spirituality, your intuitively in-touch psyche.

7 ★ Remind yourself of your mission constantly, that is by speaking, breathing and *truly living* your dreams and insights - give them form beyond simply daydreaming about them!

8 ★ Focus your energies on exploring your inner depths, and transforming yourself through your higher psychic faculties - which are strongly accessible to the acutely feeling, receptive and sensitive Piscean mind. Connect with your deep imagination and inborn creativity through any means possible.

9 ★ Use your innate powers of other-worldly awareness, pure belief and metaphysical attunement to visualise and draw that which you desire towards you. If you can develop simple faith in the positive outcome of events, you can easily use your mystical intuition to great creative effect.

10 ★ Tap into and utilise your ability to guide, heal, empathise with, and transform others through sharing your emotions, spirit and soul. But to do that, you'll need to ease yourself gently onto planet Earth where the rest of us reside! We need you here at least some of the time!

11 ★ View your dreamy nature as a strength and call forth the powers of your unusual, gifted, unique self. Be who you *really* are, without reservation or apology, and the rest will fall into place.

12 ★ Become the 'Spiritual Enlightener' of others - and yourself - that you were born to be!

13 ★ Once you have mastered purer focus, decisiveness and direction, learn to share the resulting abundance, insights and knowledge with others so they too can walk the Higher Path!

HAVE YOU PACKED YOUR MAGICAL BAG FOR THE JOURNEY?

If you wish to increase and draw more luck, love and abundance into your life, a power pack is essential. For Pisceans, I would recommend carrying or wearing the following items on you on your travels. Then just sit back and watch as magic pours into your experiences and realities, both inner and outer!

★ One of each of the following gemstones: Turquoise, Bloodstone, Aquamarine, Amethyst
★ Tarot cards The Moon and The Hanged Man (and Wheel of Fortune and The High Priestess too, if you wish)
★ A wolf in any form (use your imagination!)
★ Something made of tin
★ A fish symbol in any form
★ A postcard or image from a watery, cool, rainy or oceanic place (representing your Phlegmatic disposition). Bon Voyage!
★ A postcard from the future to yourself, proclaiming, 'Wish You Were Here!'

A FINAL WORD ★ TAPPING INTO THE MAGIC OF PISCES

There is something inherently ethereal and whimsical about Pisces the Fish. Blessed with a dazzlingly insightful and receptive mind, you need only choose to use this power. All too often you lose yourself in the pitfalls of confusion, vagueness and indirection, when you are more powerful than you ever dreamed conceivable. As a Piscean, you truly are the Magical Water-Nymph of the zodiac, affecting everyone around you with your sense of the weird, fanciful and wonderful. You are the most all-embracing and formless of the zodiac, with a well-deserved reputation for brilliant sensitivity and strong impressions. Never malicious but ever elusive and evasive, the Piscean soul seeks to connect with other like-minded souls on your own free-spirited terms. To really tap into your true magic, this soul connection is imperative to your life's spring of wellbeing. Indeed, these associations will help you become stronger, for as the saying goes, no man is an island - and no Fish need swim alone or against the current all the time. The Piscean slipperiness has its advantages, allowing you to take on whatever character or image you like, and to be all things to everyone. This is a potentially incredible strength, and fine if it makes you happy and shines a light on your path, but be mindful not to over-sacrifice yourself, be taken advantage of, or become weighed down by other people's problems; floating is always better than sinking.

Inside anyone who has a strong Pisces influence in their natal chart, is someone who is deeply emotional but who can, like a chameleon, cover it up with a watery façade and adapt to their surroundings as though nothing is brewing. To acknowledge your feeling and emotional nature is to gain easier access to the power within, for as long as you suppress it, block it or try to escape from it, cloudiness, characteristic self-sabotage or destruction may hinder your progress. The typical Piscean possesses a beautifully packaged and presented persona, but your ego and self-confidence are precarious and usually teetering on the low end of the scale. You are not a proficient self-promoter and generally shy away from attention and focus. Although dreamily reluctant to share your profound feelings, insights, talents and *true* emotional depths, Pisces is the most compassionate of all the signs; and underneath your Watery veil, you are pure spirit, just bubbling with love, inspiration, hope, belief, imagination, Universality, empathy and true magic. You are the Daydreamer, the Idealist, the Pipe Dreamer, the Drifter, the Fantasiser, the Imaginer, the Sympathiser, the Listener, the Dissolver of Boundaries, the Self-Sacrificer, the Carer, the Mystic. You are the embracer of Universal love, the force for the awakening of the higher spiritual consciousness, and above all, you are She who swims with the ebbs and flows of her own ocean.

Finally, to attune yourself to luck, harmony and success, Pisceans should wear, eat, inhale, meditate upon, create, design, and dance with any or all of the suggested luck-enhancers for your Sun sign to receive the most beneficial astral vibrations these 'boosters' can offer you. Wearing, decorating and working with the amazing powers of all your lucky guides, animals, crystals, colours, woods, cards, herbs, foods, places, talismans, planetary influences, charms, numbers, and other magical tips contained within the words of this very book, will bring you greater abundance, love, magic, energy, happiness and personal power, and attract all manner of things to you like bees to sweet flowers. This, my Piscean friends, I promise you - and Aquarians *never* lie.

Good luck on the rest of your amazing life journey, and may the LUCK be with you!

Lani is also available for personal Astrology, Numerology, Aura * & Tarot reading consultations, via post, email, Skype and in-person. Please email lalana76@bigpond.com for more information.

* In-person only

Facebook Page ★ Astrology Magic

Other Books in the **Lucky Astrology** Series

Lucky Astrology ★ Aries
Lucky Astrology ★ Taurus
Lucky Astrology ★ Gemini
Lucky Astrology ★ Cancer
Lucky Astrology ★ Leo
Lucky Astrology ★ Virgo
Lucky Astrology ★ Libra
Lucky Astrology ★ Scorpio
Lucky Astrology ★ Sagittarius
Lucky Astrology ★ Capricorn
Lucky Astrology ★ Aquarius

Order your copies now, from White Light Publishing House, at www.whitelightpublishingau.com

www.ingramcontent.com/pod-product-compliance
Lightning Source LLC
Chambersburg PA
CBHW071146300426
44113CB00009B/1099